Mastering the Supply Chain

Principles, practice and real-life applications

Ed Weenk

KoganPage

First published in Great Britain and the United States in 2019 by Kogan Page Limited

2nd Floor, 45 Gee Street
London
EC1V 3RS
United Kingdom

122 W 27th Street
New York, NY 10001
USA

4737/23 Ansari Road
Daryaganj
New Delhi 110002
India

© Ed Weenk 2019

www.koganpage.com

ISBNs

Hardback   978 0 7494 9801 6
Paperback   978 0 7494 8448 4
Ebook   978 0 7494 8449 1

British Library Cataloguing-in-Publication Data

A CIP record for this book is available from the British Library.

Library of Congress Cataloging-in-Publication Data

A CIP record for this title is available from the Library of Congress.

Typeset by Integra Software Services, Pondicherry
Print production managed by Jellyfish
Printed and bound in Great Britain by CPI Group (UK) Ltd, Croydon CR0 4YY

CONTENTS

Online resources for this book are available at www.koganpage.com/msc

LIST OF FIGURES

LIST OF EXERCISES

ABOUT THE AUTHOR

Ed Weenk founded QuSL at the beginning of 2004 in Barcelona, where he was living at the time. Currently based out of Maastricht (Netherlands), Ed has had extensive experience since the mid-1990s in managing international logistics and distribution projects at strategic and operational level.

He gained an MSc in Business Administration from Erasmus University/Rotterdam School of Management and a Professional Doctorate in Engineering (PDEng) focused on supply chain management from Eindhoven University of Technology. Ed also works as a Senior Associate Professor at different business schools, such as EADA Barcelona (Spain), Maastricht School of Management (Netherlands), Antwerp Management School (Belgium) and Centrum Graduate School of Business (Lima, Peru), on the topics of operations and supply chain, project management and intra- and entrepreneurship.

A strong believer in the principles of experiential learning based on methodologies such as the case method as championed by Harvard Business School, in-class teamwork and serious gaming, Ed is delivery partner and authorized trainer in the business simulation games of Inchainge of The Netherlands and the Palatine Group of New York.

Ed has previously written a management book titled *The Perfect Pass: What the manager can learn from the football trainer*, published in English, Spanish and Dutch, about the importance of seeing the *big picture*, having good internal and external *alignment* and achieving *coherence* at all levels.

ABOUT THE CONTRIBUTORS

Chuck Nemer CPIM CLTD MA (Leadership)

Chuck Nemer is a trainer/consultant with 40 years of experience in supply chain management, lean, leadership and APICS. He also teaches operations management at an urban university in St Paul, Minnesota (USA). He is active both locally and nationally in his APICS professional society as well, in the areas of instructor development and curriculum development. Chuck works with many schools on various business simulations, such as The Fresh Connection. He has a Bachelor's degree in Accounting from the University of Minnesota, a Master's degree in Leadership from Augsburg College in Minneapolis, MN, CPIM and CLTD certification from APICS, and online curriculum development certification from the Wisconsin Technical College System.

Corine van der Sloot CPIM

Corine van der Sloot is Director of International Sales for The Fresh Connection and a certified TFC instructor. Her focus is on bringing the world's leading SCM simulations to the DACH region (Germany, Austria and Switzerland), Scandinavia, Italy, SE Asia and Eastern Europe. She is passionate about sharing her knowledge and experience with teachers and professionals and enjoys bringing the ultimate learning experience to SCM students. Corine built an extensive background in supply chain by taking on positions in logistics, manufacturing, product management and sales. She experienced a career in large companies such as Philips and Dutch Telecom as well as taking part in independent entrepreneurial ventures. Her talent in establishing and maintaining contacts earned her the privilege of representing Bundesvereinigung Logistik (BVL) in The Netherlands.

FOREWORD

Egge Haak – Partner at Inchainge

Inchainge is a Dutch company fully dedicated to experiential learning in supply chain management based on business simulations. We constantly create new simulations and training programmes as well as enhance our existing ones, so that learners in the industry and around the world can be supported in their learning journeys. Being a small and compact organization, we take great care in developing and maintaining a large network of both professional trainers and educational teachers and professors around the globe.

The volatile and uncertain world we currently live in creates enormous challenges for companies and their supply chains. Change is the only certainty in business every day, and in order to adapt supply chains successfully, a thorough understanding of its dynamics and interdependencies is necessary. But just understanding the system as a whole will not be enough; constant adaptation also calls for leadership skills in collaboration and teamwork.

At Inchainge, we believe that such understanding and the corresponding skills can only be acquired through active experience, by which I mean the full experience of managing a supply chain with a team, of handling all dimensions in an integral way, of exploring how everything is connected, of working effectively together as a team. On top of this, our mission is to help students and companies create alignment between strategy and execution, between departments in a company and between business partners in the value chain.

We have designed and built all of our business simulations with these objectives in mind, starting with The Fresh Connection in 2008: to help learners understand relevant concepts and to provide them with a platform to experience these in a virtual company setting and thus acquire the necessary skills in order to better deal with the complexities of alignment in the competitive and fun setting of a game. But we don't stop there: we also have a wide diversity of materials to support teachers, trainers and learners in their usage of our simulations and to enrich their experience with meaningful content.

That is also where this book fits in. Apart from our existing simulations and supporting materials, we were looking for a way to further bridge the gap between theoretical supply chain concepts and their direct application, and that is precisely what you will find here. The book starts with an overview of many critical supply chain concepts, and then invites their practical application using The Fresh

Connection as an interactive case. In Part Three the book goes beyond the pure context of the simulation, providing learners with a wealth of additional supply chain challenges to think about. I therefore believe the book will be extremely useful to both learners and their instructors, be it in business or in the educational world.

At Inchainge we trust that this book will set a new standard and bring the integral experience of The Fresh Connection to a higher level.

PREFACE:
SIMPLE BUT NOT EASY (1)

Many students learn best when they are actively doing things and not only studying ideas in the abstract: when their curiosity is aroused, when they are asking questions, discovering new ideas, and feeling for themselves the excitement of these disciplines.

KEN ROBINSON AND LOU ARONICA (2015)

Truth be told, there are already many books about supply chain management and very good ones too, but it has not been our objective to add yet another textbook to the list. On the contrary, we wanted to create a textbook with a clear and strong focus on practical application by students. Albert Einstein supposedly used to say that instead of focusing on teaching and explaining theories and concepts, he preferred to put emphasis on providing the conditions in which students can practise and learn. Following suit, this book wants to provide a solid basis for students to practice and learn how to master the supply chain. *Mastering the Supply Chain* is written for people studying supply chain management. It can be used as part of courses within specialized supply chain or logistics programmes, but also links well to courses within programmes of a more generalist nature, from Bachelor level up to (Executive) MBA, as well as in-company training courses.

There are three main desires behind the topics chosen for the book and the strong emphasis on practical application:

1 The desire to put the increasing need for developing *21st-century skills* such as critical thinking, complex problem solving and coordinating with others into the practical context of supply chain management.

2 The desire to actively address the recurring theme of *simple but not easy*, ie to provide a way to make students feel first-hand the many complexities of actually applying the often relatively straightforward concepts and frameworks in supply chain management.

3 The desire to combine the *multiple dimensions of supply chain management* into one coherent and holistic view on the topic, focusing in particular on the business, technical and leadership dimensions and the way these interact.

Simple but not easy

The phrase 'simple but not easy' is one of the central threads running through the book. It refers to the fact that many of the underlying concepts and frameworks in supply chain management are relatively straightforward and therefore 'simple' to understand, but that there are a number of reasons why their application in practice is 'not easy'.

First, the supply chain area is full of concepts that describe the elements at play in certain topics. For example, when talking about outsourcing, there are frameworks that highlight the factors to be taken into consideration when a company wants to decide whether or not to outsource a particular activity. Application of such a framework will lead to a list of arguments in favour of, or against, outsourcing. Some of those arguments are quantifiable, but there are also some parts which are more qualitative in nature, and this combination of quantitative and qualitative arguments brings in the (subjective) dimension of judgement. In other words, the elements of the framework are simple to understand, but making a concrete decision on the basis of applying the framework might not always be that easy and straightforward.

Second, even though the individual concepts might be simple to understand, it is the sheer number of those at play at once and with an infinite number of interdependencies between them that makes it a very challenging area to manage, especially from a global holistic perspective. For example, we can speak about the main considerations of inventories, or the physical aspects of warehousing, or developments in transportation, all relatively straightforward at the conceptual level, but when we have to come up with an integral distribution network solution for a particular company, suddenly the puzzle becomes quite a lot more complex because we need to bring all of those aspects into the equation.

Add to this the very realistic dimension of incomplete information, assumptions, ambiguity, time pressure, different opinions and a world around us which is moving on continuously, and we get an even more complex picture.

So, in the book, 'simple but not easy' is a recurring theme. Many of the individual concepts of supply chain management are dealt with, but always with the objective of finally arriving at the point of specific and explicit decision making within a global holistic context. Indeed, mastering supply chain management is complex, but in my opinion, that's precisely what makes it such a fascinating area to work in.

The age of acceleration, 21st-century skills and experiential learning

Although, given its relevance, a slightly more extensive description of the age of acceleration, 21st-century skills and experiential learning can be found in the Appendix, a brief introduction seems appropriate here. We live in the age of acceleration; the world is changing faster and faster, calling for different skills from those that were valid in the past (Friedman, 2016). In this context, people also speak about the need for training 21st-century skills (World Economic Forum, 2016; Robinson and Aronica, 2015).

Experiential learning seems to be a very appropriate way of training such skills. I'd like to reference in particular the work of David Kolb, whose book *Experiential Learning* is a classic on the topic. Among other important contributions, for example the concept of individual learning styles, Kolb is well known for what is called the learning cycle (Figure 0.1).

The main idea behind the learning cycle is that 'knowledge results from the combination of grasping and transforming experience. Grasping experience refers to the process of taking in information, and transforming experience is how individuals

Figure 0.1   The learning cycle

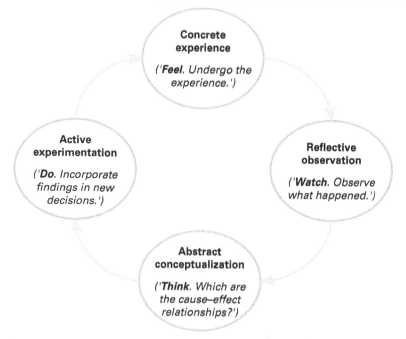

SOURCE after McLeod (2017), based on Kolb (2015)

interpret and act on that information. [...] This process is portrayed as an idealized learning cycle or spiral where the learner "touches all the bases"' (Kolb, 2015).

In experiential learning, the focus is on undergoing an experience first-hand, which allows for reflection on what happened and why, leading to forming a conceptual view of the situation, potentially reinforced by existing theories and/or frameworks. This combination will then be the basis for an improved view of the situation, which can be applied in the next experience, either in class or in another study environment, or directly in a real-world situation. In the book we will use a business simulation game called The Fresh Connection as an important tool for facilitating this experiential learning.

The multiple dimensions of supply chain management

Supply chain management has many faces and it covers a wide array of activities as far as scope is concerned. But it does have very distinct dimensions, which are very different in nature.

First, supply chain management has a clear strategic or *business* dimension. In the end, the supply chain is an integral part of a company, contributing together with the other areas and departments to overall business success. This implies that decision making within the supply chain must fit with the overall direction that the company has defined for the future. Here we speak more about the vital and direct links between the supply chain and corporate strategy and competitive positioning. Or, for example, the impact of market segmentation and value propositions on supply chain

Figure 0.2   The three dimensions of supply chain at the core of the book

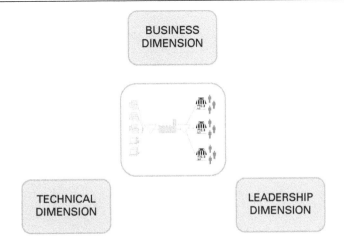

strategy and the relationships between the supply chain and the financials of the company, as expressed, for example, in return on investment (ROI).

Second, supply chain has a clear *technical* dimension, for example when dealing with aspects of manufacturing and distribution infrastructure, technology, forecasting and planning models, or supporting IT systems. This is the part that relates more to the engineering face of the supply chain.

And third, supply chain management has a clear *leadership* or people dimension. Because of its cross-functional nature, spanning activities from purchasing all the way down to sales and after-sales, there are many interrelationships with other functional areas in the company. In practice, many of the functional areas might have different objectives, leading to potential conflicts which need to be aligned and managed somehow. In this part, we speak about topics such as decision-making processes, key performance indicators (KPIs), team dynamics and stakeholder management.

Because of their importance and because of their differences, these three distinct dimensions of the supply chain, technical, business and leadership, will be dealt with explicitly and separately in the book. In fact, together they form the backbone of the structure of the book (Figure 0.2).

STRUCTURE OF THE BOOK

In line with the desires behind the book as explained in the preface, the objective of this book is to fully facilitate the '*learner touching all the bases*', using the principles of experiential learning, training 21st-century skills, while going through the first-hand experience of supply chain being simple but not easy and working with the distinct dimensions of the topic.

Parts Two and Three show students how concepts play out in the real world. This book gives free access to the entry level of a supply chain simulation game. See p 32 for details. In subsequent steps, the business simulation serves as a vehicle for grasping experience, as well as transforming experience, by offering the possibility for the simulation of rounds of gameplay complemented by conceptual frameworks, as well as active reflecting by the student, leading into a new round of simulation, creating a steep learning curve based on first-hand experience. In addition, fields of direct application outside the simulation tool will be touched upon, to widen the student's perspective even further.

To break down the complexity of the topic of supply chain into manageable parts, the book consists of three sections, each dealing with the three aforementioned dimensions of the supply chain in a different way.

In *Part One: Exploring the fundamentals* we present a helicopter view of the main important *principles*, that is, the theories, frameworks and concepts, of supply chain management, which can be found in most books on the topic. Although the list itself is quite extensive, we want to keep it as simple as possible for this book, and that is why, instead of going into much detail, we limit ourselves to brief and to-the-point introductions. Wherever relevant, reference will be made to leading textbooks from the supply chain area, as well as the most important areas touching the supply chain, such as strategy and marketing. Most of the topics covered are accompanied by some initial exercises to get the student actively working with them in order to become acquainted with them. These exercises serve to *explore* the topics at hand. This first section thus sets the scene for *practice* and *real-life application* of the principles in Parts Two and Three.

Part Two: Mastering the fundamentals focuses on applying the fundamental concepts from Part One in practice. Here, The Fresh Connection business simulation is the main vehicle that enables the application of the individual concepts that were introduced in Part One. The basic setup of the simulation used in this second part presents a relatively stable environment in which to make a wide variety of basic supply-chain-related decisions, in order to make the supply chain run smoothly and the company profitable. In this way, the student gets the first-hand experience of *analysing real company data* from different functional areas in order to *make good decisions*. Reflections and exercises in this section are thus structured in two steps:

analyse and *decide*. By running the simulation, there will be a clear and visible link between cause and effect (decisions and results).

Part Three: Imagining beyond the fundamentals elaborates on what happens if we start 'imagining beyond the fundamentals', if the status quo of a supply chain is challenged. For example, what are the implications when new products or sales channels are introduced, new geographies explored, or major supply chain risks are being taken into consideration? Reflections and exercises in the third part fall under the umbrella of *imagining the impact* of certain internal corporate directions, or external trends and developments. All aspects covered in Part Three are related to the company at the heart of the gameplay in Part Two, so, wherever possible, real company data from the simulation will be used.

In each of the three parts, the three dimensions of the supply chain (technical, business, leadership) are dealt with. This gives the book its overall structure (Figure 0.3).

Figure 0.3 Overall structure of the book

Preface: simple but not easy (1)		
PART ONE: *EXPLORING* THE FUNDAMENTALS	PART TWO: *MASTERING* THE FUNDAMENTALS	PART THREE: *IMAGINING BEYOND* THE FUNDAMENTALS
1 General introduction	**6 Knowledge in action**	**11 SC in a VUCA world**
2 Business dimension Competitive strategies Customers and value propositions Competitive advantages Supply chain and finance Business models and supply chain External environment Risk management	**7 Business dimension** Competitive strategies Customers and value propositions Supply chain and finance	**12 Business dimension** Competitive strategies Customers and value propositions Competitive advantages Business models and supply chain External environment Risk management
3 Technical dimension Supply chain strategy Physical infrastructure: *Product and push/pull* *Facilities and transportation* *Outsourcing and collaboration* *Network design* Planning & control *Uncertainty, forecasting, capacity* *Planning & scheduling,* *production & quality* *Inventories* *Payment terms & incoterms* Information & systems, organization	**8 Technical dimension** Supply chain strategy Physical infrastructure: *Product and push/pull (given)* *Facilities and transportation* *Outsourcing and collaboration* *Network design* Planning & control *Uncertainty, forecasting, capacity* *Planning & scheduling,* *production & quality* *Inventories* *Payment terms & incoterms* Information & systems, organization	**13 Technical dimension** Supply chain strategy Physical infrastructure: *Product and push/pull (challenged)* *Facilities and transportation* *Outsourcing and collaboration* *Network design* Planning & control *Uncertainty, forecasting, capacity* Information & systems, organization
4 Leadership dimension Performance measurement & targets Stakeholder management Team roles and team dynamics Trust and coordination	**9 Leadership dimension** Performance measurement & targets Stakeholder management Team roles and team dynamics Trust and coordination: external collaboration	**14 Leadership dimension** Stakeholder management Trust and coordination: bullwhip
5 Simple but not easy (2) Trade-offs and S&OP	**10 Simple but not easy (3)** Trade-offs and S&OP	**15 Conclusion: simple but not easy (4)** Final reflections

In addition, the content of the book is supported by a number of web resources containing, for example, more detailed information about The Fresh Connection business simulation, as well as some templates, supporting videos and so on.

Guided tour, web resources and business simulation game

Guided tour

In order to facilitate optimal learning, chapters in the book all have the following structure besides the content relating to each of them individually:

- Introduction and bullet-point overview of topics at the beginning of each chapter.
- In total, 80+ numbered exercises of different types, which can be done individually or as part of lecture plans:
  - Chapters of Part One: '*explore*', for example by investigating internet resources;
  - Chapters of Part Two: '*analyse*' and '*decide*', using The Fresh Connection business simulation game as an interactive case, analysing detailed data from the simulation, allowing for gameplay and seeing cause and effect relationships;
  - Chapters of Part Three: '*imagine*', using the virtual company from The Fresh Connection business simulation game as a reference and challenging its status quo.
- Summary at the end of each chapter, bridging current and next chapter.

Companion web resources

Mastering the Supply Chain is supported by companion web resources for students and for lecturers. You can visit www.inchainge.com/products/masteringthesupply-chain to see to which additional resources you can have access.

Examples of resources for lecturers:

- examples of course outlines and lecture plans;
- supporting PowerPoint slides;
- supporting videos;
- templates going with the book's exercises.

Examples of resources for students:

- reading lists;
- supporting videos;
- overview of relevant industry associations;

Access to The Fresh Connection business simulation game

In order to get access to The Fresh Connection and be able to use it as an interactive case with the book, you first need to register at the game portal via https://my.inchainge.com, by choosing the option 'No account yet? Register as a new user', and follow the steps indicated, including the instructions you get in the confirmation e-mail. After finalizing the registration process you can enter the game portal with your newly created credentials and look for the field where you can enter a so-called *course code*.

If you are going to play as part of a course in school or university, you will most likely receive this course code through your teacher. If you are working through the book individually, you have a number of different access options to choose from, ranging from a free entry-level option to premium professional access. You can choose the option that best suits your learning objectives and budget. With this book you get free entry level (watch only, free of charge). Use course code: MSC_Free. Includes full visibility of all screens and access to the Information Support Centre inside the game, thus allowing you to work through all of the exercises in the book.

Information about the pricing of the various packages, as well as the entire step-by-step process to register and enter the simulation, can be found on the following webpage: www.inchainge.com/products/masteringthesupplychain.

- *Basic level (Trial gameplay)*. Course code: MSC_Basic. Includes the same as the entry level, plus two rounds of gameplay with basic complexity, as well as Inbox explanations inside the game and the possibility of getting e-mail support during gameplay.

- *Plus level (Academic)*. Course code: MSC_Plus. Includes the same as Basic, but with extended complexity and four rounds of gameplay.

- *Full level (professional)*. Course code: MSC_Full. Includes the same as Plus, but with six rounds of gameplay and the option to participate in a professional competition based on the game.

- *Premium level (master)*. Course code: MSC_Premium. Includes the same as Full level, but with two elements of additional feedback by a certified trainer, as well as the option to do an exam and obtain an official certificate.

ACKNOWLEDGEMENTS

There are a number of people I would like to thank for their contributions to the final result you're holding in your hands now. First of all, Egge Haak, Hans Kremer and Michiel Steeman for inviting me to take on the challenge of writing this book and for critically proofreading and reviewing the content along the way. Also a big thank you to the rest of the team at Inchainge, particularly Antoon and Jochum for helping me out with the tons of queries I had about The Fresh Connection.

Second, a thank you to the team at Kogan Page for their support throughout, with special mention of Julia Swales, Rex Elston and Ro'isin Singh.

Furthermore, my gratitude goes to some of my supply chain friends who have been willing to proofread and give me their detailed and useful feedback: Gustavo Escudero and Aldo de la Cruz in Peru and Desirée Knoppen in Spain.

Thanks also to my dear contributors, who have played a big role in preparing the supporting materials for teachers that go with the book: Chuck Nemer in the United States and Corine van der Sloot in The Netherlands.

A special word of gratitude to César Mejía, who hired me for my first formal teaching assignments in Barcelona, Spain in 2004 and who was to a large extent responsible for setting me on the path of applying the principles of experiential learning in teaching and training environments – a path I still tread today on my journey as a teacher and trainer.

Last but not least, the biggest possible thank you to Marieke, Pau and Marc, for giving me continuous inspiration and energy. This one is for you.

PART ONE
Exploring the fundamentals

The first part, exploring the fundamentals, focuses on the basic concepts and frameworks of supply chain management. Step by step, these main concepts and frameworks and their importance are discussed, as well as the relationships between them. Wherever relevant, reference will be made to leading textbooks from the supply chain area, as well as the most important areas touching the supply chain, such as strategy and marketing. Most of the topics covered are accompanied by some initial exercises so that you can actively work with them in order to get acquainted with them.

These exercises serve to *explore* the topics at hand. This first section thus provides the basis for the other two parts of the book, in which you will have a chance to practise and come to *master* them, and *imagine* their application beyond the pure fundamentals.

In Part One, the three dimensions of supply chain (technical, business, leadership) are explored, each in a separate chapter.

Supply chain   01

General introduction

> In this chapter, we will start the journey of exploring the fundamentals of the supply chain and take a first look at:
>
> - the role of the supply chain within the context of a company;
> - some definitions of the supply chain and related terms;
> - how big our supply chain would need to be;
> - the impact of the size of a company;
> - the building blocks of the supply chain.

What is a supply chain?

Importance of the supply chain: technical area or business function?

What is the supply chain, and why should we bother to study the topic at all? There are many ways to answer that question, but rather than producing statistics about supply chain expenditure on a company or country level, perhaps an easy way to visualize the importance of the supply chain as an integral area of business is to see what happens if it doesn't seem to work properly.

Frequently, we read stories in the newspapers that illustrate the consequences of disruptions in the supply chain. The articles might not even use the term supply chain as such, but speak, for example, of suppliers, manufacturing or logistics. Because such supply chain disruptions are happening all the time, we'll propose an exercise about them later in this part. But first let's look at some recent examples on a larger scale that happened around the time of writing of this book in 2017–18. Examples that come to mind are the story about the apparent problematic ramp-up of Tesla's Model 3, due to a wide variety of issues ranging from production difficulties with robots, obliging the company to switch to manual labour, through continuous product design changes causing problems with tool makers, to supplier relationship management problems (Financial Times, 2017). As CNN published in March 2018 (Isidore, 2018): 'the company had originally promised it would be making 5,000 Model 3's every week by the end of last year [2017], but delivered only 222 in the third quarter, and another 1,542 throughout the entire fourth quarter. It has now pushed the 5,000 a week target back to the end of June' [of 2018]. Meanwhile, Tesla is obviously working hard to fix the issues and get back on the original track. On 3 April 2018, the company stated in an official press release that 'Tesla continues to target a production rate of approximately 5,000 units per week in about three months, laying the groundwork for Q3 to have the long-sought ideal combination of high volume, good gross margin and strong positive operating cash flow. As a result, Tesla does not require an equity or debt raise this year, apart from standard credit line' (Tesla, 2018). Independent of the questions of why and how this could have happened and who might be blamed for it, the matter is probably not that simple and straightforward. The company could run the risk of burning its cash and experience a drop in share price, should the problem persist. In addition, customer trust could potentially be harmed in the process. Hopefully, Tesla will indeed be able to turn things around, but for the moment it looks as if it's been a long and tough supply-chain ride for them.

Or take the news about global ocean shipping giant Hanjin, at the time a top-five player in the industry, filing for bankruptcy while large numbers of containers were still waiting for their ships at numerous ports around the world, and many of their ships were still at sea full of containers, but with no liquidity left in the company to bring them to shore (Guardian, 2016). Or the story about the supply problems of paper-fibre manufacturers in Brazil, plus a season with a more than average number of forest fires in Canada, leading to a toilet-paper shortage in Taiwan, with a subsequent run on the product in supermarkets throughout the country. The share prices of the manufacturing companies dropped sharply as a consequence (Horton, 2018).

Or take the example of Kentucky Fried Chicken (KFC) deciding to close 'hundreds of restaurants' in the UK due to a shortage of chicken. The reason for the shortage was that KFC changed their logistics partner and, together with the new company, they just didn't quite get the logistics operation straightened out before the go-live date. Consequently, KFC and its new logistics partner were on the news around the planet, restaurants didn't open and therefore didn't sell, customers were disappointed and restaurant staff had to be sent home (BBC, 2018).

Although there are many factors beyond the question of whose responsibility it might have been for things not working out so well in these examples, the main message for the moment is that the supply chain seems important enough for companies to worry about managing it well. The stakes if it doesn't work are just too high.

EXERCISE 1.1

Explore supply chain hiccups

Explore

The examples are dated around the time of the writing of the book in 2017–18, but such hiccups happen all the time. Go online and search for five recent supply chain disruptions, let's say from the past 6–12 months. Try to identify the reasons why the disruptions happened, and what the direct and indirect consequences for the company or companies in question might have been.

Definitions of supply chain

After this short introduction to the importance of the supply chain and what might happen if it's broken, let's try to define more clearly what a supply chain actually is. In fact, many definitions of supply chain exist: just go online and search for 'definition of supply chain' or something similar. Probably, many of the definitions you find will have something in common, but at the same time they most likely also have differences. First of all, as the examples in the previous section show, it is interesting to highlight the validity of the 'chain' metaphor. In many languages there exists a variation of the expression 'a chain is as strong as the weakest link'. Applied to a supply chain context, it puts an important emphasis on the idea of interdependencies between the various players involved. If one of my suppliers fails and consequently I'm not able to produce and deliver myself, I cannot really hide behind my supplier when responding to queries from my own customers. After all, they are dealing with me and not with my suppliers.

A widely used definition of supply chain comes from the Supply Chain Council, an industry association which some years ago joined colleague organization APICS. They are behind the development of the Supply Chain Operations Reference, or SCOR, model. It provides a 'process oriented' view of supply chain management, distinguishing the steps of plan, source, make, deliver and return in any company involved in any supply chain. See Figure 1.1 for an overview. Obviously, as we will comment upon at a later stage, the supply chain can be extended further into suppliers' suppliers and customers' customers. Stanton (2017), in his practically oriented book on the supply chain, refers to the SCOR model extensively. APICS has also recently launched an app for iOS and Android covering an overview of the entire model.

Figure 1.1 SCOR model overview

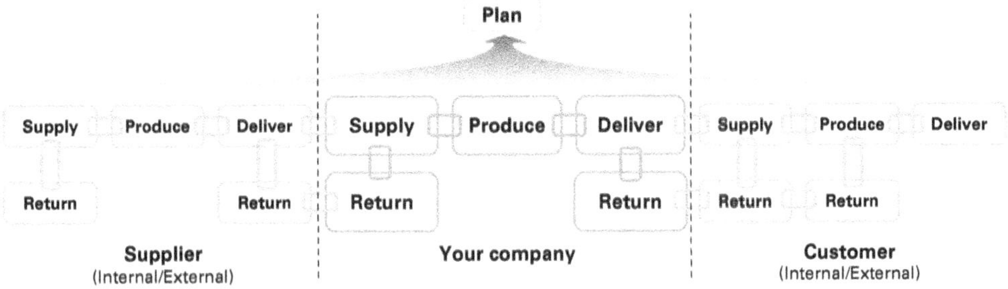

Just to take a few more examples of supply chain definitions from leading textbooks on the subject, let's look at some of them. Rushton, Croucher and Baker (2017) phrase it like this:

Logistics = Materials Management + Distribution

Supply Chain = Suppliers + Logistics + Customers

Christopher (2016) states that supply chain management is 'the management of upstream and downstream relationships with suppliers and customers in order to deliver superior customer value at less cost to the supply chain as a whole'.

Simchi-Levi *et al* (2009) define supply chain management as '[...] a set of approaches utilized to efficiently integrate suppliers, manufacturers, warehouses, and stores, so that merchandise is produced and distributed at the right quantities, to the right locations, and at the right time, in order to minimize system-wide costs while satisfying service level requirements'.

A definition I personally use in workshops and training is the one that Chopra and Meindl (2016) propose: 'A supply chain consists of all parties involved, directly or indirectly, in fulfilling a customer request.' Although it might seem a very open definition with a rather open-ended view on the boundaries, that's one of its interesting characteristics: you must define for your own case how long and how wide you want your supply chain to be.

What all definitions have in common, explicitly, is that the supply chain is about flows of goods, information and money (costs and revenues), and, maybe even more importantly, that it is aimed at satisfying the needs of a customer at the end of our chain (we call this the downstream end, as opposed to the suppliers, who are upstream). In other words, the customer, the paying figure at the end of our direct chain, is clearly part of our supply chain.

It might be interesting to note that Simchi-Levi distinguishes and explicitly connects what he calls the 'development chain' and the supply chain. The latter is covered by his definition as cited before, focusing on the stable supply, manufacturing and distribution of existing goods, while the development chain deals with new product development and the design of the processes to supply, manufacture and distribute those new products (Simchi-Levi *et al*, 2009).

More and more attention can be noted being paid to circular chains, in connection with the wider topic of corporate social responsibility and sustainability. The return processes as defined in the SCOR model already allow the possibility of including that dimension.

Please note a difference between customers and consumers. Every company along the chain has customers, but the term consumers normally refers to the final users of a product at the end of the entire chain. Retailers such as Tesco or Carrefour might be customers of mineral water producer Evian, but the consumers are the people in the stores buying the water. This distinction between customers and consumers will come back at a later stage when we discuss the concept of 'customer value' in Chapter 2, as well as when working on 'business models' in Part Three.

Importance of definitions

These definitions were presented to give you a flavour of what standard textbooks say about the subject. In my experience of working with supply chain professionals around the world, having the correct definition of supply chain is not necessarily a topic to worry about too much in practice. It doesn't often occur that we do not understand each other when talking about the supply chain from a holistic point of view, not even when we cross functional borders with other departments. In most cases this doesn't cause any serious problems.

However, this might be different in the case of definitions of areas that are part of the supply chain. There I do see more confusion about terminology, depending on background, company context or even national frames of reference. The word 'logistics' is a good example. For some, this is pretty much a synonym for supply chain, in the holistic end-to-end view. For others, logistics is more of an operational activity, for example mainly related to warehousing and distribution. One can understand potential confusion occurring when two people have a discussion, each working from a different understanding of the term. In a similar fashion, there is a difference between the functions of purchasing and procurement. Check the internet and you will find a wealth of different explanations, in some cases exactly the opposite of one another.

So even though in practice there isn't that much confusion about the term supply chain itself, in these latter examples in which less clarity exists, obviously definitions are important, not in terms of determining who is right or who is wrong, but especially from the pragmatic point of view of clarifying them with your counterpart, allowing you then to move on productively with the conversation.

What does the supply chain look like?

The length and width of the supply chain

Let's go back for a moment to the question of how long and how wide your supply chain should be. Does it make sense for you to include the suppliers of your key suppliers in your company policies? Or the customers of your customers? Obviously, answering these questions with a 'yes' doesn't come for free – it has implications on what you do and how – but if it makes sense, then include them and decide on the best way to manage those relationships. If not, then just deal with your own direct suppliers or customers.

EXERCISE 1.2
Explore how long and wide the supply chain is

Explore

In which cases do you think it might make sense to go beyond a company's own direct 'upstream' suppliers and 'downstream' customers and include their respective suppliers or customers in the company's supply chain view and policies?

What are the reasons you can think of? Another way of phrasing this question would be to think of what risks the company could run if they didn't go beyond the first-level suppliers and customers.

A similar choice would be valid for some of the internal departments in the company. For example, could the Research and Development (R&D) department be considered to be 'directly or indirectly involved' in fulfilling a customer request? Arguably, in most cases, not in the current day-to-day business, but within R&D, technologies and/or products are being developed and choices being made which sooner or later might have an impact on activities in the supply chain. The same could be valid to a greater or lesser extent for departments such as IT, Legal, Human Resources and so on. The challenge is to identify how they potentially impact on the supply chain and how best to manage that, without creating large and inefficient organizational structures and an infinite number of meetings.

The impact of size and power in the supply chain

As the term supply chain indicates, it's not about individual companies, but about the whole of which they form a part. Obviously, relationships between companies are not going to be great and wonderful just because they happen to be part of the same supply chain. An element to keep in mind is that the size of the companies involved in any bilateral or multilateral relationship is most likely going to play some sort of role in what happens between them. The exception might be the smaller company that has something special to offer in which they are so unique that even the larger ones will have to adapt, but in most cases, size is an important factor to take into consideration.

First of all, larger companies have more negotiating power than smaller ones. They move larger volumes and therefore they have the ability to impose their rules on the smaller companies. Vice versa, the smaller companies might have a more difficult starting point when negotiating contract conditions or might have more difficulties when trying to convince the larger companies to join them in improvement projects.

However, there might also be an opportunity to leverage the buying power or conditions of the large company into the schemes of the smaller one. For example, if the large company, because of its large volume, has certain favourable contracts with their transport providers, or attractive financing terms from their banks, they might allow the smaller firms to join those agreements. In other words, the conditions of the large company become available to the smaller company.

Companies such as Toyota, IKEA or Spanish supermarket chain Mercadona use their relationships with key suppliers to leverage best practices across those suppliers. So, if they see that a joint initiative with one key supplier has given good results, they might propose something similar to another supplier or even ask the two suppliers to join forces for a particular project. Such examples show that a difference in size is not by default negative for the smaller company. The way things will work out between companies of different sizes is sometimes difficult to predict. But the impact of size is something that cannot be ignored.

Building blocks of the supply chain: the pieces of the puzzle

Before going into the details of what the supply chain covers, here are a few words about how it is embedded into the company. Historical thinking is that the starting point for defining any supply chain solution is the strategy of the company, which leads to the development of partial strategies for different functional areas, among which the areas involved in the end-to-end supply chain can also be found. This would lead to the definition of logistics or supply chain targets, which then form the input for determining the right supply chain setup. Lately, a stronger notion has gained currency: that supply chain strategy is not just a consequence of strategic decisions, but a relationship that is much more reciprocal, with a two-way dependency, in which commercial strategies change due to supply chain capabilities within the company. We will come back to this at greater length in Chapter 2.

Figure 1.2   Integral logistics concept

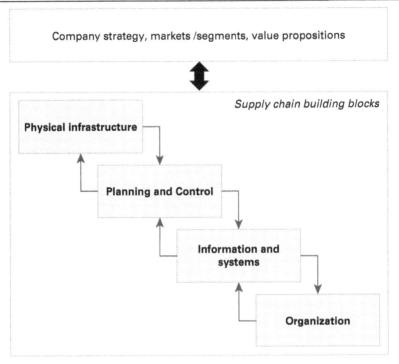

SOURCE after Visser and van Goor (2011)

So, what exactly are the building blocks we consider when talking about supply chains? To begin with, I would like to refer to what Visser and van Goor (2011) dubbed the 'integral logistics concept' (Figure 1.2). They coined the term in the 1990s but it is still widely used and, as it turns out, it covers pretty much what we would nowadays call the supply chain.

Their original concept also starts with company strategy, markets/segments and value propositions, leading then to the design of the integral supply chain. To be coherent with the notion that strategy and supply chain are not so much sequential steps but are much more intertwined, the arrow between the two boxes now goes in two directions. The building blocks of the supply chain as depicted in the model are then the following:

- *Physical infrastructure*, for example decisions about factories, warehouses, ports and other transportation hubs, the manufacturing or logistics technologies applied, having in-house or outsourced operations, pursuing a push-based or pull-based supply chain (more about this later) etc. Obviously, there is one other key element of the physical infrastructure: the materials that are moved through it.

Normally we refer to these as goods flow or material flow. A specific term used a lot in companies to identify their products is *SKU*, which stands for stock keeping unit, or reference number, or article. SKU can be applied to components as well as to finished goods.

- *Planning and control mechanisms*, such as forecasting, production planning and sequencing, inventory management, transportation planning etc. This would cover the relevant processes in the company, as well as the alignment between them.

- *Information and subsequent systems requirements*, in order to provide the relevant information for planning and execution of the aforementioned processes.

- *Organizational setup*, stating who does what and in which processes: roles and responsibilities.

As shown in Figure 1.2, the four blocks at the bottom are placed in sequence, one leading to the next, starting with making network choices. Some arrows flow backwards, thus highlighting the iterative nature of designing a coherent integral supply chain solution.

When addressing the 'technical dimension' of the supply chain in Chapter 3, we will follow the structure and sequence of the integral logistics concept. The approach of the integral concept is pretty much coherent with the building blocks of the supply chain that can be found in other textbooks.

Another distinction of decision making in the supply chain is related to the time horizon of the decisions and their impact. Typically, we would distinguish three levels of decisions in this context:

- *operational*, short-term decisions (for example for the next three months);

- *tactical*, medium-term decisions (for example, with a 3–18-month horizon);

- *strategic*, long-term decisions (for example, with a horizon of 18+ months).

How exactly short, medium and long term are defined might differ according to the company and/or industry. Owing to the speed of technological innovation, in the high-tech industry two years into the future might seem like an eternity, while in the aircraft business things simply don't go that fast (the reader interested in different speeds in different industries might want to check out Charles Fine's classic book *Clockspeed* from 1998). We will come back to the distinction between the timeframes of decisions at a later stage, in Chapter 3.

What does my supply chain look like? Supply chain mapping

A widely used technique to establish a clear view on a given supply chain (existing or planned) is called *mapping*, simply meaning 'creating a map'. Different types of

Figure 1.3   Some of the most commonly used types of mapping

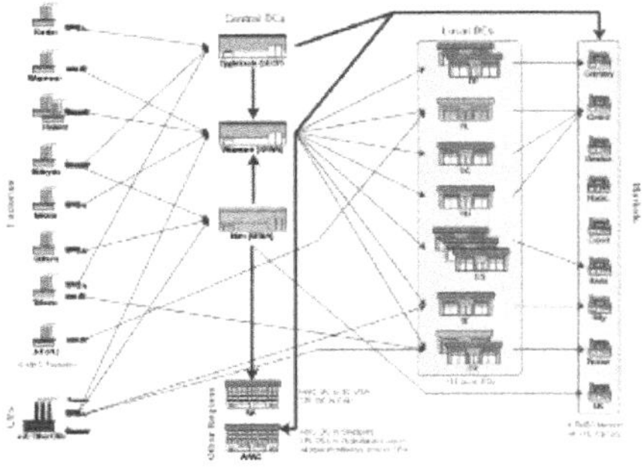

Network flow diagram
(logical connections and goods flows)

GIS diagram
(Geographical Information System)

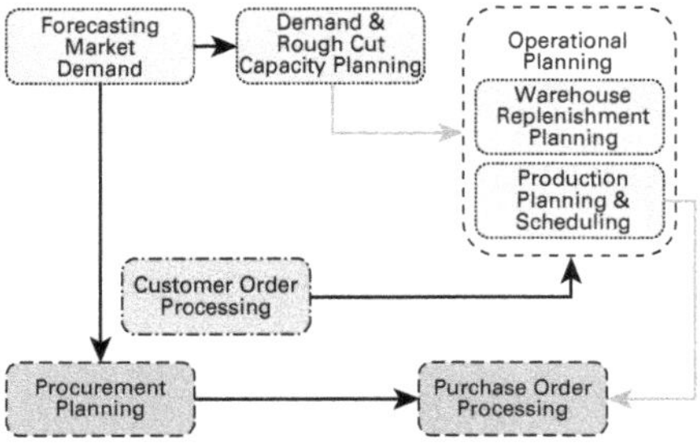

Process flow diagram
(logical connections and decision making)

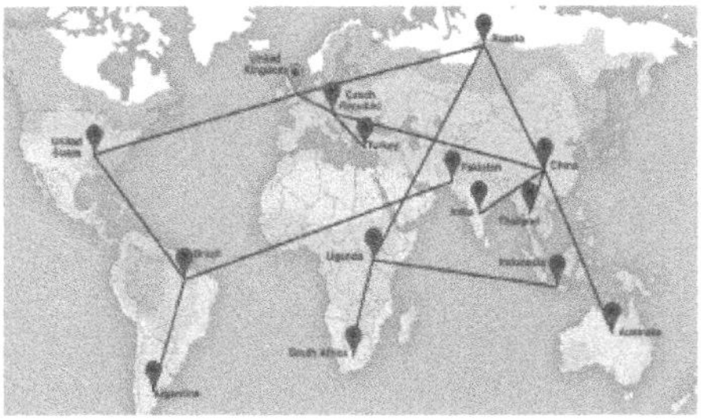

Geographical flow diagram
(flows combined with geographical zones)

map exist, all with a slightly different focus, as shown by these commonly used maps (Figure 1.3):

- *Network flow diagram*: focused on showing the logical connections between facilities in a network, so that the complexity becomes visible. The diagram can also be enriched by adding qualitative and quantitative data to it, highlighting, for example, volumes, service levels, inventory levels and numbers of shipments.

- *GIS diagram*: GIS stands for Geographical Information System, implying that certain types of data, such as demand, shipment frequencies, shipment sizes, number of customers etc, are visualized on a geographical map, for example based on postcode zones.

- *Process flow diagram*: aimed at showing logical connections in business processes and the flow of decisions. These could include a dimension related to responsibilities, for example having the flow of decisions depicted on a background representing each corporate department as a column ('swimming lanes').

- *Geographical flow diagram*: like the network flow diagram, but instead of focusing on a logical flow from left to right, this one highlights the geographical dimension on a geographical map.

Three of the abovementioned mapping types will be seen again in Part Two.

Figure 1.4 Topics covered in each of the three dimensions of supply chain management

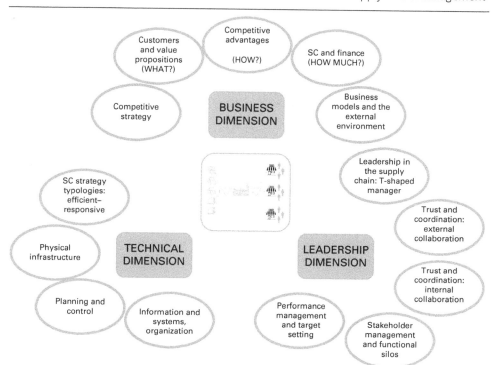

Summary

In this introductory chapter we have addressed some of the main basic definitions and building blocks of the supply chain. Now, as part of our exploration of the fundamentals of supply chain management in Part One of the book, let's take a closer look at the *business* dimension (Chapter 2), the *technical* dimension (Chapter 3) and the *leadership* dimension of the supply chain (Chapter 4). Figure 1.4 gives a high-level overview of the topics covered in each of the dimensions.

Supply chain

02

The business dimension

The supply chain is an integral part of the overall business, covering different (mainly operational) functional areas and co-existing with the other functional areas in the company. In this chapter, we are going to explore that relationship between the supply chain and a company's business more deeply.

We will address:

- the topic of competitive or corporate strategy;
- the concept of value to the customer: value propositions (what?);
- what needs to be done to deliver that value: competitive advantages (how?);
- typologies of supply chain strategies;
- the relationship between the supply chain and the financials of the company (how much?);
- an integral view on business models: business model canvas (what, how and how much?);
- the potential impact of the company's external environment on its supply chain;
- supply chain risk and resilience.

Please note that in Chapters 2 and 3, a number of exercises are featured for you to explore the different aspects of the business and technical dimensions of supply chain management. Select a few companies that match your specific interests and their corresponding industries so that you can work on those during the exercises (preferably companies involved in physical products). You can keep those at hand throughout Chapters 2 and 3.

Industry perspective: competitive strategy

About industries and markets

When defining strategy, we need to clearly distinguish between industry and market. In simple terms, *industry* refers to the competitive landscape in which a company is operating, so other companies addressing the same or similar customer segments with the same or similar products and services are competing for the same money that the customers spend.

Market refers to the group of customers a company is addressing, in other words the people or companies that would potentially buy their products or services. There is more about those in the next section of this chapter.

Starting with the industry, the first question is how much pressure there is within the industry and who the competition is, and second, how to beat them in the competitive race. Porter (1985) proposed his famous and widely used five forces framework to get a clear view on the competitive landscape by identifying the rivalry between direct competitors, the threat of new entrants, the threat of product/service substitutes and the pressures derived from suppliers and customers.

Competitive strategy

Once the industry situation is clear, a company decides how to best compete within it. Porter recognizes three basic strategies: a *cost leadership* strategy, aimed at achieving lower prices than the competition, a *differentiation* strategy aimed for example at offering better or faster products and services, and a *focus* strategy. The latter one means concentrating on a specific and relatively small, niche segment, which is ignored or at least much less actively pursued by other industry incumbents.

Another widely used framework to define competitive strategies was proposed by Treacy and Wiersema (1995). They also distinguish three basic strategies, although slightly different from Porter's:

- *operational excellence*, focused on low cost and a good service but based on a rather small product/service portfolio;
- *customer intimacy*, focused on extreme levels of customer service, large product/service portfolios and total solution provision;
- *product leadership*, focused on highest-quality state-of-the-art products based on continuous product development.

Although slightly different in their definitions, an interesting similarity between Treacy and Wiersema and Porter is that they all advocate making clear strategic choices. Porter called this avoiding getting 'stuck in the middle'; that is, if you don't make a clear choice, you're in fact trying to be everything to everyone, with the result of not being really good at anything.

EXERCISE 2.1
Explore industries, players, strategies

Explore

Take one or more industries you've chosen because of your interest in them. Do some desk research into the different players active in this market. On the basis of the information you can find, try to define which of the basic strategies the different industry players are pursuing. You are strongly encouraged to try to use the frameworks of both Treacy and Wiersema and Porter, so that you can find out how they are different, but also how well they work for you. Create a separate table for each framework, indicating the corresponding different strategy types, and allocate the companies according to their strategies.

What conclusions can you draw from the table(s) created? To what extent are strategies clear? To what extent have you found companies that look 'stuck in the middle'?

Whichever of these strategies a company chooses will ultimately also determine which actions need to be taken in the supply chain. We will say more about that after this brief look at industry and competitive strategy, but let's now look at those we are selling to – our customers.

The 'what' of the company's business: customers and value propositions

The concept of value: why would they buy from me?

A company generates revenue by selling to its customers. That is the starting point of business, and when we were speaking about definitions of the supply chain earlier on, it was clear that the customer has an important position in the supply chain. In this context, the word 'value' is also often used. A company must give its customers something they value and that they are willing to pay for. I would call that the 'what?' of the company; in other words, what is it that we promise to our customers that they perceive as valuable?

In academic literature about marketing there is a wealth of references and frameworks about the concept of value, for example in the famous work of Philip Kotler (Kotler and Lane, 2015). A generally accepted expression is that value is a function of the benefits perceived by a customer, in relation to the price paid for the product or service. In a way, this refers to the term 'price-and-quality relationship' that we are all used to in our daily lives.

Where are these perceived benefits coming from, or what are the elements of the 'value proposition'? In marketing literature there are plenty of frameworks and concepts dealing with the definition of value propositions, from the 'product levels' of Kotler (Kotler and Lane, 2015) to the value proposition canvas (Osterwalder et al, 2014) and the five value attributes and their relative degree of excellence in the market as proposed by Crawford and Mathews (2003). The latter ones go on to speak about what they call the 5-4-3-3-3 strategies: be the best in the market in one value attribute, be above average in one other and be at par in the remaining three, ie don't try to be the best at everything.

DeSmet (2018) combines the framework of Crawford and Mathews in a very original way with the basic strategies of Treacy and Wiersema as introduced at the beginning of this chapter. Lastly, Sharp (2010) also addresses the topic of value extensively, mainly from the angle of brands and branding, in combination with smart segmentation and specifically adapted marketing policies.

All the frameworks are detailed approaches with different definitions and dimensions of value. It would be outside the scope of this book to go into the detail of each of those. For our purpose we simplify a little and turn to the framework of Christopher and of Rushton *et al*, as published in their respective books on supply chain management. When considering the world of goods, which is most relevant for the supply chain, as an example, and following Christopher (2016) as well as Rushton *et al* (2017), the framework starts with the core product at the heart of its value. Some people would discuss the basic or core benefits of the product. Aspects such as the product's quality, functionality, features and durability come to mind: an umbrella should protect you from the rain, a medicine should cure a disease and mineral water should relieve your thirst.

But in some markets, especially mature ones where products from different companies are very similar to one another, those basic benefits just might not be enough to differentiate the products in the customers' minds, unless you successfully pursue a cost leadership or operational excellence strategy. For other companies, differentiation could take place at what Christopher and Rushton call the 'service surround' or 'product surround' (Figure 2.1). In this additional layer, aspects beyond the pure

Figure 2.1   Value, core product, service surround

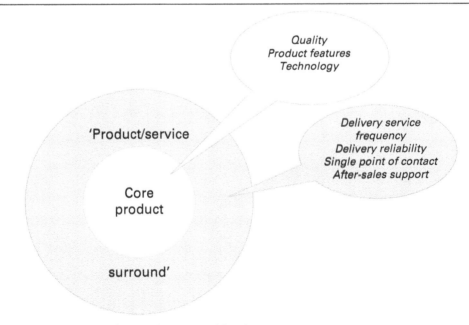

SOURCE after Christopher (2016) and Rushton *et al* (2017)

physical product come into the play, for example delivery speed, delivery reliability, flexibility to change an order before delivery, after-sales service, choice of packaging variety, or the possibility of adding customized labelling.

As we will discuss later, a proper and accurate definition of the value proposition offered to our customers is one of the key starting points in determining what our supply chain should look like.

Being everything to everyone/One size fits all? Or smart customer segmentation?

Please note that most companies do not have only one customer segment; they normally deal with various segments. In marketing literature many references to customer segmentation can be found, but the basic thought behind it is that customers are not all 100 per cent identical and that 'one size fits all' might be very efficient, but results in hardly anyone receiving exactly what they want. The opposite would be to give every individual customer exactly what they ask for, but the downside of that approach would be that efficiency and therefore prices and/or margins would be at stake.

That is where the art and science of smart customer segmentation come into the scene: how to determine as many useful segments as necessary while at the same time keeping the number as low as possible, thus optimizing between customization and efficiency. The exact concepts, methods and tools of customer segmentation are beyond the focus of this book, but for the moment it is sufficient to understand that most companies work for multiple segments and that each of these segments might call for different value propositions (even though more or less overlap might exist, they would not be 100 per cent identical). And in turn, those different value propositions might require different supply chain solutions, each playing with the same tension between customization and efficiency.

For example, think about a laptop producer such as HP or Acer. They might sell to large chains of household appliance retailers such as Mediamarkt or Curry/PC World, but also to supermarket chains such as Tesco or Carrefour. Furthermore, their products are sold directly to smaller shops, as well as via large distributors such as Ingram Micro. At the same time, their products can be found on the platforms of e-commerce retailers such as Amazon, as well as on the company's own web shops. Each of those, commercially speaking, is a different segment, sometimes even segmented into more detail according to size and/or geographical scope (international, national, regional). And as you can understand, each of those segments, although potentially interested in buying the same products, might have very distinct service requirements in terms of frequency of deliveries, repackaging, relabelling, delivery reliability and speed, electronic system connections, and a large list of etceteras.

Customer and consumer: not (always) one and the same

It was briefly hinted at already earlier on, but in any given company situation there might be a difference between characteristics that are important to the direct paying customer of a company and those that are important to the (final) consumer. When considering a local convenience store owner in the city or town centre, their customers in most cases would be the same as the end consumers, so there is no need to differentiate between customer and consumer.

But in the case of a pharmaceutical company, for example, the final consumer is the patient and they are obviously interested in what a medicine will do inside their body, that is, the core benefit of the product provided by the so-called 'active ingredient(s)' it contains. However, the pharmacy, which is buying the medicine from the pharmaceutical company, is probably not interested in the core benefit because in the end they will not use the medicine themselves. For them, the core benefit of the product is mainly important because they know it represents a potential sales volume of patients – for example, looking for a medicine to combat headaches. In addition, the pharmacy will most likely be very interested in delivery-related aspects, such as delivery lead time, flexibility, packaging types, product availability and so on.

So even though it is tempting to focus only on why a consumer might want to buy a certain product from a company, it's crucial not to forget the aspects that provide value to those who pay us directly, our customers, especially when these aspects are not the same. From a supply chain perspective, we need to make this distinction explicit and include both points of view, since they might have different implications for the different supply chain building blocks. In literature about industry types, business models and marketing, the distinction is commonly made between business-to-consumer (B2C) and business-to-business (B2B). However, even a B2B company selling to other businesses will ultimately have a consumer at the end of the chain, so it might be tempting to mix up the concepts of customer and consumer.

EXERCISE 2.2
Explore market segments

Explore

For the industry you chose in the previous exercise and the players you identified there, try to find more detailed information about the different market segments they supply.

For each of the segments you have identified for a specific company, try to find information about their respective value propositions offered to these customer segments.

Our viewpoints on the industry, the competition and the value propositions offered to the different customer segments give us a starting point for defining what the supply chain should look like.

The 'how' of the company's business: competitive advantages

On how to create value: the value chain

As soon as a customer has expressed interest in what the company promises, and this customer has decided to buy, then ultimately a delivery needs to take place, according to or even exceeding the expectations of the customer. Everything needed to deliver successfully on the promise is what I would call the 'how?' of the company.

If a company competes by promising shorter lead times than its competitors, it effectively needs to find ways to become faster than them. If it promises better delivery reliability (also called service level), it has no choice but to become more reliable than the others. If it offers lower prices, it would need to become cheaper. At the highest level, it's as simple as that.

Now the real supply chain puzzle starts, and serious doses of creativity are required. Because how do you become fast? Or more reliable? Or cheaper? And above all, consistently being able to carry out the job day after day? Once more, we turn to Porter for a reference, since he also addressed the 'how' side of the story when he described his famous 'value chain' (Porter, 1980). Although the concept is wider than just supply chain, there are many overlapping elements. On the one hand, Porter distinguishes primary activities, such as marketing and sales, production and logistics, all directly involved in the creation and delivery of the product or service concerned. On the other hand, there are the supporting activities, such as human resources, research and development, and so on.

According to Porter, a company can make a competitive difference by achieving excellence in any (combination) of the areas, leading to achieving competitive advantages. Obviously, in which areas it must excel will be defined by the decisions made with respect to corporate strategy. For example, to be a world leader in fundamental research aimed at new material discoveries and new product development is mostly relevant for product leadership strategies and not so much when aiming at becoming a cost leader.

As I noted in my previous book, *The Perfect Pass*, Porter talks first about the objective of performing strategically important activities cheaper and/or better than the competition. In other words, Porter says that one must understand that for improving the competitiveness of a company, a difference can be made in any one or more of the strategically important activities. Competitiveness is related to the operational capabilities of the company. It is also something that is perceived by their customers, and ultimately is at the heart of a company's profits. The implication of this is that each of the activities in the value chain can be used to create a competitive advantage and that a view of the big picture is required to put everything into perspective.

Second, Porter stresses the fact that activities are interdependent and not isolated. Consequently, anyone who achieves a good alignment of these activities would create either optimization or improved coordination between areas. This could manifest itself in a set of high-quality and smart business processes across different areas, leading to cheaper and/or better performance. At the same time, given the interdependency of all areas, one would have to make sure that action or initiatives in one area were coherent with the actions and initiatives in another (Weenk, 2013a). We will return to both the abovementioned aspects of Porter when talking about the integrated view of business models later in the chapter.

Key to superior performance: competitive advantages

The key idea of competitive advantages is to identify in which areas the company is or should be better, faster or cheaper than competitors, as well as knowing why. Is it because of more well-developed processes? Because of more advanced technology or patents, because of better qualified or more motivated people in one or more of the primary and/or support activities? This combination of distinguishing factors is called the 'competitive advantage' of a company; it describes why the company is able to compete successfully with the other companies in its industry, hopefully in a sustainable way, over the long term. The more elements it has as part of its competitive advantage, the more difficult it will be for competitors to copy and catch up, and the more likely it will be that advantages can indeed be sustained into the future.

Any of the elements mentioned when dealing with the building blocks of the supply chain earlier on, as part of the integral logistics concept (physical infrastructure, control structure, information and systems, organization), would potentially be on the list as part of a company's competitive advantage. For example, Amazon can achieve its same-day delivery service because it has invested in having many local storage facilities and applying advanced robotics technologies in most of them. Amazon is able to provide reliable information about availability of products or the status of deliveries because of extensive investments in the development of advanced IT systems, as well as having the processes and contracts in place to manage an enormously wide portfolio of suppliers. All of those ingredients of their supply chain taken together, and probably more, explain how Amazon has created an overall competitive advantage, difficult to copy for others, at least in the short to medium terms.

EXERCISE 2.3
Explore competitive advantages

Explore

Go back once more to the industry you chose in the previous exercise and the players you identified there. Try to find more detailed information, for example in their annual reports, about the elements of their competitive advantage. In what are they better, faster, cheaper than the competition?

Why are they better, faster, cheaper – what's their secret?

How sustainable do you think the different competitive advantages are? How easy or difficult would it be for competitors or even new industry entrants to copy them?

The supply chain and a company's financials: the 'how much?'

It's clear that in order to survive, all businesses need to make a profit and so spend less than they earn, at least in the long run. At the same time, there needs to be a healthy balance between the profits generated and the investments made in order to achieve them. This part of financials I would call the 'how much?' of the business. We will now look at the impact of the area of supply chain on profit and loss and on investments. Although all major supply chain textbooks write about the supply chain and finance, Christopher (2016) and Rushton *et al* (2017) even dedicate an entire chapter to the topic in their respective books. In part, we will refer to their work here. The same goes for DeSmet (2018), mentioned earlier, whose recent book is entirely dedicated to the links between supply chain strategy and financial metrics.

Receive and spend: the income statement

The first important financial statement in the annual report of a company is the income statement, or profit and loss statement (P&L). It shows whether a company has made a profit or a loss and shows the details of how it's built up, starting with the revenue and subtracting all expenses (Figure 2.2).

Figure 2.2   Items on the income statement (P&L)

Revenues	
–/ –	**Costs of goods sold**

Gross profit

– / –	**Operating expenses**
	Selling expenses
	Research and development expenses
	General administration expenses
+ / –	Other operating income/expenses

Earnings before interest and taxes (EBIT)

– / –	Interest and taxes

Net income

As can be seen in the overview above, there are plenty of direct links between the supply chain and the income statement. First, it can be argued that superior supply chain performance in terms of delivery service, speed or flexibility will lead to sustainable revenue, or might very well lead to additional sales if performance is better than the competition. Furthermore, there are obviously very clear links between the supply chain and the money spent, as expressed in the costs of goods sold (for example, purchasing of raw materials, inbound transportation, energy and labour costs for manufacturing and warehousing). In addition, there are the costs for distribution to customers, which are normally to be found as part of the sales expenses.

All in all, the income statement gives us a clear view on what is called the top line (revenue) and the bottom line (profit). From this statement it can also be deduced that a market strategy aimed at top-line growth is not necessarily the same as one aimed at bottom-line improvement.

EXERCISE 2.4
Explore top line and bottom line

Explore

Strategically speaking, in which cases do you think that the focus of a company might be on 'top-line growth'? And in which cases on 'bottom-line improvement'?

What specific actions can you think of that would fit well with a top-line growth focus? And with a bottom-line improvement focus?

How are these two strategies different and/or similar?

Now that we can see what earnings and expenditures have been like, let's look at the investments that have been made in order to make that happen.

Own and owe: the balance sheet

The second important financial statement in the annual report of a company is the balance sheet, also sometimes called the 'financial position'. It shows the assets, liabilities and equity of the company; in other words, the resources that the company owns, as well as the money it still owes to others (Figure 2.3).

Although the financial position includes more than just supply-chain-related items, the main ones from a supply chain point of view are the snapshots of inventories, trade accounts receivable (A/R) and property, plant and equipment (PPE) on the asset side and the trade accounts payable (A/P) on the liabilities side. One could potentially also add cash as related to the supply chain when thinking about the relationship between deliveries made, delivery reliability and even invoice accuracy. A/R and A/P have direct links with topics such as payment terms, order sizes and so on. Inventories are relatively straightforward to understand, and together with the accounts receivable and accounts payable they make up the working capital of a

Figure 2.3   Items on the balance sheet (financial position)

Current assets	Current liabilities
Cash and cash equivalents	Accounts payable
Accounts receivable	Notes payable
Inventory	Accrued expenses
Other	Deferred revenue
Total current assets	*Total current liabilities*
Property, Plant and Equipment (PPE)	**Noncurrent liabilities**
Land	Long-term provisions
Buildings and improvements	Long-term debt
Equipment	
Less accumulated depreciation	
	Equity
Other assets	Capital stock
Intangible assets	Capital and other reserves
Less accumulated amortization	Retained earnings
Total noncurrent assets	*Total noncurrent liabilities and equity*
Total assets	**Total liabilities and shareholders' equity**

company (see next sub-section). PPE has a direct link with the supply chain infra-structure, production and logistics technologies and equipment applied.

Hot topic: working capital and supply chain finance (SCF)

Over the past few years, increasing attention to the topic of working capital can be noted. It has even led to the rise of an almost totally new field of expertise: supply chain finance. The first conference by the international Supply Chain Finance Community was organized as recently as 2013. It would be outside the scope of this book to go into too much detail about it, so for the moment we restrict ourselves to clarifying why attention to this subject has increased.

A company's net working capital (NWC) is defined as follows:

NWC = Inventories + Trade accounts receivable – Trade accounts payable

When expressed in days rather than in amounts of money, we speak about the cash-to-cash conversion cycle (CCC):

CCC = Days of inventory + Days of accounts receivable –
Days of accounts payable

Days of accounts receivable is sometimes called 'days of sales outstanding' (DSO), and days of accounts payable is sometimes called 'days of purchasing outstanding' (DPO).

As can be deduced from the formula, the way a supply chain is designed and oper-ated, the use of inventory, having shorter or longer delivery lead times, achieving better delivery reliability, agreeing shorter or longer payment terms or different Incoterms, and so on, generates more or less working capital.

For example, if I have high levels of inventory of finished goods in my company, then the money for this inventory has already been spent, because first I bought the components from my suppliers and then I spent money on producing the finished goods, but I have not had any return on it yet, because the goods are still in my in-ventory ready to be sold (this is also why we call inventories 'tied-up capital', that is, money invested, and I cannot use this money anymore because it's been used al-ready). On top of that, the invested money has to have come from somewhere, for example a loan or credit line from my bank, for which the bank will charge me an interest rate as well as fees for making the arrangement.

That's why finance people are becoming so much more involved in the supply chain, since decisions taken there will have a direct impact on the actions they have to consider to finance those activities.

For example, think of a leading supermarket chain. When people shop there for supplies, they normally pay on the spot, so the supermarket has a number of days of accounts receivable that is very low or even zero. Those same leading supermarkets normally put a lot of effort into optimizing their product portfolio in such a way that they maximize the sales per metre of shelf space, which also leads to focusing on products with high rotation, which in turn facilitates having a lower overall number of days of inventory. Finally, they usually pay their suppliers on the basis of fairly long payment terms, for example 90 or 120 days, leading to a reasonably high number of days of accounts payable. In this way, their working capital or cash-to-cash conversion cycle is as low as they can possibly get it (or sometimes for some retailers even negative): relatively low inventories + a relatively low number of receivables – a relatively high number = a relatively low amount of net working capital, reducing the need to spend money on financing.

The framework in Figure 2.4 shows a recent interpretation of supply chain finance (de Boer *et al*, 2015). Currently, much attention is focused on the operational level related to working capital, but the tactical and strategic levels are also getting more and more attention.

Integrated financial view: ROI

Bringing the income statement and balance sheet together, we arrive at an overall indicator that is widely used in companies in general, but also specifically in the supply chain area: *return on investment (ROI)*. In fact, different definitions of ROI exist, but for the purpose of this book we use one that reflects a clear relationship between supply chain decisions and financial impacts. Figure 2.5 contains elements from both the P&L statement (earn and spend) and the balance sheet (own and owe) in a company's annual report. In addition, it indicates how the supply chain can have an impact on the different elements.

Another interesting feature of ROI as an indicator is that it is applicable across industry sectors and across strategies. DeSmet (2018) highlights this point. He uses

Figure 2.4   Supply chain finance instruments

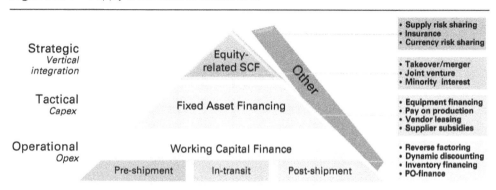

SOURCE de Boer *et al*, 2015

Figure 2.5   Supply chain and ROI

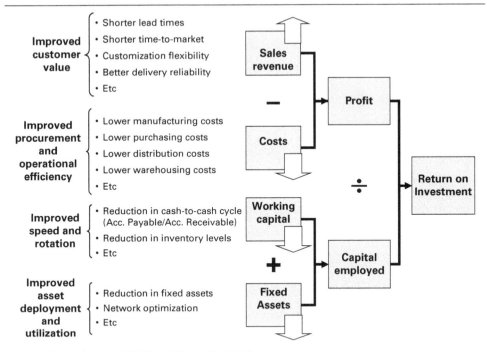

SOURCE after Rushton *et al* (2017) and Christopher (2016)

return on capital employed (ROCE) as an indicator, which is in fact comparable to ROI, and argues that different corporate strategies might have a very different operational focus, but that this should not affect ROI or ROCE in the end. In other words, there are different ways of being successful, if strategic choices are implemented coherently.

Given its relevance to the company and the supply chain, as well as the relative simplicity of the concept of ROI, in The Fresh Connection business simulation game it will be used as a central key performance indicator in Parts Two and Three.

EXERCISE 2.5
Explore annual reports and financial KPIs

Explore

Go online and find a few recent annual reports from a number of companies. It might be interesting to look at different companies from the same industry, as well as looking across different industries. Analyse the income statements and balance sheets and see how the numbers and ratios are similar or different between companies and industries.

For example, specifically compare:

- cost of goods sold as percentage of total revenue;
- number of days of inventory and/or inventory as percentage of revenue;
- the cash-to-cash conversion cycle;
- the PPE ratio (revenue / PPE);
- ROI or ROCE.

Try to find plausible explanations for the similarities and differences between these ratios in different companies. This exercise will give you a better understanding of the structure of the different businesses.

EXERCISE 2.6
Explore the financial impact of the supply chain

Explore

What do the indicators you analysed in the previous exercise tell you about the financial impact that the supply chain can have on a company?

The supply chain as part of a sustainable business

Outside-in: 'what' and 'how' together as part of the business model

Let's try to bring 'what?' and 'how?' as well as 'how much?' together in one integral view, so that the underlying connections and interdependencies between these different aspects become as clear as possible. In an earlier book I phrased it using a number of reflections (Weenk, 2013a):

> What is the promise to your clients ('what')? What are you particularly good at to fulfil the promise consistently, day-in day-out ('how')? Why do the answers to the previous questions form a winning combination, or in other words: why are you different [from]/ better than your competitors [leading to a profitable business ('how much?')]?

Since the above reflections were written, I have been concentrating on business models, using a framework called the 'business model canvas', as developed by Osterwalder and Pigneur (2010). According to Osterwalder and Pigneur, 'a business model describes the value an organization offers to various customers and portrays the capabilities and partners required for creating, marketing, and delivering this value and relationship capital with the goal of generating profitable and sustainable revenue streams'. In practice, the business model concept and the corresponding canvas provide an excellent basis to work from.

Osterwalder and Pigneur propose a canvas consisting of nine different areas, which together make up the business model. Figure 2.6 shows the canvas.

They refer to part of the canvas as the 'front stage' (this would be the 'what', on the right-hand side), and part as the 'back stage' (the 'how', on the left-hand side) (Figure 2.7).

Please note that the business model canvas is nicely coherent with the integral logistics concept introduced in the preface (Figure 0.2), whose different elements are discussed in detail in Chapters 2 and 3. The part referring to strategy, markets and value propositions can be related to the '*what?*' in the canvas, whereas physical infrastructure, processes, information and systems, and organization can be located on the side of the 'how?'.

Figure 2.6 Business model canvas

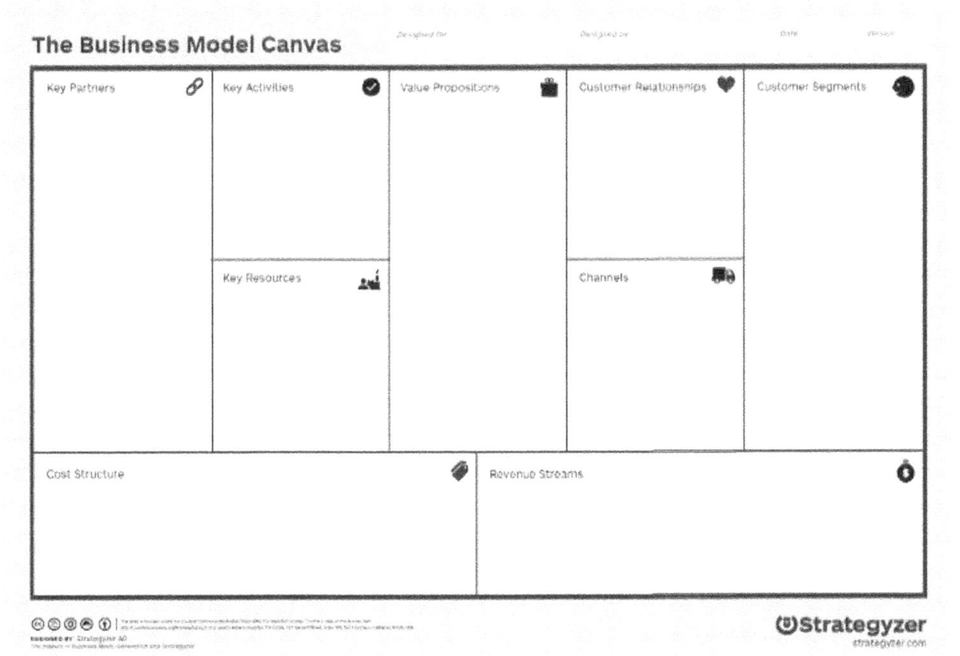

SOURCE Osterwalder and Pigneur (2010), www.strategyzer.com, under Creative Commons Attribution Share Alike

Figure 2.7 The 'what?', 'how?' and 'how much?' of business models

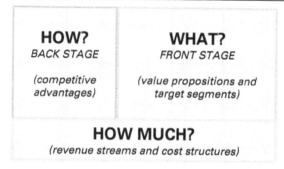

SOURCE After Osterwalder and Pigneur (2010)

In my opinion, there are various attractive dimensions to the business model canvas, which also makes it a fine tool from a supply chain point of view:

- It shows the connections between *what* and *how* in one integral simple image.
- Joint development of the canvas by different departments of a business forces them to discuss and create one 'agreed' version of the business model.
- The canvas allows for checking whether all elements of the *what* are indeed supported by elements of the *how*, thus testing the strength and coherence of the business model. At the same time, discussions might also raise relevant questions about elements of the business model which are perhaps not so clear ('*know what you don't know*').
- It allows people active in the supply chain area to position themselves in the wider scheme of things, ie clearly showing their role and purpose within the (strategic) context of the company.
- In addition, as a tool, it provides an excellent basis for effective discussions, since its empty boxes, which need to be filled with content, act almost like a checklist. In my experience, conversations consequently become much more to the point, leaving more time for searching for answers to the questions raised.

EXERCISE 2.7
Explore business models

Explore

For a few of the companies you chose for the previous exercises, try to develop a view of the entire business model using the business model canvas.

We will come back to the business model canvas in Part Three, in relation to The Fresh Connection.

Inside-out: the external environment

Apart from looking at a particular market and the industry in which a company is active, every business is also part of society at large, in which many things are happening that might have an impact in the shorter or longer term on any of the company's activities, and the supply chain is no exception. One of the most widely used frameworks for looking at the external environment is the PESTEL analysis. The results of this analysis lead to identification of the opportunities and threats a company might face in the future. Like so many things in business studies, PESTEL is an acronym, the elements of which are explained below, along with some generic examples relevant to the supply chain. Since we will deal with this topic more extensively later, at this stage we give just a brief introduction:

- P = *Political*, such as trade bans, tension in relationships between countries, the application of import/export quota etc.

- E = *Economic*, such as ups and downs in the economy, the economic growth or decline of countries or regions, cyclical industries that react strongly to upswings or downswings in the economy etc.

- S = *Societal/sociological*, such as the trend towards increasing individualism, generational trends such as the changing preferences of Generation X or millennials versus older generations, but also increasing environmental awareness or sensitivity to human rights in developing countries etc.

- T = *Technological*, such as the wider trend of Industry 4.0, new technologies appearing, blurring barriers between technological areas that used to be separate etc.

- E = *Ecological*, such as global warming, changing weather patterns, increasing issues with scarcity of raw materials, the 'plastic soup' in the oceans, recycling etc.

- L = *Legal*, such as stricter legal rules, eg regarding waste, pollution, total lifecycle responsibility, requirements for product registration etc.

For each of these factors, at a strategic level companies have the task of identifying relevant trends and developments and deciding what they are going to do about them. As we have said, this will in many cases ultimately affect the supply chain in some way or another, not only in terms of products, services and markets, but also in relationship to what a company can and maybe cannot do anymore in its supply chain. This will become all the clearer in the next two sub-sections, about the triple bottom line and risk and resilience.

The triple bottom line: how responsible is your supply chain?

Although arguably connected to a number of factors in the external environment, as might have become obvious through a PESTEL analysis, over recent decades corporate social responsibility (CSR) has gained a lot of attention. The key message of CSR is that companies should not only focus on maximizing profit, but at the same time behave as if they were responsible citizens.

John Elkington (1997) was allegedly the first to speak in this context of the 'triple bottom line' or TBL, or sometimes 3BL. The first bottom line is the one we have spoken about before, the financial bottom line, but Elkington suggested complementing these by a social bottom line as well as an ecological bottom line, thus coming to the three Ps of 'People, Planet, Profit'. We have already touched upon the relationship between the supply chain and finance, but it is easy to see that the supply chain has large potential connections to the People dimension (own workers, staff of suppliers, fair trade, local communities, people in society at large etc), as well as with the Planet dimension (use of natural resources, use of land, energy consumption, waste, pollution etc).

A more recent trend in the same vein, taking things one step further, is proposed by Kate Raworth (2017) in her recent book *Doughnut Economics*. After working at the United Nations for a number of years, she moved on: 'I left to fulfil a long-held ambition and worked with Oxfam for a decade. There I witnessed the precarious existences of women – from Bangladesh to Birmingham – employed at the sharp end of global supply chains.' This ultimately led her to create a new vision for economics, starting not from financial profit but from the human side, basically asking herself: if we want to improve human welfare, what would the economy need to do to help achieve that? From the collapse of the Rana Plaza Building in Bangladesh in 2013 to reports in 2017 that companies in the UK that manufacture clothes for high-street fashion retailers pay their factory workers only half the legal minimum wage, it seems that in company supply chains all is indeed not well and that the push for lower costs has had important negative side effects.

In terms of the supply chain, part of Raworth's original thinking, apart from the sourcing and off-shoring dimension, also pays much attention to concepts such as circularity: the reuse and recycling of materials. It is clear that such ideas might or will have lasting impacts on supply chains, from alternative raw materials down to return flows and changed activities in manufacturing (see Figure 2.8). Indeed, the *'circular economy'* and the related term *'cradle to cradle'* seem to be gaining a lot of attention recently in the wider supply chain community. Figure 2.8 shows the Ellen MacArthur Foundation Circular Economy model, which includes a number of corresponding concepts, building on work by Braungart and McDonough (2002).

Figure 2.8 'Butterfly diagram' of the circular economy

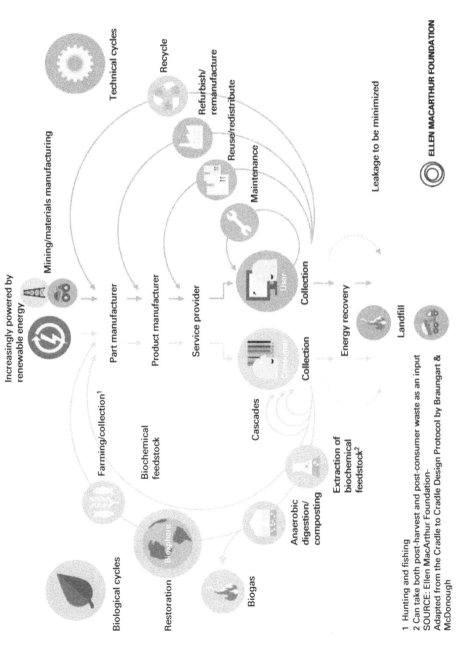

CIRCULAR ECONOMY - *an industrial system that is restorative by design*

Technical cycles

Recycle

Refurbish/
remanufacture

Reuse/redistribute

Maintenance

Leakage to be minimized

Mining/materials manufacturing

Increasingly powered by
renewable energy

Part manufacturer

Product manufacturer

Service provider

User

Collection

Consumer

Collection

Energy recovery

Landfill

Biological cycles

Restoration

Biosphere

Biogas

Farming/collection[1]

Biochemical
feedstock

Anaerobic
digestion/
composting

Extraction of
biochemical
feedstock[2]

Cascades

1 Hunting and fishing
2 Can take both post-harvest and post-consumer waste as an input
SOURCE: Ellen MacArthur Foundation-
Adapted from the Cradle to Cradle Design Protocol by Braungart &
McDonough

ELLEN MACARTHUR FOUNDATION

SOURCE Ellen MacArthur Foundation www.ellenmacarthurfoundation.org. Adapted from *Cradle to Cradle* (Braungart and McDonough, 2002)

Catherine Weetman, in her book on the circular economy for business and the supply chain, also builds on this concept. She argues that to facilitate true circularity, the design of products should already take return, reuse and recycling into consideration, thus leading for example to the concept of '*D4D – design for disassembly*'. Given the importance of the topic, she dedicates an entire chapter of her book to the 'design and supply chain', providing the basis for the many examples later in her book. 'The "design and supply chain" is fundamental to the circular economy, with major implications for business strategy and future success. It can reduce operating costs; buffer against resource risks (cost and security of supply); help create safer, healthier products; contribute to ecosystem restoration; and create desirable, well-designed and durable products for customers' (Weetman, 2017). Recall Simchi-Levi's connection between the development chain and the supply chain to see that Weetman's approach is perfectly coherent with that, taking it one step further, into the circular economy,

We will look more in detail at the triple bottom line and the circular economy in Part Three.

About things that can go wrong: risk and resilience

As tends to become clear from a thorough PESTEL analysis, the world is getting more and more complex, and this undoubtedly has an impact on company supply chains. This leads to the wider topic of supply chain risk management, which increasingly appears under the heading of *corporate resilience*, particularly in the notable work of Sheffi.

The first step in risk management is to identify the risks. Sheffi cites an interesting framework developed by Debra Elkins at General Motors, distinguishing four risk categories:

- *Financial vulnerability*, ranging from more internal policy factors such as debt and credit ratings and provisions for health care and pension plans to macroeconomic factors such as interest and currency fluctuations, economic recessions and so on.

- *Strategic vulnerability*, ranging from internal aspects such as ethics violations, budget overruns and ineffective planning to external factors such as attacks on the brand, new competitors, mergers and acquisitions, and so on.

- *Operations vulnerability*, ranging from internal risks such as theft, harassment and discrimination, the vulnerability of manufacturing equipment, and staff, to more external factors such as supplier or service provider failures.

- *Hazard vulnerability*, referring to both random and malicious disruptions, such as intentional damage to property, intentional land or water pollution, and terrorism as well as weather- or nature-related risks such as earthquakes, plagues of insect, flooding and so on.

Figure 2.9　Risk management dimensions: concentric vulnerability map

Financial vulnerability

Strategic vulnerability

Risks that tend to come from outside the organization

Risks that tend to come from within the organization

Hazard vulnerability

Operations vulnerability

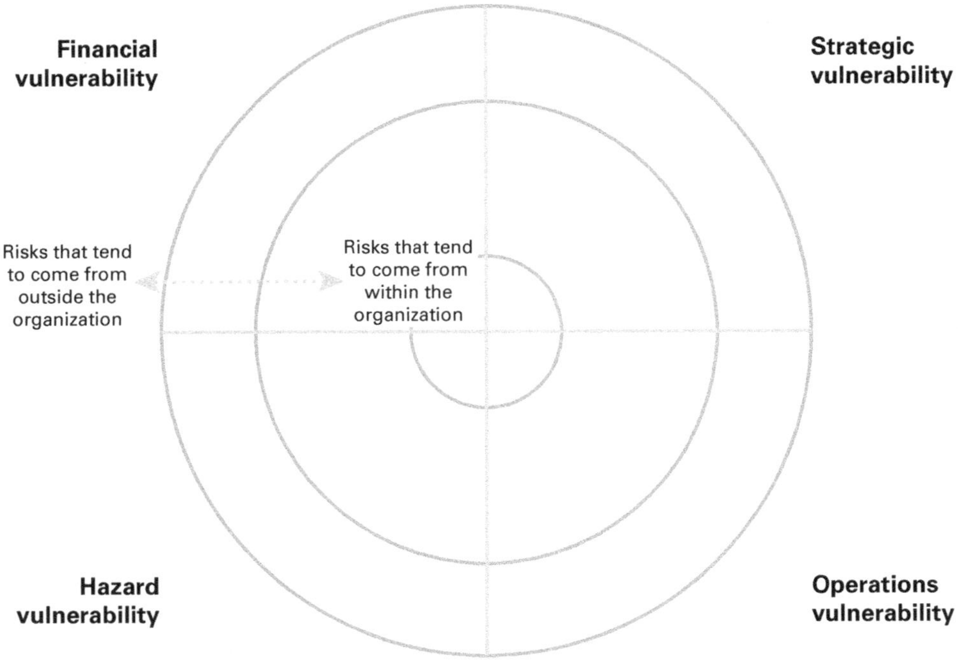

SOURCE adapted from Sheffi (2007)

These dimensions together lead to a diagram dubbed the 'concentric vulnerability map', in which the risks represented towards the outside of the circles are coming from outside the company, whereas the risks towards the middle come more from within the company (see Figure 2.9).

After identifying the risks, they need to be classified, allowing priority setting. Traditionally, the probability and the impact of risks are looked at when classifying risks. High-probability risks, which, in addition, have a high impact when they occur, should receive a higher priority when thinking about countermeasures and mitigations than lower-probability and/or lower-impact risks. Sheffi reports on another dimension from more advanced risk management practice, which he calls 'detectability':

> Some types of disruptions can be forecasted or detected well before they have an impact, while others hit without warning. Detectability adds a time dimension to the classification of disruptions and is defined as the time between knowing that a disruption event will take place and the first impact. Note that the detectability of an event can be positive (detection before the impact), zero (realization at the instant of occurrence), or even negative (detection after the disruption has taken place). (Sheffi, 2015)

Risks are part of (corporate) life and companies will have to make choices about where to put their priorities. We will return to this topic later in Part Three.

Summary

The objective of this chapter has been to explore the fundamentals related to the business dimension of the supply chain, in other words the role that the supply chain plays within the context of the entire business and its financials, as well as the potential impacts from the external environment (Figure 2.10). In the next chapter we will continue the journey of exploring the fundamentals, now shifting attention to the 'technical' dimension of the supply chain, zooming in on the details of the many different building blocks it has.

Figure 2.10   Recap of topics of Chapter 2, the business dimension of the supply chain

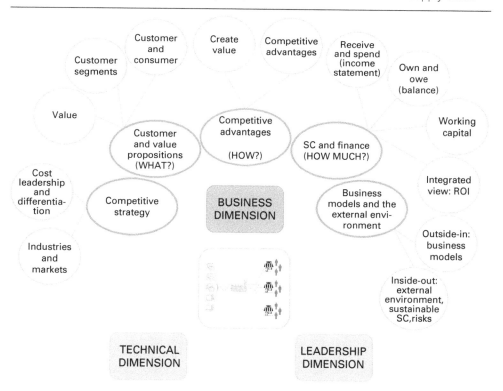

Supply chain   03

The technical dimension

From the topics of the business dimension of the supply chain, as discussed in the previous chapter, the company's direction is now clear, product–market combinations have been decided and the way to compete against the other incumbents is defined. Now it's time to work out the technical details of the supply chain. In this chapter, we are going to explore the following topics more deeply:

- typologies, or archetypes, of supply chain strategies;
- the physical infrastructure (push and pull, facilities and transportation, outsourcing and collaboration);
- planning and control (processes, forecasting, inventories, production);
- information and systems, organizational aspects.

From corporate strategy to supply chain strategies: typologies

Predictability and volatility drive supply chain design: efficient or responsive

You might have heard the term *efficient supply chain*, or mention of 'lean', 'low cost' or 'cost-driven' supply chains. At the other end, we have *responsive supply chains*, which some people might call 'agile' or 'flexibility-driven' supply chains. By the way, please note that the term 'lean' in the context of a typology of a supply chain strategy isn't the exact equivalent of the same term in the context of the 'lean management' approach, which is more about a process-oriented methodology for continuous improvement (and in fact applicable within the context of any supply chain strategy).

Arguably, a cost-driven supply chain is very different from a responsive supply chain, even though in both cases there will probably be production, as well as inventories stored in warehouses and trucks driving around to deliver things. But the way they are structured physically, the rules that apply in planning and control, the way systems are used or how the organization is set up are probably very different in one case versus the other.

The way we use the different building blocks of the supply chain will to a large extent depend on the chosen company strategy. If my customers want high delivery reliability from me, I might want to decide to keep slightly higher levels of inventory so that I always have product available, or invest in very fast production machinery which allows for quick make-to-order policies. On the other hand, if my customers prefer low cost over reliability, then this picture will obviously change, the focus shifting to producing larger production batches or buying larger quantities from cheaper suppliers.

So, the first thing we need to do is to establish a clear link between corporate strategy and supply chain strategies. A famous and ground-breaking article addressing this topic was written by Fisher (1997), who basically took a product-based view, stating that some products have more unpredictable demand, either because they are newer to the market and their success has not been proven yet, or for example because they have more variety in their final versions since there are many different features to choose from, causing many different possible combinations, or because there are many product promotions taking place in the retail channels. Fisher coined the term *innovative products* for those.

Other products have more stable and therefore predictable demand, because they have already been around for some time and demand is pretty much known, or because they have fewer features to choose from, or fewer promotions. Fisher called those the *functional products*. Fisher's point was that innovative products require a different supply chain approach from the functional products. He labelled the two extremes *physically efficient supply chains* for the functional products and *market-responsive supply chains* for the innovative products.

The world is changing: more refined supply chain typologies are required

Since Fisher's article, many other scholars have built on this first concept of supply chain differentiation. Chopra and Meindl (2016) also follow the terminology proposed by Fisher in terms of efficient or responsive supply chain. However, citing also the work of Lee (2002), they have widened the scope of the uncertainty dimension from pure demand uncertainty or variability of a product to include supply uncertainty, caused by machine breakdowns, lack of supplier reliability, lack of supplier and/or production flexibility, use of immature technologies and so on. They speak in this context about achieving strategic fit between demand and supply uncertainty on the one hand and supply chain capabilities expressed on the responsiveness spectrum on the other (see Figure 3.1).

Christopher (2016), besides a variation on the abovementioned strategies dealing with demand and supply uncertainty, presents another dimension to take into consideration: demand volume. He then comes up with a framework that in terms of supply chain strategies stays within the spectrum of efficient supply chains versus

Figure 3.1 Supply chain differentiation based on demand uncertainty and supply uncertainty

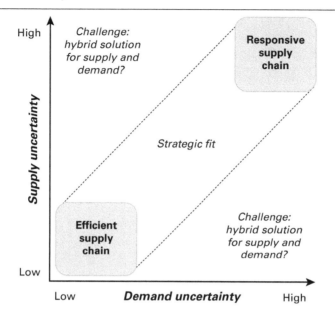

SOURCE adapted from Chopra and Meindl (2016)

Figure 3.2 Supply chain differentiation based on demand volume and demand variability

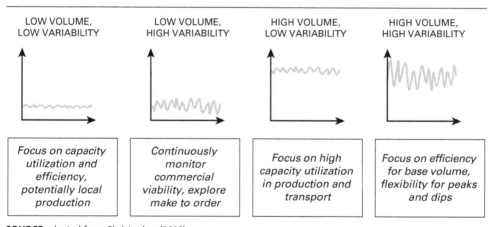

SOURCE adapted from Christopher (2016)

responsive supply chains, but seen from another perspective, as can be appreciated in Figure 3.2, which is an adaptation of Christopher's work.

Another interesting and slightly more recent development, building further on frameworks and the principal supply chain strategies, was developed by Pérez (2013) in his book *Supply Chain Roadmap: Aligning supply chain with business strategy*. He proposes a step-by-step approach, including the use of a number of predefined templates, with a number of elements similar to those used in the other approaches we have seen so far. This leads to what he calls the 'business framework', consisting of the *sourcing view* (sourcing complexity and the impact on the economics of sourcing), the *technology* view (technological factors and the economics of manufacturing and/or assembly) and the *demand* view (customer behaviours and the economics of the target market). Pérez defines six major supply chain models (he refers to them as *archetypes*) as a starting point: Efficient, Fast, Continuous replenishment, Agile, LeAgile and Flexible.

Gattorna follows a similar terminology, but taking into consideration a few additional variations: collaborative, lean, agile, campaign and fully flexible. He goes into depth when describing the different typologies, dedicating a full chapter to each one. A very interesting addition by Gattorna to general thinking about supply chain typologies is that, for him, these configurations will have to become even more dynamic in the future due to increasing volatility, ultimately impacting not only the supply chain area but the entire firm. In his most recent book, *Dynamic Supply Chains*, he presents a compelling company-wide view, with supply chains as an integral part of it (Gattorna, 2015).

Finally, a more recent contribution by Martijn Lofvers links supply chain typologies directly to the corporate strategies as defined by Treacy and Wiersema, which were touched upon briefly in Chapter 2. This 'strategy compass' can be seen in Figure 3.3, including some examples of companies that fit with certain supply chain strategies (Lofvers, pers. comm., 2017).

For the sake of argument, as well as in order to make things manageable, and because they are in fact the cornerstones of the overall typology framework and therefore very important for any supply chain student and practitioner to know about, for the remainder of the book we will work on the basis of the two extremes that all of the aforementioned approaches have in common: the *cost-driven* and the *responsive* supply chain. We should then be in a position to define what a cost-driven supply chain or a responsive supply chain could actually look like, a topic we will work out more actively in Part Two.

Decision making at various levels: strategic, tactical, operational

Before taking a more detailed look at the technical building blocks of the supply chain, I would like to go back to a topic that's been touched upon both explicitly and more implicitly on a number of occasions, which is that decision making takes place on different levels. In this case, we are referring to the strategic, tactical and operational levels.

Many of the topics and decisions mentioned in this chapter on the technical dimension of supply chain, following the structure of the integral logistics concept, are of a more strategic nature if a company is in the process of defining a new supply

Figure 3.3   The strategy compass

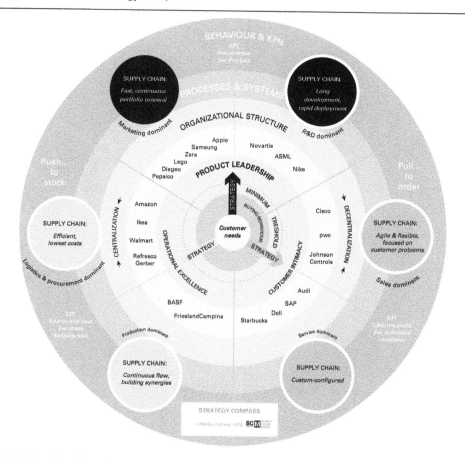

SOURCE courtesy of Martijn Lofvers. © Martijn Lofvers, 2017

chain, or redefining an existing one. In most cases, the decisions to be made involve building a new solution that should hold for at least a number of years.

Once the new or redesigned supply chain starts operations, the decision frame becomes more tactical and operational, and time horizons shorten accordingly (Figure 3.4).

In the gameplay using The Fresh Connection, starting in Part Two, you will be focusing on making strategic and tactical decisions, since the operational decisions and execution will be taken care of inside the simulation engine, within the tactical parameters you have set.

But now, let's first look in more detail at the building blocks of the supply chain, which were introduced briefly in Chapter 1. Most of the concepts that will be re-ferred to can be considered relatively standard supply chain theory, that is, the

Figure 3.4   Supply chain decisions (strategic, tactical, operational)

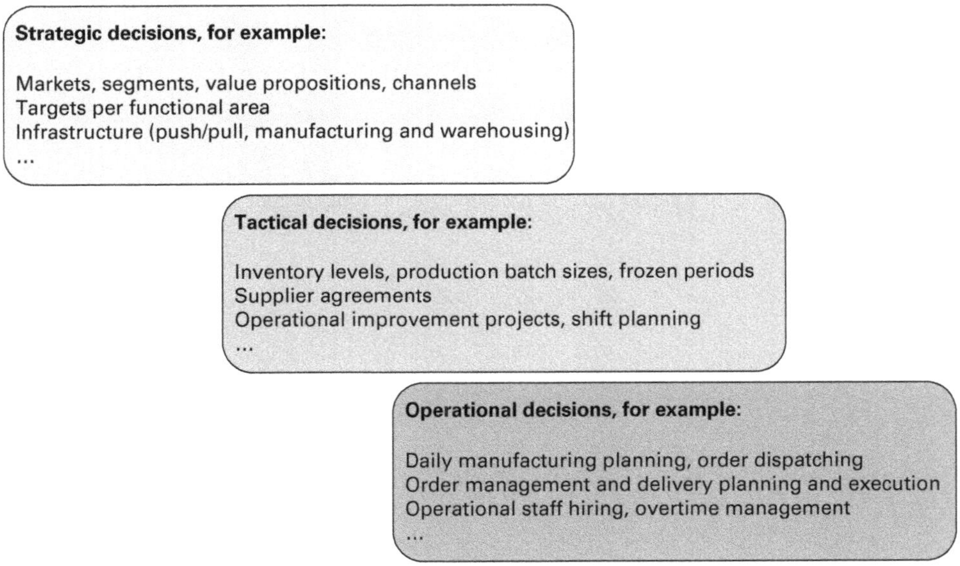

Strategic decisions, for example:

Markets, segments, value propositions, channels
Targets per functional area
Infrastructure (push/pull, manufacturing and warehousing)
...

Tactical decisions, for example:

Inventory levels, production batch sizes, frozen periods
Supplier agreements
Operational improvement projects, shift planning
...

Operational decisions, for example:

Daily manufacturing planning, order dispatching
Order management and delivery planning and execution
Operational staff hiring, overtime management
...

'fundamentals', and can be found in more detail in most of the supply chain text-books mentioned already on a number of occasions (Rushton *et al*, 2017; Christopher, 2016; Chopra and Meindl, 2016; Simchi-Levi *et al*, 2009; Visser and van Goor, 2011; Gattorna, 2015). Where there is a need to reference a specific concept or framework from one of the textbooks, this will be mentioned explicitly.

The structure we follow in the coming paragraphs is that of the integral logistics concept, introduced in Chapter 1 (Figure 1.2). The same structure and items will come back in Part Two: Mastering the fundamentals, in connection with The Fresh Connection gameplay, as well as in Part Three: Imagining beyond the fundamentals, using The Fresh Connection as a case example.

Physical infrastructure or network: push/pull, facilities and transportation

Once a company has decided which customer segments it wants to target, and knows what the corresponding value propositions are, including the specific products, strategies for growth, geographical expansion, changes to the product/service portfolio and so on, it needs to think about the physical infrastructure to support the plans. The final setup of a physical infrastructure consists of a number of interrelated items, which will be dealt with in the following sub-sections.

Products: physical characteristics and the development chain

Product characteristics play an important role in the setup of a supply chain. It's easy to see, for example, that the sourcing of raw materials, manufacturing and the transportation of plastic soccer balls for small children, to be sold to toy stores even without packaging materials, is very different from the supply chain for dangerous liquid chemicals, or for complex technological products such as cars, or large and heavy products such as cranes.

From a logical perspective, there are three different steps in the sequence of getting from idea to production: the first is product design, in which the specifications of the product are defined. This is followed by process design, in which it is defined how the designed product can be best produced. In this stage, decisions are made about which production process types to apply (job shop production, batch production, continuous process production and so on), leading to decisions about types of machinery and human labour as well as detailed production process flow design. This is then followed by the operational execution step; in other words, the product and process designs are put into daily use in manufacturing and distribution.

Besides their logical sequence, it is not strictly necessary that one step needs to be 100 per cent finished before the next one can start. The so-called concept of 'concurrent engineering' exploits this idea: I can already start making my first sketches for the production process event even though the design of the product I will be producing hasn't been finalized.

Following the logic of the steps mentioned above, a first defining factor of what our supply chain should be like is determined by the product characteristics, such as:

- size/volume (large, small);
- weight (heavy, light);
- value (cheap, expensive);
- fragility (easy to break);
- type of material (solid, liquid, gas, dangerous or not);
- perishability (for example related to shelf life);
- complexity (number of components, 'Bill of Materials – BoM');
- and so on.

A specific concept related to the above is the 'value density' of products, the value in money of product per cubic metre (see Figure 3.5). This is especially relevant in transportation, warehousing and inventory policies. For a cheap, large product, the logistics priorities will be different from those for a small, expensive product. Value density will also explicitly come back later in Part Two.

Figure 3.5   Value density of products and supply chain priorities

	HIGH VALUE, LARGE ITEMS	**HIGH VALUE, SMALL ITEMS**
High	Focus on delivery speed and inventory rotation, optimization of warehousing space, transportation and handling	Focus on delivery speed and inventory rotation
	(industrial equipment, cars, flatscreen TVs, etc)	(shaving knives, smartphones, electronics, cosmetics, etc)
	LOW VALUE, LARGE ITEMS	**LOW VALUE, SMALL ITEMS**
	Focus on delivery frequency, optimization of warehousing space, transportation and handling	Focus on Availability
Low	(washing machines, refrigerators, furniture, etc)	(toilet paper, shampoo, potato crisps, mineral water, etc)

Value per m³ (vertical axis)

Number of items per m³ — Low ... High (horizontal axis)

SOURCE (after Visser and van Goor, 2011)

A item among the abovementioned product characteristics is related to the bill of materials (BoM): the components out of which a product is made. For example, a chair might be made from one seat, one back, and four legs, whereas the seat might consist of one piece of wood, one leather cushion, and so on. The reason to mention this here is twofold:

- First, the BoM defines whether assembly is needed for a certain product, and if so, how complex the assembly is, and in which sequence the product needs to be assembled. As such, it is the basis for the time-phased sourcing of components and planning for timely delivery as well as the assembly activities.

- Second, there has been increasing attention paid to the relationship between product design and the logistics aspects of the product, summarized under the term 'design for logistics', with the objective of simplifying product architectures while increasing flexibility for late-stage customization.

As touched upon briefly earlier on, Simchi-Levi (Simchi-Levi *et al*, 2009; Simchi-Levi, 2010) speaks in this context about the development chain of new products, with product architecture (BoM) being part of that. One ongoing trend, which began some time ago, was the push for a smart modular design for products. The sourcing structure in the car industry, with Tier-1 suppliers providing modules and Tier-2 suppliers delivering sub-modules or components to the Tier-1 suppliers, is a clear example of this. Product modularization has a number of advantages to facilitate such supply chain structures:

- First, it reduces complexity during final assembly because now a relatively small number of different modules will have to be put together, rather than individual components. In a way, part of the complexity will be moved up the chain, because assembly will already be done at the Tier-1 supplier upstream.

- Second, it reduces the sourcing and planning of incoming materials, because the number of modules is lower than the number of components, so fewer items will have to be planned and fewer suppliers will need to be managed directly.

- Third, if the modules are designed cleverly, and made up of relatively few sub-modules, many combinations of different finished goods can be created. Since inventory management now takes place at the modular level and not at the finished goods level, less risk is incurred.

Arguably, one of the better examples of exploiting modularity and the principles of design for logistics in the development chain is Swedish furniture retailer IKEA. In terms of product design, IKEA allegedly tell their designers to ensure that various components of different variations of a piece of furniture fit well together, so that, for example, with two types of seat, three types of leg and three types of back, 18 different chairs can be made.

Supported by their business model, in which customers themselves actually assemble the final products in their own homes, this allows IKEA to forecast demand at the module level (2 + 3 + 3 = 8 modules), rather than for each of the 18 possible chair types individually. The same goes for storage: only 8 modules in the store warehouse, rather than 18 different chairs. Thus, modularity of the product design, in the case of IKEA a very deliberate design policy, allows for 'late customization', as well as for space savings. In addition, IKEA designers make sure that the individual modules or components are as flat as possible, enabling transportation without unnecessary space inside the packaging.

EXERCISE 3.1
Explore the development chain and design for logistics

Explore

Of a few companies you chose for the exercises in the previous chapter, try to think of examples of how the principles of the 'development chain' and 'design for logistics' might work.

Please note that linked to the topic of design for logistics and the development chain, but then extended to sustainability and the circular economy, is the concept of D4D – design for disassembly, mentioned in Chapter 2. Not only should a company find smart ways of putting together many product variations from a limited number of components or modules, but the later stages of return, disassembly, reuse and recycling should also be considered.

Push/pull: economies of scale versus market flexibility

Once products and product designs are clear, the next decision has to do with the concepts of *push* and *pull*, as expressed by the *Customer–Order Decoupling Points* (CODPs), Hoekstra and Romme (1993), and also to be found in other textbooks such as Rushton *et al* (2017)). Or, as some people say, the *order-penetration point* or the *push/pull barrier* (remember the discussion about the importance of clarifying definitions from Chapter 1!).

Instead of using the term CODP, as suggested by Hoekstra and Romme, in practice most people are more familiar with the names or the acronyms of the different CODPs. Following the example in the simplified Figure 3.6:

- *CODP 1*: Make to local stock (MTS)
- *CODP 2*: Make to central stock (MTS)
- *CODP 3*: Make to order (MTO).

The difference between CODPs 1 and 2 can serve as an example of the concept of '*risk pooling*' as described by Simchi-Levi (Simchi-Levi *et al*, 2009; Simchi-Levi, 2010), who states that 'demand variability is reduced if one aggregates demand across locations'. Because of this reduced variability, for example, less safety stock is needed. The application of risk pooling implies centralized inventory (CODP 2).

Hoekstra and Romme, having a background in Dutch tech firm Philips, used an industry in which assembly plays a major part as the basis for their work, so their proposed terminology obviously reflects that particular background (they actually positioned 'assemble to order' (ATO) between CODPs 2 and 3 in Figure 3.6). Since then, other diagrams expressing the same principle have been suggested by others, introducing, for example, terms such as 'make to forecast' (MTF) and 'engineer to order' (ETO). These terms were later expanded further to include the concept of postponement, which has gained a lot of popularity given the potential for supply chain optimization it promises.

Postponement can be explained as being a variation on ATO, but with specific customization of product taking place at a very late stage in the chain, normally

Figure 3.6 Customer–order decoupling points (CODPs)

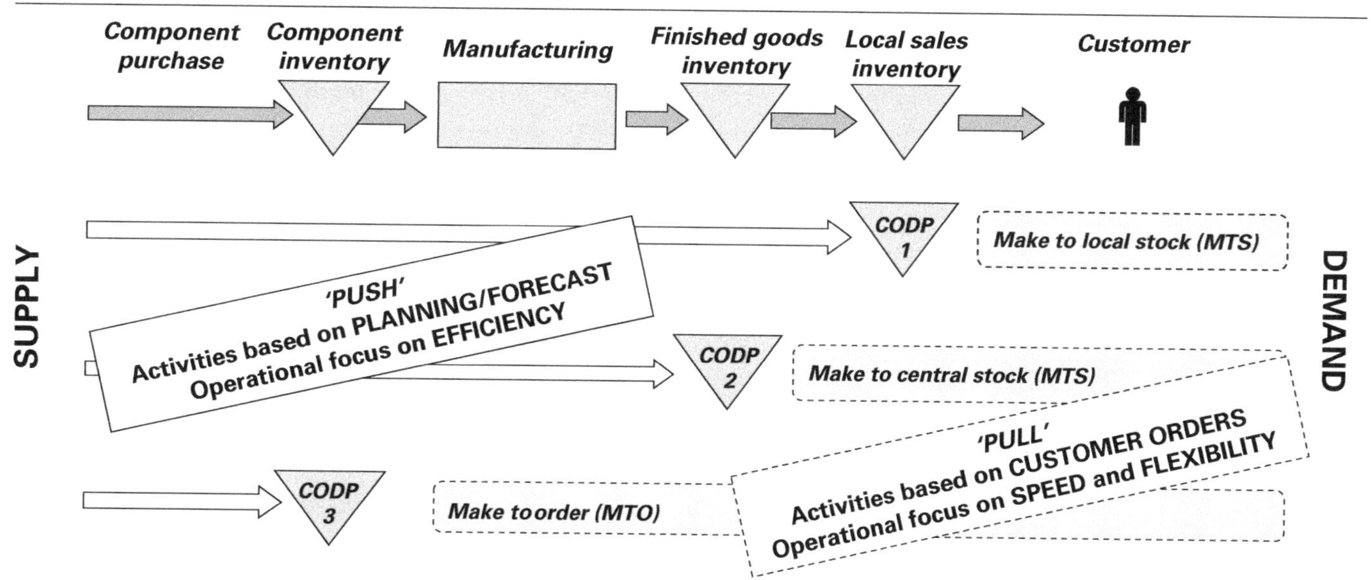

DEMAND

SUPPLY

Component purchase | Component inventory | Manufacturing | Finished goods inventory | Local sales inventory | Customer

Make to local stock (MTS)

Make to central stock (MTS)

'PULL'
Activities based on CUSTOMER ORDERS
Operational focus on SPEED and FLEXIBILITY

Make to order (MTO)

'PUSH'
Activities based on PLANNING/FORECAST
Operational focus on EFFICIENCY

CODP 1

CODP 2

CODP 3

SOURCE adapted from Hoekstra and Romme (1993) and Rushton et al (2017)

somewhere between the original CODPs 1 and 2. A typical example would be bringing components or semi-finished products, manufactured according to the forecast requirements for those components or products, to a specific region, and then assembling those into customized customer- or country-specific finished goods as soon as a specific order comes in.

The concept of postponement is very powerful, for example in cases where a limited number of components can be used in different combinations to form a wide variety of finished goods, because of the aforementioned principle that forecasting demand at the component level is less complex than forecasting demand at the finished goods level (and linking back to the 'design for logistics' principles at the same time). This supposes, at least partially, that the time needed for the activity of customization, be it assembly, packaging or similar, fits within the lead times the customer expects.

Take the example of a certain non-prescription drug, or so-called over-the-counter (OTC) drug, sold in pharmacies worldwide. The pills are packaged in blister packs, and then, together with a brochure in the local language, they go into a box, again with local branding and/or language on the box. Traditional concepts were to forecast local demand and have inventories in each country to supply to pharmacies in different countries. However, since the medicine and the blister packs are the same for all the countries in the world, and only brochures and packaging are country-specific, it could also be decided to have a regional stock of already blistered pills, plus a separate stock of local boxes and brochures. Since boxes and brochures are relatively cheap in comparison to the medicine, and since the activity of bundling blister, brochure and box can be done relatively quickly and cheaply, this activity can be postponed until there is more certainty, or even a fixed customer order from a specific country.

Returning to the topic of physical infrastructure, the relevance of the CODP concept lies in the fact that a decision to choose a CODP lays the foundation for the integral logistics concept; for a start, it determines the physical infrastructure. For example, if make to order is my chosen CODP, I wouldn't need any central, regional or local finished goods warehouses in my network because I would ship out the product to the customer as soon as it had been produced. Also, it defines the starting point for the planning and control approach, because the medium-term materials requirement forecasting would need to be at the component level, rather than at the finished goods level. The operational focus of activities upstream of the CODP would normally be on scale and efficiency, and the operational focus downstream of the CODP would normally be on speed and flexibility.

In other words, determining the CODP is a major design choice for any supply chain.

EXERCISE 3.2

Explore customer–order decoupling points (push/pull)

Explore

It can be argued that in an 'ideal world', CODP 3 (make to order) or even a potential CODP 4 (buy and make to order) would be the perfect option; there is no risk of getting stuck with an excess stock of components, nor would finished goods exist, since activities start only when an order has been received from the customer. However, this ideal scenario is in many cases not possible. What reasons can you come up with that 'push' companies in the direction of having to choose CODPs further downstream than CODP 3? Try to find at least five different reasons.

Facilities: the warehousing and manufacturing hubs in a network

Once the CODP has been determined, the physical infrastructure can be designed. In terms of facilities, we need to think about production or assembly plants, warehouses, and transportation hubs such as ports and airports or cross-docks. Decisions for each of these types of facility include, for example:

- number of facilities;
- locations;
- physical sizes;
- operational capacities in terms of volume to be handled;
- machines or equipment technologies to be used;
- human resources availability required, and the desired number of working hours;
- whether the operation should be in-house or outsourced.

Decisions about the reliability of the estimated volumes coming out of the facilities could even be entered into the equation, independent of whether they are owned or outsourced, but considering factors such as technology maturity, the political situation, the risk of strikes, the qualifications of the labour force and so on.

Obviously, many of these factors are very much geographically determined, even sometimes influenced by specific local circumstances such as legal regulations, trade blocs and government subsidies. Cost calculations can be made for many of the dimensions of the available alternatives, allowing for comparison of the different scenarios. Most likely, a number of qualitative arguments also exist, which do enter into the equation.

EXERCISE 3.3
Explore possibilities for capacity expansion

Explore

Imagine that your company, on the basis of future expectations, would require additional manufacturing capacity. What would be the options you think exist for providing such additional capacity?

What are the pros and cons related to each of the options?

Which of those pros and cons can be quantified and which not? How time consuming would quantification be? Where would inputs need to come from? How reliable would they be?

What does that tell you about the final decision?

Transportation: the spokes between the hubs

At the same time as looking at the facilities, the available options for transportation need to be investigated. In the end, if the facilities are the '*hubs*' in the network, whereas transportation represents the '*spokes*', so both dimensions are directly connected, and it could be that the (in-)availability of certain options in transportation might have an impact on the choices of facilities and vice versa.

Decisions need to be made about modes of transportation, taking into consideration their respective characteristics in terms of capacity, speed, security, flexibility and costs. Decisions also need to be made about making transportation an in-house activity or whether it's preferable or even necessary to outsource. Like facilities, many of these factors are very much geographically determined. Transportation infrastructures, the available alternative transport modes, specific legislation and transportation industries might vary a lot between different countries.

EXERCISE 3.4
Explore transportation in a geographical context

Explore

For a number of different countries, preferably on different continents, analyse the topic of transportation. For example, take a look at:

- population density across the country, indicating distribution patterns;
- available infrastructure (roads, rail, river, sea);
- available transport modes (road, rail, ship, air);
- maturity of the service provider industry.

What conclusions can you draw from the comparison?

Forward and backward integration: outsourcing and external collaboration

When deciding on facilities and transportation, one aspect that needs to be covered is whether to outsource a certain activity. This is the famous make-or-buy decision, valid for manufacturing and storage as well as transportation, freight forwarding, distribution and logistics services.

EXERCISE 3.5
Explore outsourcing

Explore

What pros and cons can you list in terms of outsourcing to a third party? Make separate lists of pros and cons for:

- manufacturing;
- storage;
- transportation;
- freight forwarding services;
- distribution and logistics services.

What differences and similarities have you found?

In the exploratory exercise, you will have found a number of arguments that appear under the pros as well as the cons, the exact answer depending on the specific product or service and the company considering outsourcing. For most products or services, the decision whether to outsource is a very strategic one, not least because the implications can be long-lasting, meaning that the consequences of the decision will make themselves felt for a number of years. This is in terms not only of financial consequences, but also specific competencies will need to be built up (managing a factory is not the same as managing a supplier contract and relationship), and changing back to the initial situation if things don't turn out so well is not that easy.

Once the decision has been made, the company needs to decide how to manage the relationship. Not all components are equally important, nor are all supplier markets the same, and in managing the supply we obviously want to spend our time and effort where it makes most sense. Kraljic, in a classic article written in 1983, suggested a framework for segmenting suppliers and defining supply and supplier management policies accordingly. Over time, different variations of the initial concept have been suggested, based on different criteria, although the original thinking that segmentation makes sense because different items require different policies has remained. See Figure 3.7 for an example.

The diagram distinguishes between the importance of purchasing for the business (cost of materials versus total cost; value-added profile; profitability profile; and so on) and the complexity of the supplier market (supply monopoly or oligopoly conditions; pace of technological advance; entry barriers; logistics cost and complexity; and so on). Simply put: the business impact of a certain component or service versus the supply risk.

Figure 3.7   Supply and supplier policy matrix

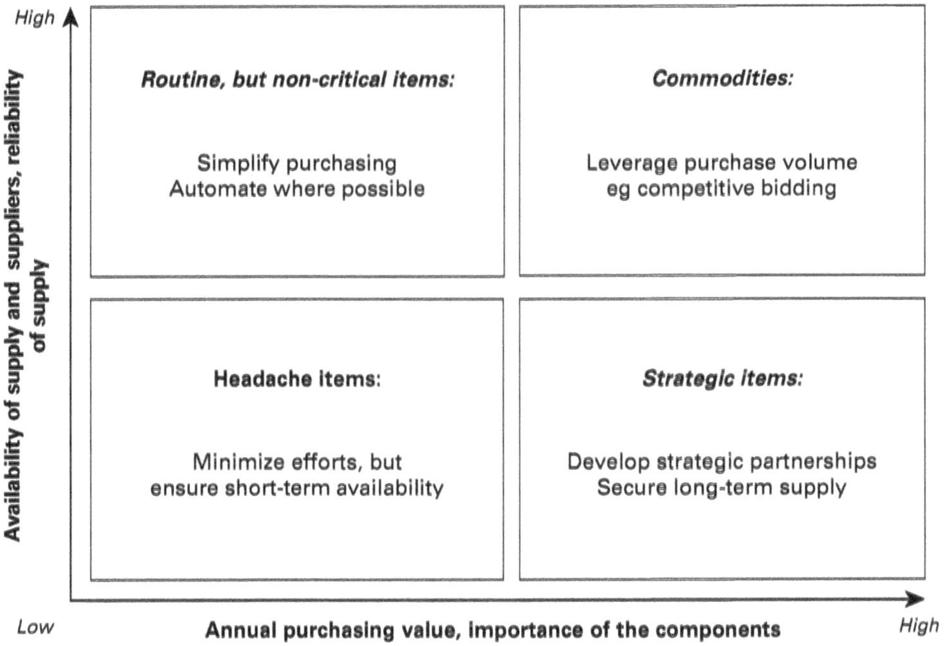

SOURCE after Kraljic (1983) and Rushton *et al* (2017)

The different quadrants suggest applying different policies. For example, on the supply of components that represent only a very small cost compared to the total expenditure of the company and that can be bought anywhere (business impact low and supply risk low), you would want to minimize your management attention. On the other extreme, if you spend a lot of money on a certain component or service and there are only a few suppliers in the market that can do the job for you, then you want to treat that relationship in a special way, because the breakdown risk is just too high. So once again, segmentation is very helpful to establish priorities for putting your time and effort where it makes most sense.

Please note that the quadrant of high value, high risk would be directly linked to the key partners area of the business model canvas we looked at earlier.

EXERCISE 3.6
Explore strategic long-term relationships

Explore

What elements would you see as possible parts of a 'strategic, long-term relationship' with a key partner? What activities or projects would you propose that go beyond pure and simple buying and selling?

What costs and benefits would you expect?

What would be the implications of the proposed initiatives in terms of human resources on both sides? How much time do you think the implementation of such projects would require?

Network design: connecting the dots

The activity of defining the optimal infrastructure for a specific supply chain is normally referred to as *(distribution or logistics) network design*. Nowadays, with the help of sophisticated software, different network structures can be modelled and the impact of different scenarios, in terms of, for example, costs and delivery service levels, can be analysed. Parameters to play with are number and location as well as sizes and costs of facilities, transport modes, inventory levels, demand volumes and so on.

It is vital to keep an end-to-end holistic view on total costs and resulting service levels. This implies that the scope of supply chain activities included in the network study should be sufficiently wide to cover this. In this context, sometimes the terms *total cost of ownership* (TCO) or *total cost to serve* (TCS) are used. In most cases,

Figure 3.8 Network optimization of different scenarios with advanced software

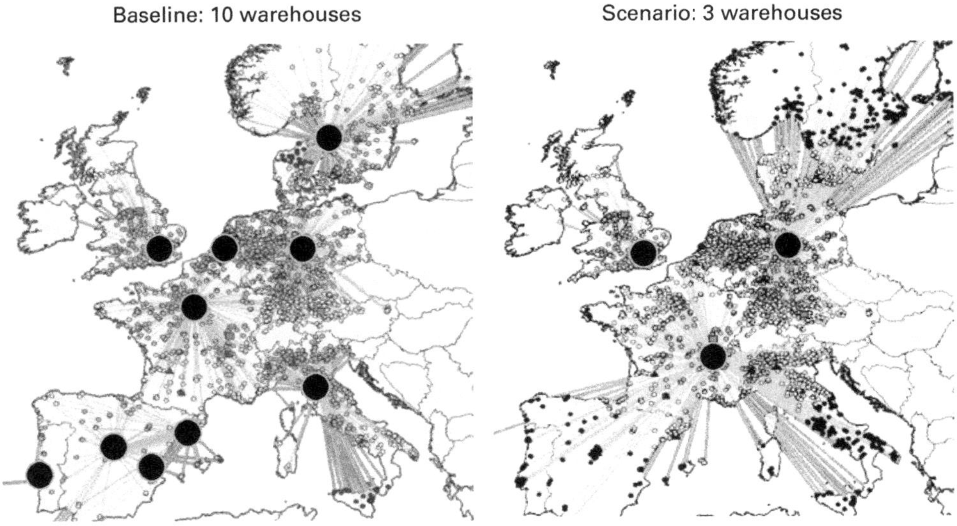

Baseline: 10 warehouses   Scenario: 3 warehouses

SOURCE from own project using advanced network optimization software

these refer to including not only goods-related operationally oriented costs such as transportation and warehousing (space and people), but also inventory-related costs (financing, insurance, security, obsolescence), overhead costs, production-related costs, and even costs beyond the boundary of the company, for example costs at suppliers (material costs, space costs, transportation costs and so on).

Obviously, widening the scope in this way calls for much more information and probably slows down the process of modelling, but the alternative is simple: missing part of the picture, which is fine if it's a deliberate choice, taking into consideration the associated risks. The final decision about scope, in the light of complexity, level of detail, information availability, resources required and time pressure, is therefore a typical trade-off.

As a last step in this part of the chapter, let's try to get a grasp of the challenge of dealing with the complexity and the need for alignment in relation to the elements of the supply chain strategy and the physical infrastructure we have just seen. Using Figure 3.9, you can express your thoughts on who is involved (directly or indirectly) in the various decisions regarding strategy and infrastructure.

Once filled out, what conclusions can you draw from Figure 3.9? What does it tell you in terms of interdependencies, in terms of the complexities of alignment? Which potential solutions would you see dealing with this in the best possible way? Write down your notes; we will get back to the topic later in Chapter 10.

Now that the network structure is defined, the appropriate setup for planning and control can be decided upon.

Figure 3.9   Matrix of strategy and infrastructure decisions and functional departments

	SALES	OPS	SCM	PURCH	HR	FIN	...
Supply chain strategy (typology)							
Decoupling points (push/pull)							
Facilities (warehousing/ production)							
Sourcing & outsourcing							
Transportation							
Network design							

Planning and control: processes, forecasting, inventories, production

Getting things done via supply chain processes: O2C, P2P, D2S

Supply chain activities consist of many different steps. Normally, those steps are clustered and organized into 'logical' processes. How many processes are distinguished in a company and what names they have is very different from one company to another. However, there are some main processes that seem to be becoming part of 'standard' process nomenclature. Also, companies that work with one of the larger enterprise software systems such as SAP or Oracle tend to adopt the terminology of the processes as named in the IT system.

The main high-level supply chain processes at the tactical and operational level are:

- *Purchase-to-Pay* (or Procure-to-Pay, or P2P), which contains the steps involved from the moment we send a purchase order to our supplier to the moment the corresponding payment is made.

- *Order-to-Cash* (or O2C), which contains the steps involved from the moment an order is received from our customer to the moment we receive payment from them.

- *Demand-to-Supply* (or D2S), which contains the steps involved from forecasting future demand to the moment the materials are ready to be shipped to the customer. Sometimes also referred to as Forecast to Fulfil (F2F) or Forecast to Delivery (F2D).

Figure 3.10   High-level overview of the main tactical and operational supply chain processes

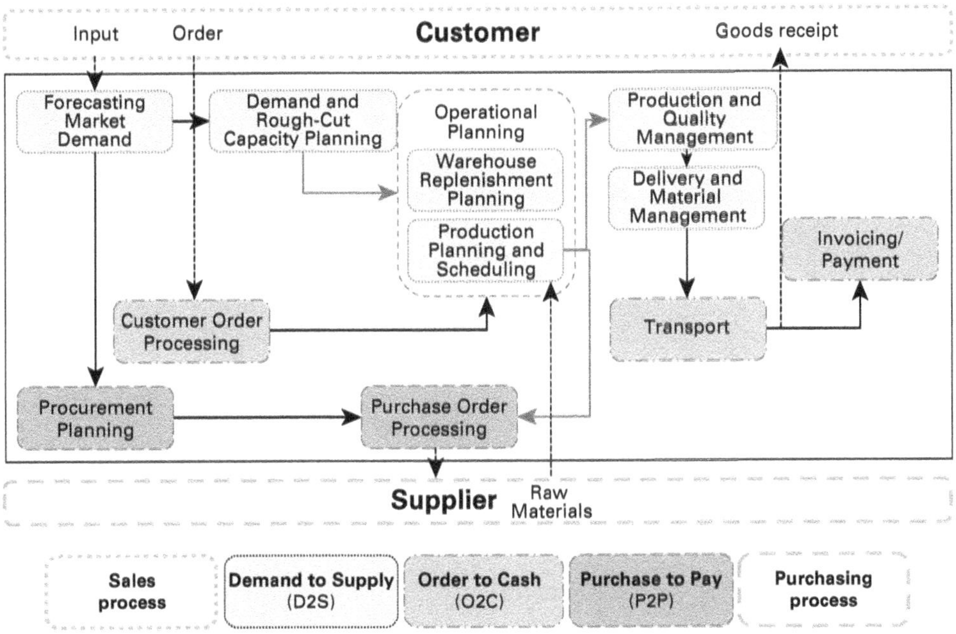

From an overall business point of view, the processes related to Sales and Purchasing can be added:

- *Sales process*, in which negotiations with customers take place, in order to sell them goods on the basis of agreed product and service specifications. Typically, an increased service promise will lead to higher prices paid by the customer. The outcome of the sales process are concrete customer orders.

- *Purchasing process*, in which the appropriate suppliers are identified and service level agreements are negotiated, specifying component and service specifications. Typically, a better service required from the supplier will lead to higher prices to be paid by you. The results of the purchasing process are concrete purchase orders.

Figure 3.10 gives a representation of the high-level tactical and operational supply chain processes, complemented by the sales and purchasing processes.

As can be seen in Figure 3.10, the first two processes, P2P and O2C, have slightly more focus on the material and money flowing between customers and the company and between the company and suppliers, whereas the third, D2S, is more focused on the internal activities involved in producing and storing raw materials and finished goods.

Uncertainty in demand and supply

The first factor to take into consideration when thinking about the planning and control of a given supply chain is the impact that uncertainty in demand and supply has. Rather than listing the reasons why demand or supply is more or less predictable here, I'd like to propose this as an exercise, since you can probably come up with the main important considerations yourself. Keep in mind that uncertainty can potentially come from each of the boxes in the diagram: sales process, purchasing process, D2S, O2C and P2P.

EXERCISE 3.7
Explore uncertainty in demand and supply

Explore

What reasons can you think of that make demand less predictable?

And what reasons can you think of that make supply less predictable?

The answers to these questions determine in large part how you deal with forecasting, inventories and the size of production batches. For example, the more uncertainty on either side, the more difficult is the important task of balancing supply and demand in a cost-efficient way, and probably the more justified is the effort and sophistication put into people, processes and systems.

In the following sections, a number of key activities within these major supply chain processes are highlighted.

Key 1 to D2S: forecasting market demand

Referring to the choices made in terms of the customer–order decoupling point, we now know that materials requirement forecasting needs to be done at the level of components, intermediate or semi-finished products or finished goods. In terms of forecasting, I'd like to highlight a few aspects:

1 As the saying goes, rule number 1 of forecasting is that 'forecasts are always wrong'. Despite this, forecasts will never be perfect and probably not even when in the future we have the support of artificial intelligence.

2 Many mathematical formulas and heuristics exist for making forecasts, such as the moving average model, exponential smoothing, regression analysis and so on

(the classic book by Silver *et al*, 1998, provides a wealth of those, as nowadays so does even Wikipedia). And even a basic tool such as Microsoft Excel nowadays contains a number of built-in formulas, and plenty of advanced planning and optimization software exists to provide even more alternatives. However, the reality is that most approaches still have one fundamental underlying assumption: that history will repeat itself. In other words, what happened in the past will somehow be representative of what will happen in the future. In some cases that might be true, but there are also indicators that this assumption might be more and more challenged in the future (think back to the discussion about the age of acceleration in the preface).

3 There seems to be plenty of proof that clever human interaction with advanced planning systems is the key to more accurate forecasting.

4 In company life, there is an enormous challenge with respect to forecasting, which is the level of priority that accurate forecasting has for the people best positioned to provide those forecasts. In many cases, marketing and sales people probably have the best actual insights for providing accurate forecasts based on mathematical projections, enriched by practical knowledge about customer and competitor movements, planned promotions, new product introductions and so on. However, in many cases they don't see sufficient benefits in actually spending time and effort to make those forecasts. And let's face it, the reality is that they have much to lose. If rule number 1 of forecasting is indeed true, then they will always be at the risk of being held personally responsible for providing wrong information. That, of course, is not a very attractive starting point.

Key 2 to D2S: capacity planning

In many production environments, machine capacity is expensive. Recently, a client of mine told me about a new factory his company was building in order to be prepared for dealing with future expected demand, as well as anticipating future new technologies: an investment of €750 million (as you will remember from the discussion on finance in Chapter 2, a large portion of this would go into the PPE item on the balance sheet; just think about the impact on ROI if you increased PPE by €750 million). Once such money is spent and production capacity is available, it should be used well, and this is where capacity planning and production planning and scheduling come into the picture.

Where we have multiple factory locations worldwide capable of producing the same goods, we need to make sure that overall world demand will be allocated to the different production locations. Such allocation decisions are normally part of what is called rough-cut capacity planning. This decision becomes particularly important when overall demand is expected to be higher than available capacity. In widely used terminology, a certain product or component will then be 'under allocation', meaning that the different local markets might be competing to get part of the production pie. Companies are then forced to have set rules for deciding which market would get which part of the total production volume.

Key 3 to D2S: production planning and scheduling, batches, frozen periods

Once allocation to factories has been done, production planning and scheduling at machine level can be done. The key decision here, to align expected time-phased output in terms of products produced on the one hand and maintaining a good level of production efficiency on the other, is to decide on the size of the *production batches*, sometimes also called *production lot sizes* or, when expressed in time rather than quantity, the *production intervals* (every how many days do I launch a production batch of a certain article?). The larger the production batches, the more economies of scale can be achieved. The shorter the production batches, the more times the machine will switch from making one product to another. This will obviously increase responsiveness to changes in demand, but at the expense of efficiency, since the machine will have to be stopped, cleaned and started up again more frequently. Compare the two diagrams in Figure 3.11 and assess the differences in terms of:

- Number of times production capacity is 'lost' because of switching to another batch. This impacts available net production capacity, but also the number of start-up losses of new production batches.

- Number of times new product arrives at the next stage in the supply chain.

- Average amount of inventory as a consequence of the batch size (this is called the 'cycle stock') and the implications of this.

- The average degree of freshness of the product.

- Number of times you're getting into the dangerous area of running out of stock.

Please keep in mind that in the figure, no reference is made to a particular article. As you can imagine, the situation becomes more complex when the variety of articles produced on the same machine is larger. Typically, in large-scale production, a fixed sequence in which the articles are produced is defined, which has implications for the time that elapses before a particular item is produced again. This concept is often referred to as the 'production wheel'.

Another important concept to be taken into consideration during production planning is the so-called 'frozen period', meaning for how long into the future do I not allow any changes to the production plan and schedule, whatever happens. Think of it this way: we prepare a production plan that covers, for example, the next three months, and a more detailed production schedule covering the next month.

Figure 3.11   Comparison of large batches versus small batches

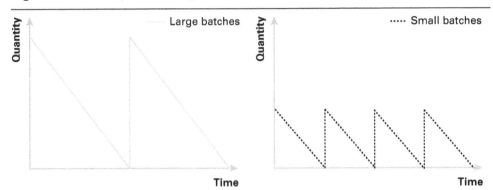

If we set the frozen period to be one month, the implication is that whatever happens during the first month will not affect my detailed production schedule. After one month, we once again prepare a detailed schedule for the next month and we update the production plan again for the next three months (in other words, we have a rolling horizon). In a way, even though external uncertainty (market demand) is, of course, not impacted by the frozen period, setting it for a longer time does reduce internal uncertainty by 'freezing' the production schedule.

While the disadvantage of the frozen period might be that no immediate changes can be made in order to respond quickly to changes in the market, its advantage is that everyone involved (production managers, machine operators, team leaders, HR managers, suppliers, maintenance people) know exactly what needs to be done every day during this period. This creates stability, giving the possibility of better preparing for something that is already fixed and therefore enabling greater efficiency in the chain.

Key 4 to D2S: production and quality

Once production planning and scheduling has been taken care of, we move to the actual execution of the plans. Now we need to deal with operational hiccups, such as lack of staff availability, machine breakdowns, the necessity to running into overtime, and supply interruptions from suppliers. Many different functional disciplines interfere here. In order to buffer against such hiccups, inventories can be built up, which is the topic of the next sub-section. An important indicator used to measure the number of hiccups is called 'production plan adherence'; it measures to what extent the original production plan has actually been carried out.

Key 5 to D2S: inventory management (warehouse replenishment)

From the earlier section on finance in Chapter 2, you might remember the financial importance of managing inventories effectively. The management of inventories has a number of different dimensions, which we will deal with in the coming paragraphs. The cornerstone of inventory theory is formed by two decisions: *how much* to order and *when* to order, as expressed by Figure 3.12.

The diagram shows the main concepts of inventory management:

- *Inventory level*: expressing the amount of inventory over time.

- *Re-order point*: the level of inventory at which an alert indicates that new materials must be ordered (when to order?).

- *Order quantity*: the amount of inventory ordered each time an order is placed, either to internal production or to external suppliers (how much to order?). A basic theoretical concept called the economic order quantity (EOQ) states that the optimum order quantity is a trade-off between the costs of ordering versus the costs of having product in inventory. For example, if I order once for the whole year, I will spend little time and money on ordering but I will have a high average inventory. In the opposite case I will order smaller quantities very frequently, so that average inventory will be lower, but more time and money will be spent on ordering, checking, invoicing, etc. Note that the amount of inventory due to the specified order quantity is called the '*cycle stock*', mentioned earlier under Key 3

Figure 3.12　Sawtooth diagram of inventory management

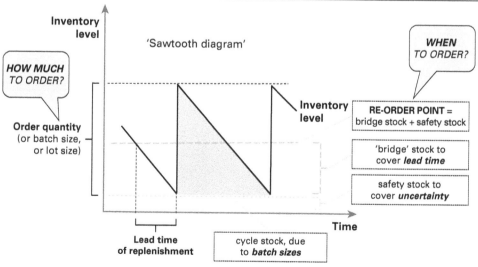

to D2S. Note also that the concept of order quantity also appears there when referring to batch sizes from a production perspective.

- *Replenishment lead time*: the time between placing an order to replenish inventory and the actual delivery.

- *Bridge stock*: the amount of inventory needed to cover average demand or consumption of the product or component during the replenishment lead time.

- *Safety stock*: the amount of inventory needed to cover uncertainty in supply or demand during the replenishment lead time.

As in the case of forecasting, there is a wide range of sophisticated formulas to calculate the optimum order quantity and particularly the amount of safety stock (Silver *et al*, 1998). Normally, each formula takes into consideration one or more specific factors at play, thus providing a partial view on possible outcomes. The perfect all-inclusive formula doesn't seem to exist (yet...).

In addition to the sawtooth diagram, there are a few other reasons why inventory might be held at a particular time. Whereas the sawtooth diagram deals mainly with aspects of inventory and ordering costs as well as storage efficiency and supply and demand uncertainty, other elements in the equation might be related to production efficiency or purchasing strategy. We speak in this context about two additional types of inventory, apart from bridge stock and safety stock already mentioned:

- *anticipation stock*, for example due to a strong seasonality effect on demand, or planned maintenance or holiday shutdowns in production;

- *strategic stock*, for example if there is a possible supply shortage of specific components or to hedge against material price fluctuations.

EXERCISE 3.8
Explore order quantities

Explore

In Exercise 3.7, you thought about the reasons that make supply and demand less predictable. These reasons would, as a consequence, lead to higher safety stocks to cover this uncertainty. Now think of arguments that would influence the optimum order quantity.

We have already explained the reasoning behind the EOQ, but what arguments can you think of that would make order sizes in purchasing and/or production different from the EOQ and larger than justified by the short-term demand? For example, if the EOQ calculation told you that you should order 105 units of product from your supplier each time, what reasons could there be to actually order more than that quantity each time? Or less? Think of the concepts of cycle stock, anticipation stock and strategic stock, and try to find examples of those online. In which industries are you likely to find examples of each of these three types of inventory? Why is that so? How big can the impact be (eg peak season sales as a percentage of annual sales)? Or think of aspects such as perishability, obsolescence, fluctuations in production and component costs, and try to find examples of those online. In which industries are you likely to find examples of these aspects?

Please note that the sawtooth diagram shown in Figure 3.12 is based on what we call a 'continuous review' model of inventory, based on a re-order point. The continuous line of the inventory quantity implies that the inventory level is monitored and known continuously, in real time, and that a replenishment order is launched as soon as the inventory level crosses the line of the specified re-order point. Another type of review method is the one based on 'periodic review', meaning that inventory levels are checked at certain (fixed) moments. This would be like the traditional shop owner, taking stock once a week when closing his shop on Saturday evening and then deciding on whether and how much to order from his suppliers, who doesn't know the exact inventory levels at any time during any day. The longer the review period and the higher the demand, the more differences there are between the continuous and periodic review systems. In practice, the following inventory policies can be found frequently:

- (s,Q): continuous review, re-order point, fixed order quantity. s expresses the re-order point, ie whenever the inventory level crosses this point a replenishment order is placed. Q expresses the replenishment order quantity.

- (s,S): continuous review, re-order point, order-up-to level. s expresses the re-order point, ie whenever the inventory level crosses this point a replenishment order is placed. S expresses the quantity of the order-up-to level, ie the total desired level of inventory when the replenishment arrives.

- (R,S): periodic review, order-up-to level. R expresses the review period, ie how often the inventory level is checked. S expresses the quantity of the order-up-to level, ie the total desired level of inventory when the replenishment arrives.

- (R,s,S): periodic review, re-order point, order-up-to level. R expresses the review period, ie how often the inventory level is checked. s expresses the re-order point, ie when the inventory level has crossed this point at the time of checking, a replenishment order is placed. S expresses the quantity of the order-up-to level, ie the total desired level of inventory when the replenishment arrives.

In Chapter 8, we will take a look at which inventory policies The Fresh Connection applies for their components and finished goods.

Keys to O2C and P2P: payment terms and Incoterms©

Although much more can be said about the O2C and P2P processes, from the perspective of this book I will limit myself to only a few basic concepts that appear in both processes, although in O2C these are aimed at the customer and in P2P at suppliers.

Starting with payment terms, these specify the amount of time that a buyer has before they have to pay the seller. A payment term of 60 days means that the buyer has 60 days to pay the seller. It is quite common practice to give a discount to the buyer if the payment term is shorter, since the seller will have the cash available quicker. Think back to the concept of the cash-to-cash conversion cycle in Chapter 2 to understand why faster payment could be of interest to the seller. Payment terms are agreed between a company and its suppliers at one end, and between a company and its customers at the other.

The second concept is about when the payment-term clock starts ticking, which is specified by the Incoterms© (International Commercial terms, as defined and registered as a trademark by the International Chamber of Commerce – the ICC). These terms specify at which point in the chain between seller and buyer the transfer of risk (ie ownership) takes place and who is responsible for which part of the costs, for example of transport, port and customs handling, intermediate storage and so on. In the most recent version of the terms, in total 10 different possibilities are specified. See Figure 3.13 for three examples of widely used terms:

- *EXW* – ex works (named place of delivery): in its most extreme form the seller leaves the goods ready for pickup at their premises (factory, warehouse or similar). The buyer is then responsible for pickup, transport and so on. In supply chain terms this is sometimes also known as factory gate pricing, since the price quoted by the seller ends at the factory gate (ie no further services or delivery are included).

- *FOB* – free on board: the buyer indicates a ship on which the goods must be loaded. Until the goods are on the ship, ownership and costs are with the seller. These transfer to the buyer when the goods are on board the ship.

- *DDP* – delivery with duty paid: the seller takes care of everything until delivery in the country of the buyer, to a site indicated by the buyer, for example their factory or warehouse, or a third-party location. The buyer or their third party takes responsibility from unloading onwards, as this is the moment when cost and ownership pass from the seller to the buyer.

Figure 3.13   Examples of three widely used Incoterms©

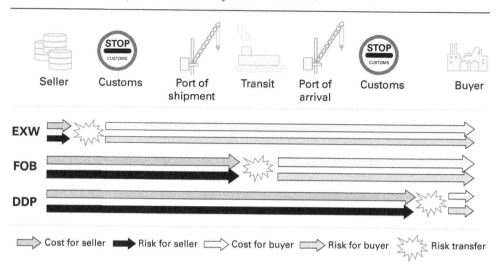

Please note that in all three examples the transfer of costs and risks takes place at the same point. This is not the case for all the specified terms. In some cases, ownership of the goods shifts to the buyer while the costs for transport still are in the hands of the seller.

Among other things, these Incoterms specify the moment when the responsibility and ownership of a product shift from seller to buyer. Which Incoterms are used between a specific buyer and a specific seller is normally a result of either standard common practice in an industry, or a negotiation between the companies involved. Given the size and market power of a company, and/or the volumes they buy or sell from a supplier, they might be interested in applying a specific Incoterm.

A third concept, which has an impact on the O2C and P2P processes, is a scheme called *consignment stock*. It basically refers to the fact that components or products remain inside the customer's facilities but are still the property of the supplier until the moment that the customer sells or uses them. For example, in the automotive industry it is quite common that components are stored in a warehouse at the car brand's assembly site, but the supplier only gets paid for those components once they have been used to assemble a car. The amount of time that these components have been in stock before they are used has a serious influence on the amount of time that the supplier must wait for their money, so effectively risk is shifted.

Lastly, there is the topic of credit limits and credit risk. There is, of course, a direct relationship with the O2C and P2P processes and therefore with supply chain execution, since credit limits or certain credit ratings might, for example, stop a customer order being accepted at a given moment. However, since decisions about credit limits and policies of dealing with credit ratings are normally outside the scope of the supply chain operation, we will leave it here and not dive deeper into the topic, apart from saying that The Fresh Connection has another family member in the suite of simulations, called The Cool Connection, in which such financial aspects do need to be addressed by participants in the game.

Before moving to the next section, let's look for a moment once more at the challenges of dealing with complexity and creating alignment. Similarly to the discussion of strategy and infrastructure, we can now take a view on the roles of the various functional departments in relation to the more tactical and operational processes we have just seen in detail. The matrix shown in Figure 3.14 could help you to visualize your ideas on who is (directly or indirectly) involved in the various O2C, P2P and D2S processes.

Figure 3.14   Matrix of O2C, P2P and D2S sub-processes and functional departments

	SALES	OPS	SCM	PURCH	HR	FIN	...
Forecasting Market Demand							
Demand and Rough-Cut Capacity Planning							
Warehouse Replenishment Planning							
Production Planning and Scheduling							
Production and Quality Management							
Delivery and Material Management							
Procurement Planning							
Purchase Order Processing							
Customer Order Processing							
Transport							
Invoicing/Payment							

What conclusions can you draw from the matrix? What does it tell you about inter-dependencies, and the complexities of alignment? What are the potential solutions in dealing with this? Write down your notes, as we will return to this topic in Chapter 10. The following section covers topics such as information, systems and organizational aspects.

Information and systems, and organizational aspects

Information at the heart of decision making: ERP-suite systems

Now that the physical infrastructure and the planning and control setup have been defined, we know what information would be required to carry out the planning at the various levels as well as operational execution. This information need is insepa-rable from important choices to be made in terms of IT systems. As mentioned before, many companies today work with enterprise resource planning (ERP) systems. The promise of such integrated systems is that by working with aligned data structures, different parts of the business can work with the same interconnected sys-tem, thus uniting, for example, sales with HR with finance with production and the supply chain.

Although within the context of this book we do not go much into detail on the subject of systems, it is important to mention the differences between various types of system:

- *Planning systems*, or decision support systems. These are aimed at calculating different scenarios for the future, so that a more substantiated choice can be made about what to do. Within the context of the supply chain, separate planning modules typically exist, for example, for production planning and scheduling, transportation and route planning, forecasting and demand planning, and network design.

- *Execution systems*. These are normally the core of ERP-suite systems. This is where the real-time information related to goods flows and the corresponding administrative aspects is created and processed. Within the context of the supply chain, this would be related to customer orders, transport orders, production orders, purchase orders and so on.

- *Analytical or datamining systems*. These normally have a large data repository at their heart, sometimes called a data or business warehouse, containing historical data about past transactions derived from the execution systems. These data repositories can either be part of the datamining systems or, more commonly, connected to them via IT interfaces. Analytical systems are aimed at carrying out user-defined queries, data visualization and the creation of specific reports and 'dashboards' with key performance indicators (KPIs).

In The Fresh Connection game the execution system will be taken care of by the game's engine, but in terms of planning and analytical systems you can develop your own 'intelligence' using standard tools such as Microsoft Office or Apple Office and/ or more advanced software. As you will notice during the gameplay, availability of data is one of the keys to effective decision making. We will come back to this in Part Two.

A last comment about information and systems: currently, there are myriads of new developments in terms of technology and they are moving really fast, digital transformation is a trend in itself and some people's expectations of, for example, artificial intelligence are sky-high. Although there is plenty of speculation, no one really knows what will come out of these trends and exactly how quickly.

Organizational aspects: the supply chain department and the chief supply chain officer (CSCO)

After defining the network, the planning and control setup, and the systems to be put in place, as a last step we need to think about who will do what, which people will take on which tasks, and what will be the exact roles and responsibilities of each person involved?

All companies involved in some way in the creation, transformation and/or movement of materials are executing supply chain activities. However, in practice, many different organizational models exist for shaping these activities. Although organization by functional areas seems to be the norm in most companies, it is not always clear whether the supply chain is a functional area in itself or is part of other areas.

Some companies have supply chain departments, others do not. For some, the supply chain is part of the wider area of Operations, for others these are functions at the same level in the organization chart. In some companies, the supply chain is not represented on the Board of Directors, while at companies such as Apple and GM, people with a supply chain background have already made it to CEO. In an article on Forbes.com, Hans Thalbauer, a senior VP from SAP, even raises the question, 'Is Chief Supply Chain Officer most important role in executive suite?' (Thalbauer, 2016).

For now, the main conclusion is simply that many different models of organizing the company exist, and that, given the differences between companies, it seems very difficult to determine whether 'a best way' exists.

Figure 3.15 Recap of topics of Chapter 3, the technical dimension of the supply chain

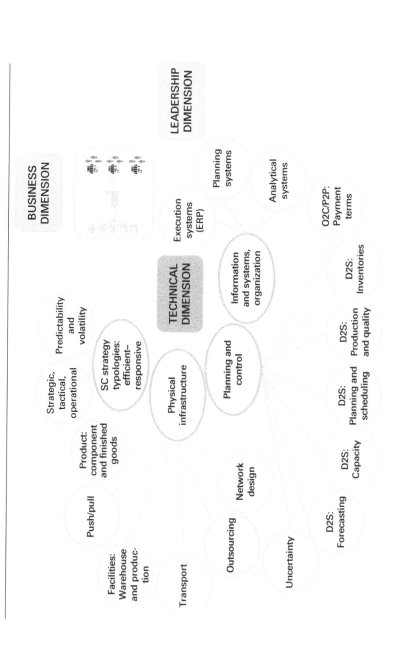

Summary

After covering the fundamentals of the business dimension in Chapter 2, in this chapter we have looked in detail at the technical dimension of the supply chain, taking the chosen corporate strategy as a starting point; the technical dimension comprises the physical infrastructure, processes, information systems and the organizational model (Figure 3.15).

Now, let's continue the journey of exploring the fundamentals and move on to the third dimension of supply chain management: the leadership dimension.

Supply chain

04

The leadership dimension

After dealing with the business and technical dimensions in the previous chapters, in this chapter we will look at the last of the three dimensions of the supply chain: the leadership dimension. We will explore the following aspects of leadership more deeply:

- performance management and target setting;
- stakeholder management, functional silos and corporate culture;
- trust and coordination from the perspective of internal collaboration and team performance;
- trust and coordination from the perspective of external collaboration and end-to-end transparency.

Even if the role of the supply chain in the overall business of a company is understood and the technical dimensions have been worked out in detail, there is still another dimension that cannot be ignored: the leadership, or people, dimension. Many process designs seem perfect – until people appear. People come with moods, opinions, irrationality, motivations, backgrounds, family situations, health complexes and many other things that simply cannot be denied. This leadership and people dimension poses additional challenges for successful execution of supply chain operations, so let's look at them.

Making people move: performance measurement and target setting

In the end, companies are made up of people, and the supply chain is obviously no exception. Since the corporate mission and vision statements are in most cases not enough in themselves to have people move in the 'right' direction, companies put in place certain performance measurements and targets in order to set a goal to be reached within a certain time frame. Sometimes these targets form part of individual annual plans, sometimes they are also connected to (financial) incentives. Although performance indicators and target setting is considered by many to be more of a 'technical' topic (as in the case of measuring the outcomes of the operational process as the starting point for defining potential process improvements), we deal with targets under the umbrella of the leadership dimension. This is because, in my opinion, how to go about performance measurement and target setting is a leadership decision. The role and importance a leader gives to KPIs and targets define how that leader is going to work with their people; it will be an important, visible part of the working climate that will be created. The manager in question has an impact on whether these performance indicators create a healthy challenge to make things happen or put intense pressure on staff, leading to a stressful situation. This is particularly the case when such indicators and targets are connected to individual (financial) bonuses.

A widely used concept in the context of KPI development is that of 'SMART' KPIs, alluding to the fact that KPIs should be chosen intelligently; each letter of the word SMART represents a specific aspect to be taken into consideration. Although different explanations of each letter exist, the following typically work well:

- S = *Simple*: meaning, for instance, that the name of the indicator, as well as the formula to calculate it, should be clear and understandable to users. If not, people might simply not trust the outcome, because they don't have a grip of the underlying concepts.

- M = *Measurable*: meaning that it should be possible to capture the concept in a number, a percentage or a value (eg yes/no). Since most things can be measured in some way or another, a second dimension of 'measurable' should be considered, namely whether it can be measured in a timely and cost-effective way. If a certain indicator should be tracked on a weekly basis but measuring it and getting results takes more than two weeks, either because data are difficult to obtain or because producing reports requires a lot of work, or because the suppliers of those data take a relatively long time to make them available, then perhaps another KPI should be considered.

- A = *Acceptable*: meaning that the audience for whom the indicator is intended accepts it as being representative of what it is supposed to measure. If someone proposes to measure delivery performance based on the number of complaints received from customers, but another colleague is of the opinion that that would be measuring customer satisfaction rather than real delivery performance, then the proposed KPI would not be acceptable to both, and therefore not suitable, since every time new results were reported the discussion about their validity would start all over again.

- R = *Realistic*: meaning that the target value should be within reach. If not, it is very likely to result in demotivation, instead of stimulating people to reach the objective.

- $T = Time$-$constrained$: meaning that there should be a deadline of some kind, otherwise people will lose interest, or they will say 'it's OK, we will reach it someday'.

Kaplan and Norton (1992) came up with their concept of the balanced scorecard long ago and nowadays, in practice, probably because we are technologically in a better position to do so than in the past, we see more and more *KPI dashboards* appearing, presenting a 'balanced' collection of KPIs together creating a multidimensional view of their performance for the user in question. We will say a bit more about those dashboards when addressing data visualization software in Chapter 8, as well as in Chapter 9 when we come back to the leadership dimension of the supply chain, applied to The Fresh Connection.

An element to keep in mind when developing meaningful KPI dashboards is to distinguish between KPIs that measure the desired final result and KPIs that measure in some way the path to getting to the final result. For example, if I want to lose weight, my individual KPI for the desired result could be my actual weight. The KPI expressing the path could be the number of steps I have walked in a given period. Obviously, to be able to define both types of KPI presupposes a good understanding of cause and effect relationships between parameters.

EXERCISE 4.1
Explore KPIs and dashboards

Explore

Using the means you have at your disposal, such as the internet, libraries, course textbooks, databases, magazines and so on, explore the topic of KPIs. What can you pick up from these publications?

Since performance indicators and targets will be involved in the gameplay in Part Two, I don't want to expand too much on them at this stage, but I should say that creating KPIs and corresponding targets that provoke and stimulate internal collaboration is quite difficult to do. Unfortunately, some of most widely used targets, usually defined according to functional department, do quite the opposite. More about this in Part Two.

Having targets in place can be a great thing, but be aware that it doesn't necessarily guarantee great outcomes and might have a significant impact on the working climate. Let's now look at some other aspects that will also have an impact on the working climate and decision making in the company.

Stakeholder management, functional silos and corporate culture

Independent of whether 'supply chain' is a separate department or not, the activities within the scope of the supply chain have a bearing on many other departments in the company. Decisions in the supply chain area will often have an impact on what other departments are doing and vice versa, which immediately implies the need for alignment and managing stakeholders. Remember the discussion about those directly and indirectly involved in the supply chain, when looking at definitions in Chapter 1.

However, typical organizational structures are still in most cases centred around functional departments (sales, finance, human resources, and so on), and while this might be totally understandable from the specialization point of view of putting functional experts together, it might also have a slightly trickier side effect. Ashkenas (2015) notes that 'many organizations still have hierarchical, siloed, and fragmented processes and cultures. In fact, having to cope with a fast-changing global economy has led many companies to create even more complex matrix organizations, where it's actually harder to get the right people together for fast decision-making'.

Strong organizational silos reinforce an 'us versus them' feeling between departments, which is obviously a barrier standing in the way of cross-functional alignment. Ashkenas goes on to argue that Jack Welch's approach, when he was the CEO of GE, would still be worth recommending: create cross-functional forums 'bringing people together across levels, functions, and geographies to solve problems and make decisions in real time'. Apparently, this has proven less easy for most companies than it looked. GE started doing this in the 1990s, but it seems to be one of the few to have figured out how to do it. Or can it be that others just don't see it as important and haven't even tried?

Whichever way it is, functional silos are apparently going to be around for some time, and having more institutionalized cross-functional platforms and mechanisms still seems rather far away in most cases, which implies that from within the supply chain area there is going to be a strong need for active cross-functional stakeholder management. This requires strong characters who are not afraid of functional borders and who have other traits such as a sense of empathy, negotiation skills and so on.

For sure, *corporate culture* also enters the equation. If people across a company share the same (strong) corporate culture, cross-functional boundaries become less relevant, because there is another and joint 'us' that might be stronger than the 'us' of the functional departments. As Campbell (2011) states, citing James L Heskett, a famous Harvard professor of service and logistics, 'effective culture can account for 20–30 percent of the differential in corporate performance when compared with "culturally unremarkable" competitors'. However, the reality is that not all companies have such 'effective' cultures, and in those cases cross-functional alignment might be more up to the individual supply chain manager's talents for stakeholder management.

Trust and coordination: internal collaboration and team performance

Team attributes: what successful teams seem to have in common

Even in cases where an effective corporate culture is in place, that still amounts to no more than a lower barrier to establishing communication and alignment in a company at large or, at the micro level, in the team involved in specific decision-making processes. Recent research by MIT and RSM/Delft University of Technology, based on the gameplay of students with The Fresh Connection, highlights two very interesting and important aspects of team characteristics and behaviour:

- *Trust between team members* seems to have a significant impact on team performance. Teams in which the individual team members, independently of one another, indicate high levels of perceived trust between them create a good working atmosphere leading to better results. The MIT research also indicates 'the fragile nature of trust' and, in the case of virtual working teams where individual team members are located in physically different places, 'the sharp improvement after the team-members had met face-to-face', suggesting that team members who did not know each other previously, and who until then had only communicated via e-mail, telephone, videoconference and the like, started working together much more productively after actually having met in person. According to the research, meeting face to face gave an important boost to mutual interpersonal trust between the team members (Phadnis *et al*, 2013).

- *High levels of reflexivity* also seem to have a positive impact on team performance. 'Team reflexivity is a team's ability to consciously and reflexively react to changing and fluid situations and adapt accordingly' (Schippers *et al*, 2011). According to research at RSM/Delft University of Technology, this ability plays particularly to the benefit of teams whose mix of team members tends to favour seeking 'accomplishment and attaining positive outcomes, and where individuals are more inclined to explore all possible means [to] the goals they desire' (Schippers *et al*, 2011). This is in contrast to teams in which team members, rather than focusing on attaining positive outcomes, tend to focus mainly on avoiding negative outcomes.

So, what can we pick up from this? Even if we could say that the abovementioned conclusions can be relatively easily understood conceptually, unfortunately, trust and reflexivity cannot really be designed, and can certainly not be imposed. In a specific team trust needs to be earned, it needs to be developed over time, and the same might go for reflexivity. There seem to be very few shortcuts, if any. So, what do these factors depend on? In the following paragraphs I'll try to shed light on some of those.

Characters and personalities: team composition, team roles, and team dynamics

Before going on, it's important to mention that the composition of a 'team' in a company, whether a formal team put together for a specific purpose or 'just' the accidental mix of people from different departments involved in a specific decision-making process, is in practice hardly ever the consequence of a thorough analysis of candidates based on technical knowledge and skills, nor of character traits and mindsets. In my experience, in most cases, the 'team' is simply the mix of available people at a moment in time.

First, there is the mix of technical skills and experience that people bring to the table, which has an impact on the dynamic that will follow. The MIT research into team performance also highlights in this context that 'the ability of the individual team members, namely the analytical reasoning skills and overall intellectual competence [...] also attribute to team performance' (Phadnis *et al*, 2013). However, there are more dimensions at play. Five relatively inexperienced junior people meeting with a senior colleague who's been around for 20 years might generate an ambience that is quite different from six senior managers meeting to discuss an important decision. By the way, in my own experience, neither the first nor the second team would provide a guarantee of better results.

Another factor at play here is the character and personality of each person. We are who we are, and we're not all the same. That might work out well if personalities are complementary, but might also cause conflicts if personalities match to a lesser extent.

There are plenty of frameworks to describe an individual's team roles, for example the one proposed by Belbin (2010). By putting different individuals' team roles together, the overall strengths and weaknesses of the team can be assessed. Or there is the Thinking Hats approach as developed by De Bono (1999), which also exploits the topic of team roles. The key message here is that each team, whether a formal team working on a project or an informal team of colleagues meeting to agree on some important topics, is a mix of personalities that is to a certain extent totally random, and independent of process design. And this mix of personalities can play an important role in the outcome of the team process. In similar fashion, Gattorna

(2015) puts the well-known framework of Myers-Briggs' individual leadership styles in the particular context of supply chain management.

Stages in the life of the team

A second dimension to take into consideration is related to how long the team has been together and how well they have developed as a team. The famous psychological framework of Tuckman (1965) from the area of group dynamics describes this as a four-phase evolution: forming, storming, norming and performing, later complemented by an additional closing stage called adjourning, transforming and mourning. The basic thought behind the framework is that all groups go through the same stages of development, from chaotic initial stages in which people are getting to know each other, profiling themselves and taking position within the group as a whole, to stages in which the group establishes its own internal rules and ways of working together and really starts performing. In order to highlight this phenomenon, many teachers involved in gameplay with The Fresh Connection prefer to create mixed teams of people, who preferably have not often worked together, in the constellation of the team for the gameplay.

Motivation

The next aspect to take into consideration is motivation, in this case of the individuals in the team. In a way it starts with whether team members have chosen to be in the team or not. If they haven't, but they still like the team and/or the activity, they might end up being happy; if they don't like the task and/or the team, it will most likely have a negative impact on their behaviour, ultimately affecting team performance.

Libraries are full of books explaining many more aspects of people's motivation. Let's highlight a few dimensions in order to create a little awareness and to enable useful reflection on the topic later on. An interesting angle is to look at intrinsic and extrinsic motivation. Intrinsic motivation comes from within the individual and represents a drive to learn new things, to meet new people, to deal with new challenges. Extrinsic motivation has to do with other people giving either rewards (positive) or punishment (negative) to the individual, thus causing an external motivation to do certain things.

There seems to be plenty of scientific evidence that intrinsic motivation is a much stronger driver for positive behaviour than extrinsic motivation. It can easily be observed in schools and universities: students who are there because they are genuinely interested in learning something new and useful and who have a much more positive mindset than those who are mainly there for getting the diploma or because their parents told them to go. In companies this is not very different. Some team members are just there because they need a job to pay the bills and their boss told them to go to the meeting, whereas others might be driven by intrinsic motivations and come with a very positive mindset, ready to get things done. So in any team in any setting you might find one or both of these sources of motivation to be more or less present, with the potential to impact the team's performance.

Communication: questioning, listening, using common language

But there is yet another dimension to team performance, also very relevant, which is communication. The risk is that this topic becomes very vague. Often, I hear people in companies say that communication is perceived to be insufficient and/or ineffective, but most of the time it's much less clear what exactly that might mean and, more importantly, what can be done about it. For one thing, better communication doesn't necessarily mean talking more.

There is a simple and straightforward role play in communication and decision making between sales and production that I often do in my company training sessions. Pairs of two people, each assuming a different role and having received a description of the hypothetical situation, are sent out for a meeting and must reach an agreement to solve the issue at hand. Obviously, the issue can potentially cause conflict between the two roles. Afterwards there is a debrief of the activity in which potential solutions that have come up in the meeting are explored, but above all in which we try to put our finger on the key success factors in reaching an agreement. I've done this activity many times in training sessions, and in the debrief the same factors almost always appear as key success factors, for example and in random order:

- Active listening, giving explanations and asking for explanations.
- Empathy and willingness to listen, attitude.
- Clarity on expectations and ways of working.
- Try to work based on facts, avoiding unsubstantiated opinions.
- Try to establish a 'common language'.
- Willingness to solve the issue.
- Contextualize, explore alternatives.
- Come to the meeting prepared, with your homework done.
- Try to avoid seeing questions as criticism of a person.
- Create an atmosphere that allows for challenging the assumptions.
- Look for mutual interest, and be prepared to make compromises.

I find it very interesting that this list turns out to be very similar every time I do this activity (and obviously without me pushing or imposing any inputs). Apparently, most people, intuitively and/or from personal experience, know the key success factors in making such potentially conflictive conversations work, but we are also very successful at failing to do it well. For me, it's another clear example of 'simple but not easy'. The mix of people, their backgrounds, skillsets, characters, personal situations, motivations, bosses, career perspectives, the stress of a particular day, and so on, all play a role in making it work.

Overall team performance: tasks and relationships

The fact that the supply chain is full of such potentially conflictive issues within and between different functional areas is what makes leadership such an important aspect of the supply chain. So, after all the previous paragraphs talking about elements of team performance, now we're coming back to evaluation of the leadership dimension: how well is it going in our case?

To measure the outcomes of the team process and understand how the 'leadership', implicitly or explicitly, has worked, we can, on the one hand, look at how the team actually achieved the results and, on the other, at how good the team atmosphere has actually been. We can use a methodology proposed by Management Worlds, Inc, who developed questionnaires for mapping two interesting dimensions of team performance: one oriented to the *tasks* (are we getting things done?) and one oriented to *relationships* (are we OK as a team?). In a way, all dimensions, such as the technical and intellectual skills of the individuals, their characters and personalities and social skills, the trust in the team, the degree of reflexivity, and the implicit and explicit manifestations of leadership, come together in this analysis. These questionnaires will come back later in Part Two, connected to The Fresh Connection gameplay and applied to your own team.

EXERCISE 4.2
Explore team performance

Explore

Delve into your own practical experience. This could be experience of working in a company, an internship, workgroups at school, teams in sports or other hobbies, and so on. Try to recall to what extent you have noticed the influence of the topics discussed above, such as functional silos, 'corporate' culture, team roles, communication, team performance in terms of tasks and relationships. What are your observations? How could these observations be useful to you when gameplay starts?

Trust and coordination: external collaboration and transparency

Let's go one step further. We defined the supply chain, including other companies upstream and downstream. Now link that to the topic of trust and coordination. If establishing trust and coordination internally within the company is already an important challenge, as shown in the previous paragraphs, imagine doing the same with external parties, for whom at the outset it might not even be clear to everyone involved what they have in common with you. In principle, since it's about establishing relationships between people, all the aspects dealt with in the last section on internal collaboration are equally valid in the case of external collaboration. But there is an additional dimension: in the end, between-companies' relationships are more formal, you're not colleagues reporting to the same boss, and goals and objectives are not necessarily the same. So, as part of this chapter on the leadership dimension of the supply chain, I would like to come back to the topic of trust in particular.

Lack of transparency: bullwhip effect

One of the most famous phenomena in the supply chain, which is at least partially due to lack of trust and therefore lack of transparency in terms of information between companies, is called the bullwhip effect. If my customer doesn't want to share their views on their future demand forecasts with me, then the only thing I can do is guess, to the best of my abilities. As sound and extensive academic research into the bullwhip effect shows, I then will tend to build in more security than strictly necessary. In every stage of the supply chain upstream, the effect becomes stronger, leading to 'excessive inventory investment, poor customer service, lost revenues, misguided capacity plans, ineffective transportation, and missed production schedules' (Lee *et al*, 1997).

See Figure 4.1, which was generated based on the results of playing a famous supply chain game with MBA students in a business school. In the graphics, in each of the stages in the supply chain the quantities of product ordered by the company from their direct supplier week by week are shown. So the graphic of the shop shows the quantity of product as ordered by the shop week by week from their supplier, which is the wholesaler. One can easily imagine the negative aspects as highlighted by Lee, because how do you build up inventory in such a situation, if the behaviour of your customer is so erratic and unpredictable? How much operational capacity in terms of warehousing, or production, or transportation should each stage in the supply chain build up? What are the consequences for cost efficiency and ultimately profit? What are the consequences for my delivery reliability to my customer and ultimately their loyalty to me?

There are a number of causes for the bullwhip effect to occur, one of them clearly related to the aforementioned lack of transparency between suppliers and customers. We will come back to the topic in Part Three.

Figure 4.1 The bullwhip effect

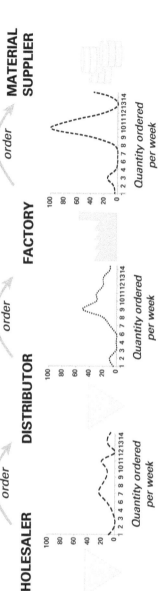

SHOP   *order*   WHOLESALER   *order*   DISTRIBUTOR   *order*   FACTORY   *order*   MATERIAL SUPPLIER

Quantity ordered per week

SOURCE own observation from beer game simulation game as done in class

Vendor managed inventory (VMI): a potential solution to lack of transparency?

For now, let's take the concept of vendor managed inventory as an example of establishing or improving information transparency between suppliers and customers. It has been around for quite a while and can be considered one of the possible (partial) solutions to reducing the impact of the bullwhip effect. At the heart of the concept is the shift of responsibility from the customer ordering product from their supplier to the supplier taking responsibility for maintaining sufficient stock in the customer's warehouse.

In order to do this, the supplier needs reliable information about existing stock levels in the customer's warehouse and the level of sales made by the customer. Ideally speaking, this information would be complemented by a sales forecast from the customer. With this, the supplier should have all of the information needed to be able to 'proactively' replenish inventory in the customer's warehouse and thus guarantee availability of product within the agreed range of quantity (Figure 4.2).

Figure 4.2   VMI versus 'traditional' order-based systems

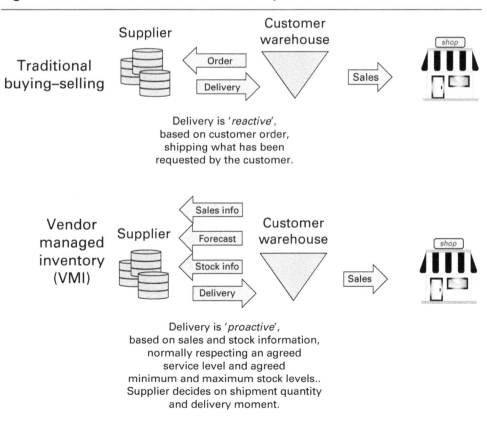

EXERCISE 4.3

Explore VMI

Explore

What key success factors for a successful VMI implementation can you think of? For example, think of:

- product characteristics: size, weight, packaging;
- product portfolio: number and diversity of SKUs;
- sales volumes and sales patterns;
- supplier size versus customer size;
- importance of supplier for customer;
- importance of customer for supplier;
- systems sophistication of supplier;
- systems sophistication of customer.

In which situations would VMI be more likely to work well? And how would 'leadership' fit into the equation?

At the conceptual level, initiatives such as VMI are all fairly straightforward. But as it turns out, such types of project, apart from the technical side of process design, implementation and connection of systems, definition of roles and responsibilities, and fine-tuning of parameters, do actually require an important dose of trust, especially if the initiative is suggested and pushed by the supplier.

Why would I share (confidential) information about my sales with my supplier? Why would they need to know in real time what is selling well and what is not? Why would I open up my books and tell them how much inventory I have? How would I make sure that they would not overstock my warehouse, just to make it easier for themselves? How would we deal with new product introductions? And why would my supplier be able to do a better job at forecasting and replenishment than I could do myself: am I not the expert in my own products and sales instead of them? And besides, even if all this worked well, with how many suppliers could I do this in parallel – my resources are limited, aren't they?

Although most people would intuitively understand that mutual trust leading to more open communication between companies would enable improved performance and a reduced bullwhip effect, via solutions such as VMI, apparently this is a bit harder in practice than the concept itself would suggest. Unfortunately, also in the context of external collaboration, mutual trust cannot be imposed; it requires a lot of time and effort to establish, but above all a positive predisposition to begin with.

A friend of mine works at a well-known multinational company and he told me that recently his company had won an industry award for supply chain innovation. Part of the project was to establish forward integration with key customers, including the integration of processes and systems. When I asked how many customers they had been successful with so far and how much time that had taken, it turned out that they had achieved launching the implementation of customer number 4 after about 18 months down the road in the project. And none of the previous three customers could really be considered a 'finished implementation' yet. Change is indeed slow. And by the way, a fair number of their customers had actually, in a friendly but firm manner, declined the invitation to participate.

In summary, the benefits of such changes are sometimes easy to see at the conceptual level, but they require a lot of vision, persistence and leadership to get them done. In that sense, many elements of the example of VMI can be extrapolated into any collaboration project crossing borders between suppliers and customers. This then also links back to the topic of supplier segmentation and particularly collaboration with strategic suppliers, as discussed in Chapter 3.

The role of leadership in the supply chain

As the topics in the chapter so far have hopefully illustrated, making things happen in the supply chain is not an easy task. The technical complexity can be quite overwhelming, but then getting all the people involved, both internally and externally, on board poses quite an additional challenge. This is why leadership is called for.

The concept of the T-shaped manager was allegedly first coined by David Guest (1991), possibly after certain principles as applied at the time by McKinsey and Company, and its principles have been promoted a lot since then by famous design firm IDEO, the company behind much of the 'Design Thinking' school of thought. The central idea of the T-shaped manager is that they combine the benefits of deep (technical) knowledge and problem-solving skills in a particular functional or business area with broad communication skills across different areas, within or across firms.

Interestingly enough, in an article in the *Harvard Business Review*, Hansen and von Oetinger (2001) give a slightly different, and in my opinion compatible, interpretation of the T-shaped manager. For them, it's not so much about the mix of deep functional and wide cross-functional skills, but about the mix of moving oneself and spreading knowledge and experience vertically within one unit of the firm, and doing the same horizontally between units of the firm, a concept that can be expanded to places outside the firm in order to reach more of the supply chain's end-to-end way of operating. In other words, they focus a bit more on behaviour rather than on pure skills. From my point of view, both views are very relevant to the nature and character of what's going on in the end-to-end supply chain.

Christopher (2016) places the T-shape in the context of the supply chain from a very high-level perspective, and supply chain recruitment company Inspired-Search has taken the concept of the T-shaped manager a big step further and has actually created a detailed supply-chain-specific version of it (Figure 4.3). This has been the starting point for a series of blogposts I wrote in 2013 titled 'The supply chain manager's daily decathlon', which were published on the website of magazine SupplyChainMovement.com.

The central idea of the blogs was to use a number of well-known and some self-invented games requiring very different skills to create a supply chain decathlon,

Figure 4.3   The T-shaped supply chain manager

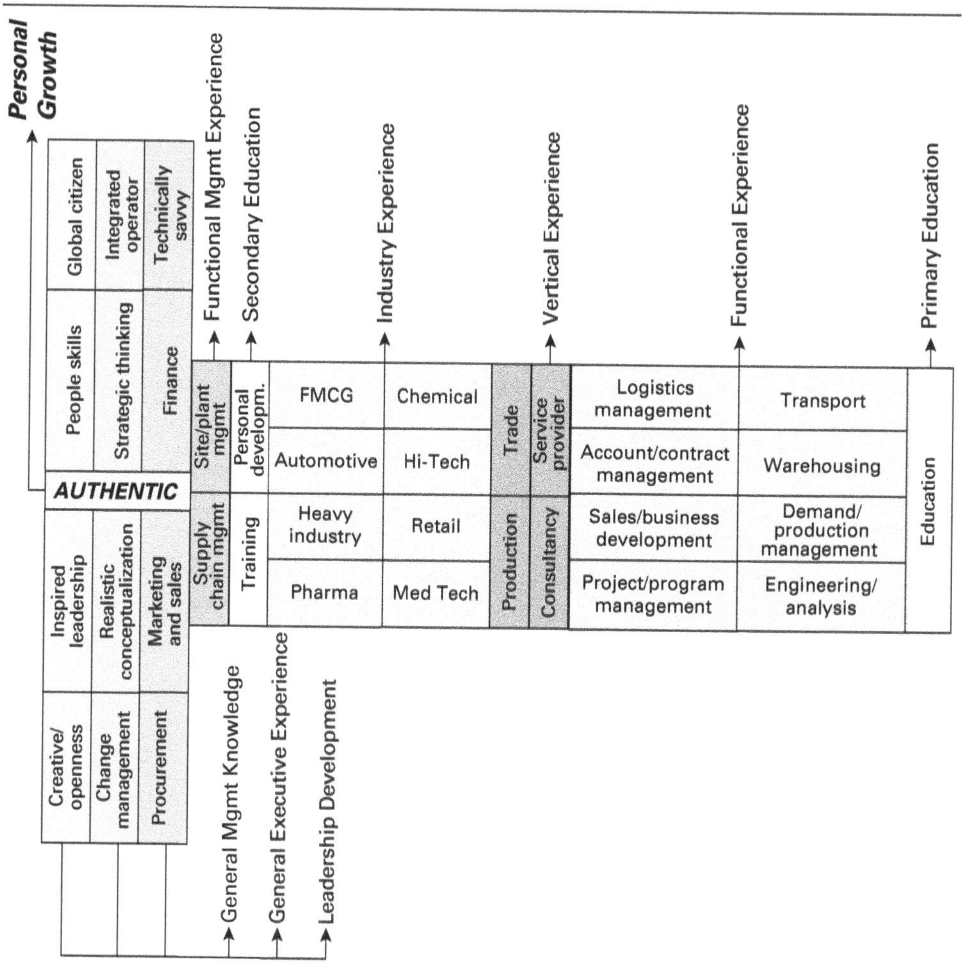

alluding to the fact that 'given the diversity of the challenges in their job, supply chain managers need to be versatile, multi-skilled people, chameleonic in a way. A bit like the decathlon athlete, they need to perform well on a lot of different disciplines, not necessarily the best at each, but good enough to have a good shot at becoming the overall number 1 in the tournament' (Weenk, 2013b). The games and skillset dealt with were the following:

- SimCity™ – holistic thinking, big picture, perspective;
- Mighty Materials Monopoly – business sense, financial expertise;
- Rush Hour® – logical thinking, problem solving, targets;
- Power Pit-Stop Project – analytics, technical skills, project management;
- World of Warcraft® – negotiation, stress- and uncertainty-resistance;
- High-hope Tightrope – trade-off sensitivity, balancing objectives;
- Dragons' Den – elevator pitching, verbalize and visualize;
- Diplomacy® – alliance building, political sensitivity;
- Who are you? – sensibility for people, creating ambience;
- Mega Marathon – endurance, while enjoying the ride.

Although not written from the perspective used in this book, of the skills mentioned in the blog as required for being successful at the 10 different games of the decathlon, at least half can be seen as part of the leadership dimension, the others as more related to the business and/or technical dimensions of supply chain.

To end this chapter I would like to go back to Jack Welch, former long-time CEO of General Electric. There is a wonderful video of him speaking about the role of a leader, focusing particularly on the people aspects of that role. According to Welch, there are four vital angles to leadership. As a leader you have to be the Chief Meaning Officer, not only explaining to people where you want to go, but also showing clearly what's in it for them if they join you on the journey. Furthermore, you need to be the Chief Broom Officer, getting rid of the organizational clutter, removing the silos. Then, you also need to be the Chief Generosity Officer, enjoying your colleague's successes, not focusing only on yourself. Finally, Welch distinguishes the role of the Chief Fun Officer, celebrating small victories with the team and making them into big victories, having fun at the job every single day (JWMI, 2015).

Linking back to the central principle of the learning cycle of experiential learning, I would invite you to track the way you apply the skills mentioned in this chapter, for example during the gameplay. This will help you first of all to identify their appearance and their importance, as well as enable you to assess your own performance in each of them.

Figure 4.4 Recap of topics of Chapter 4, the leadership dimension of the supply chain

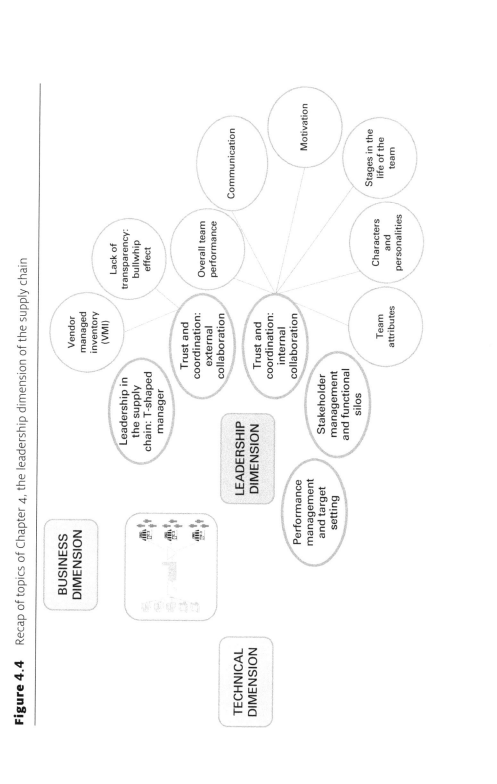

Summary

The topics of performance measurement, stakeholder management and corporate culture, team roles and team dynamics, and trust and coordination bring us to the end of the third dimension of the supply chain, the leadership dimension (Figure 4.4). In the next chapter, we will finish our journey of exploring the fundamentals and look at the overall complexity of managing the business, technical and leadership dimensions of the supply chain all at once.

Simple but not easy (2)

05

Complexity and alignment

In this last chapter of Part One: Exploring the fundamentals, there will be a few closing remarks about the complexity of the supply chain when combining its business, technical and leadership dimensions, and highlighting two keys to dealing with this complexity:

- the art of making trade-offs;
- the process of sales and operations planning (S&OP).

Both these topics, in addition to the previous chapters, should put you in a good position to kick off gameplay in Part Two.

Complexity!

I hope that you will have seen by now that the individual concepts relevant to supply chain management are relatively straightforward. I'm quite sure that you have noticed that most of them are not that difficult to understand, from a conceptual point of view. However, it would probably be a big mistake to think that it is therefore all easy, because it's not. There are a number of reasons why supply chain management as a business area is so enormously complex from a strategic and holistic, as well as from an operational, point of view:

- The sheer number of individual elements which together form supply chain management makes it complex to have the full view at all times.
- The *interdependencies* between the different elements make it complex to grasp the impact that decisions in one part will have on the other parts. The supply chain is a complex system of processes, people, companies and so on.
- *Objectivity* is not always that straightforward. Although much can be calculated and analysed, there is plenty of room, and need, for opinion, debating, convincing, putting another layer of complexity over the previous points.

- Now add *uncertainty* into the equation. Uncertainty about supply, uncertainty about demand, uncertainty about operational performance, uncertainty about what competitors will do, uncertainty about the pace and content of technological developments, uncertainty about what will happen in business and society, and a large list of etceteras. More complexity to be considered.

All of the above, and probably more, are at play at the same time. And to me, this is precisely what makes the supply chain such a fascinating area to work in. The supply chain is complex and has need of alignment on many dimensions:

- between the short term and the long term;
- between the strategic and the operational;
- between supply chain execution and bottom-line results;
- between the big picture and the details;
- between the pros and the cons;
- between the internal and the external;
- between facts, assumptions and opinions;
- and, ultimately, between demand and supply.

Before finally going to the gameplay in Part Two, let's finish with two very important topics, one a concept and the other a process, which are absolutely critical to dealing with all of the complexity and alignment challenges in the supply chain in a practical way and getting to effective decision making in order to move the company forward. This is the concept of '*trade-offs*' and the process of *sales and operations planning* (S&OP).

Trade-offs: you can't have it all

It will have become clear by now that many of the decisions to be taken in the supply chain area are multifaceted and that the context is one of interdependencies between functions and areas. Most of the decisions will always have pros as well as cons, so the perfect solution satisfying all dimensions and all stakeholders most likely doesn't exist. Probably, in most cases we will need to trade off and find some sort of acceptable balance between the different parameters, options and interests.

Some of those trade-offs can be approached from within one and the same decision area, such as transport or warehousing, but many of them in practice have some cross-functional aspects ('if I change something in transportation, it might have an impact on warehousing as well, or on customer service'). In addition, some elements in the equation can be quantified, but others maybe not so much, which implies that not all of the arguments in favour or against can be added up in a very straightfor-ward mathematical way.

Furthermore, on most occasions information to support the decision will not be 100 per cent complete, so assumptions will have to be made to fill in the gaps. Then mix in the people dimension and a bit of time pressure because the boss is waiting, and it is obvious that good decision making requires a holistic view, as well as per-sistence, a well-structured approach and a fair dose of pragmatism.

This is the real juggling act of trade-offs, for which people working in the supply chain have to develop a good degree of sensitivity: if we are changing one thing in the supply chain, where could other impacts be expected? In fact, this is one of the skills from the daily decathlon as mentioned in the previous chapter. In addition, one will have to develop a pragmatic approach to how to deal with these trade-offs in practice.

Let's first take a quick look at a widely used view on the elements at play in supply chain trade-offs, which is in a way similar to the famous '*iron triangle*' of project management: cost versus time versus quality. If in a project designed under reason-able assumptions I would need to take certain measures to speed up the final delivery of the project, for example because the customer has changed their mind and wants the results sooner than agreed, I might well have to jeopardize the previously esti-mated budget, or the actual quality of the deliverables, in order to realize the earlier deadline. Similarly, in the supply chain we could translate this to a trade-off between the dimensions of *fast*, *good* and *cheap*. Most supply chain textbooks speak in some way or another about the classical trade-off between promised service to customers, operational costs and the required inventories (Figure 5.1).

Coherent with the increasing attention to supply chain finance aspects dealt with in Chapter 2, the associated impact on working capital or even total capital em-ployed is taken into consideration more and more, bringing us in fact very close to the KPI of return on investment as discussed earlier in the book. Good and fast would have an impact on revenue, cost obviously on the expenses, with the overall

Figure 5.1   Classical trade-offs in the supply chain: better–faster–cheaper

cost supported by the working capital. Getting very familiar with these elements of the trade-offs when thinking about choices to be made will be very helpful to you in developing the required sensitivity for the pros and cons at stake.

Second, a pragmatic approach to thinking about trade-offs in the context of supply chain decision making is to take a holistic view of the choice at hand and simply follow the steps below, thus creating a business case for a specific decision:

- List the pros and cons that could occur as a consequence.

- Quantify as many of the identified pros and cons as possible.

- Where assumptions need to be made, specify as much as possible the reasoning behind them. If it makes sense, develop different scenarios.

- Make qualitative descriptions of those parts that cannot reasonably be quantified within the given timeframe or based on the available data.

- Make sure that the implementation aspects to go from the as-is situation to the future situation are addressed as well.

- On the basis of the entire picture, try to formulate a convincing argument supporting the decision that can be defended to others in the company. In this step, the chosen corporate strategy should guide you in making the final decision and formulating the argument: decisions should be coherent with the overall strategy.

In Parts Two and Three, plenty of examples of trade-offs will become visible and the topic of business cases will come back explicitly in Chapter 10.

Cross-functional alignment: S&OP and IBP

In line with the phenomenon of trade-offs, combining the business and the technical as well as the leadership dimensions while making decisions for the supply chain requires strong alignment between different functional areas of the company. Think back to the reflections you did using Figures 3.9 and 3.14, looking respectively at interdependencies between the different functional departments in relation to the definition of supply chain strategy and the infrastructure, and the interdependencies in relation to the sub-processes of the overall O2C, P2P and D2S processes. Now put these two views together to get a clearer overall view on the complexities involved in the decision making and the challenges of actually aligning the functional departments.

In fact, the process of S&OP has been developed over time to give a response to precisely those challenges. Some people also speak about integrated business planning (IBP), taking the initial S&OP philosophy to next level of sophistication. On the internet, other maturity models for S&OP can be found, the one developed by consultancy company Gartner being a well-known example. According to Tom Wallace, one of the leading people behind the important initial development of S&OP, 'Sales & Operation Planning (S&OP) is a set of decision-making processes to balance demand and supply, to integrate financial planning and operational planning, and to provide a forum for establishing and linking high level strategic plans with day-to-day operations' (Wallace, 2009).

Nowadays, S&OP has made it into the top-level agenda of most leading firms on the planet, even though many companies still struggle to get it right. On the one hand, this might be surprising, since the process steps are really not that complicated (see Figure 5.2). On the other hand, S&OP also reflects the combination of the business, the technical and the leadership dimensions of supply chain, so maybe we shouldn't be that surprised at the difficulties with its implementation after all.

EXERCISE 5.1
Explore S&OP/IBP

Explore

Using the means you have at your disposal, such as the internet, libraries, databases, magazines and so on, explore the topics of sales and operations planning/integrated business planning. What can you pick up from these publications?

Figure 5.2   S&OP process: sequential monthly steps

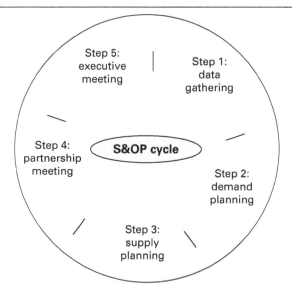

SOURCE after Stahl (2009) and Dougherty and Gray (2006)

Figure 5.3 The three dimensions of supply chain management

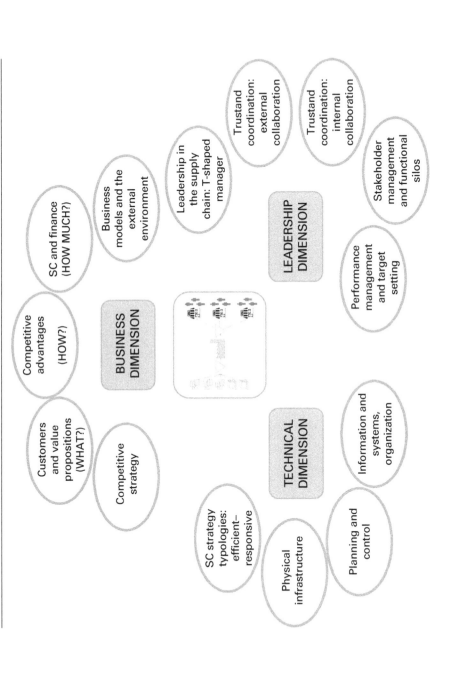

In Part Two, when playing The Fresh Connection, you will have the challenge of developing your own S&OP process and experiencing its complexities.

Summary

The topics of complexity, trade-offs and sales and operations planning bring us to the end of the journey of exploring the fundamentals of supply chain management, and thus also to the end of Part One. As a recap, in Figure 5.3 you can see an overview of the concepts that have been discussed so far. All of these will come back in some shape or form and be connected to The Fresh Connection in Parts Two and/or Three.

Again, lots of topics, not that difficult individually, but all at play at the same time. I have said it before on a number of occasions already: *simple but definitely not easy*. And that's precisely the fun part of it. After finishing the journey of exploring the fundamentals in Part One, we will now move on to Part Two, in which we start a second journey, the journey of mastering the fundamentals.

PART TWO
Mastering the fundamentals

After exploring the fundamentals in Part One, in Part Two we will focus on the practical aspects of applying these concepts with the aim of truly mastering the fundamentals. Here, The Fresh Connection business simulation will be the main vehicle that will serve for the application of the individual concepts that were introduced in Part One. The basic setup of the simulation used in this second part presents a relatively stable environment in which to make a wide variety of basic supply-chain-related decisions, in order to make the supply chain run smoothly and the company profitable. By running the simulation, there will be a clear and visible link between cause and effect (decisions and results). In this way, the student will get the first-hand experience of *analysing real company data* from different functional areas in order to *make good decisions*. Exercises in this section will thus be structured in two steps: *analyse* and *decide*. Furthermore, each chapter will end with a final *reflection*, in order to close the learning cycle.

Also in Part Two, the three dimensions of the supply chain (technical, business, leadership) will each be dealt with in a separate chapter.

Knowledge in action with a supply chain simulation: Game on!

06

In Part One, the focus has been on presenting a helicopter view of the main frameworks, theories and concepts in connection with each of the three dimensions of the supply chain: the business dimension, the technical dimension and the leadership dimension. In Part Two, we will shift our attention to the practical application of the concepts from Part One, using The Fresh Connection business simulation as an interactive case study, which will allow you to get first-hand experience of the complexities involved. In this chapter we kick off Part Two by getting to know the simulation and its business situation, as well as providing a thorough step-by-step analysis of the starting point and an action plan for round 1 of gameplay.

The Fresh Connection business simulation game

The Fresh Connection (TFC) business simulation game is developed by Dutch company Inchainge. The company already had an important track record of using a variety of board games in their training and consultancy activities when TFC was launched in 2008, bringing 'serious gaming' to another level.

At the heart of TFC is a *lossmaking producer of fresh fruit juices*, located in northwest Europe (let's say The Netherlands), which needs to be returned to profitability by making strategic and tactical decisions over the course of a number of rounds of gameplay, each round representing six months in the life of the company. The attractiveness of such business simulation games is that students can play in a fun, competitive, risk-free, yet realistic environment in which a direct relationship between cause and consequence (decisions and results) can be experienced.

What makes TFC stand out in comparison to other business simulation games is that it has a clear focus on the value chain and the flow of materials from upstream suppliers to downstream customers. Furthermore, by splitting the decisions to be made into the clear functional areas of sales, purchasing, production and supply chain, and with a different team member responsible for each area, the experience gets very close to real corporate life, in which a functional split of responsibilities is the norm, rather than the exception.

Beyond the pure functional decision making, this leads to the need for finding effective and efficient mechanisms to ensure *cross-functional alignment*. Add a little bit of time pressure into the pressure cooker and we have a combination of all the ingredients required for a wonderful learning experience.

The Fresh Connection business simulation game allows for customized configuration, based on its modular setup, with each module having a different thematic emphasis. In addition, typically a game setup would start with a slightly lower level of complexity at the beginning of the game (round 1), followed by increasing complexity as the gameplay advances in subsequent rounds. In the context of educational programmes, the decision of which configuration to use would normally be taken by the lecturer in charge of the course, taking into consideration the course's specific content and learning objectives. The key points to keep in mind at this stage are:

- TFC is a juice company that is currently making a loss.
- Gameplay is in teams, each team member taking charge of a different functional role.
- Gameplay will be in rounds of decision making, each round representing six months in the life of the company.
- Game setup, timings and so on will normally be defined and communicated by the course lecturer.

In the remainder of this chapter we will get started by:

- exploring the simulation;
- analysing the company's starting point;
- starting to think about an action plan for round 1 of gameplay.

Please note that Part Two, and to a lesser extent Part Three, is based on a game configuration that corresponds largely to what most schools and universities are using in practice. This goes for the configuration of complexity in the game, as well as the number of entities and their respective names. So, it might be that the specific configuration you will be playing in your own course is a bit different from what you will find in the book. If this is indeed the case, don't worry, because the topics, exercises and reflections are equally valid and applicable for any configuration of the game.

Introducing: Team SuperJuice

Team SuperJuice is formed by a team of students and they are going through the same experience as you are. In Figure 6.1 you can see the team in action preparing their first round of gameplay.

Throughout Part Two you will find bits and pieces of the work done by Team SuperJuice that can serve as an inspiration for your own work.

Introducing: Bob McLaren, the owner of our company

Bob McLaren has prepared a few videos for your information. Please go and watch the videos, which you can find on the web portal connected to the book. These videos will give you a brief overview of TFC and its current state of affairs.

After watching the videos, please continue reading the description below.

Figure 6.1   Team SuperJuice

Figure 6.2   Introducing the company's owner

Hello there, my name is Bob. I'm the CEO and owner of The Fresh Connection Group.

We are thrilled by the current market outlook and projections on future growth, but nevertheless one of our recently acquired companies is struggling to be profitable.

I want you to help me turn it around. Are you and your team up for the challenge?

TFC: the company, the mission, the experience

Company and customers. TFC is a producer of fruit juices, which it sells to a limited set of retail customers. TFC supplies its customers directly. If sufficient product of the agreed specifications is in stock, the delivery is made on the next day after the customer places an order.

Products. TFC provides a modest range of flavours, such as Orange or Orange-Mango, in different pack sizes, such as 1-litre cartons and 0.3-litre PET bottles. The finished goods have a shelf life of 20 weeks from the date and time of their production. The customers claim a significant part of these 20 weeks, usually between 60 and 80 per cent. This leaves TFC with a total shelf life of between 20 and 40 per cent of these 20 weeks. If the shelf life expires, the product will unfortunately have to be destroyed.

Product storage and distribution. TFC products are stored on pallets in the finished goods warehouse, also called the outbound warehouse. They stay there until a delivery is made, or until their shelf life has expired. TFC does not have its own fleet to deliver to its customers' distribution centres and instead outsources transportation to an extremely reliable partner.

The production process. TFC manufactures all the products it sells. The fruit juices are mixed in a mixer and then immediately bottled using a bottling line. The mixer and the bottling line are part of TFC's equipment. The different pack sizes are bottled on the same line.

The components. A finished product consists of two main components: the packaging and concentrated fruit juice (pulp). A bill of materials that can be found within the system lists what quantity of which component is used in a finished product. The formula – the fruit-pulp mix and additives that give the fruit juices their unique flavour – has been one of the most closely guarded Fresh Connection secrets for over a century.

The suppliers. The components are purchased from suppliers. The packaging material is bought from local and regional suppliers. Pulp is acquired either from fruit traders or from producers across the globe. Each supplier has its own characteristics regarding, for example, size, basic component price, lead time and reliability.

Component storage. The components that are delivered to TFC cannot always be used immediately in production, which is why the company has a raw materials or inbound warehouse to store them. Packaging material is delivered on pallets and stored in this warehouse. The warehouse also holds fruit pulp, if it is delivered in drums or IBCs (intermediate bulk containers: small tanks that hold 1,000 litres of pulp and are the floor-size of a pallet). The fruit pulp that arrives in tank trucks is pumped into a tank yard. The pulp also has a restricted shelf life, although much longer than the shelf life of the fruit juices (once water is added, the shelf life reduces drastically). Once expired, the pulp will be destroyed.

Teams and roles. Together with your teammates, you will be in charge of TFC. If you make the right decisions, you will save the company from going under. Things have been going badly at TFC for some time now – it's running at a loss, customers are complaining bitterly about poor service levels and, in the meantime, the warehouses are bursting at the seams with stock. In short, something's got to be done. Will you be the one to save TFC?

Each team member has a specific role: Vice-President (VP) Purchasing, VP Operations, VP Sales or VP Supply Chain Management. All team members have their own responsibilities in terms of the role they assume, allowing them also to make their own decisions. However, as a great philosopher once said: 'Together is not alone.' Cooperation is the key to saving TFC from going under.

The *VP Purchasing* is responsible for purchasing the components. They negotiate the terms of supply and the price with suppliers, and can terminate existing contracts and conclude new ones. The VP Purchasing plays a crucial role in the game. By choosing suppliers who offer favourable terms, low prices and a high level of reliability, the total purchasing costs are kept under control, stocks stay low and the reliability of delivery of components to production is high.

The *VP Operations* is in charge of the production facilities and the warehouses. They orchestrate the work shifts and ensure that the staff are trained. They also decide on the space and staff deployed in the warehouses. The VP Operations can make or break the game for the entire team. By ensuring that the production system remains flexible, production costs are low and reliability high, the total production costs are controlled while product availability is high.

Product sales are overseen by the *VP Sales*. They negotiate TFC's terms of delivery with customers. Things such as the service level, promotional pressures and the sales volume rebate are all negotiable. The VP Sales plays an extremely important role in the game and their bargaining can result in a high sales price – as long as TFC can keep its promises. And sales are, of course, the launch pad for profits!

The *VP Supply Chain Management* is the glue that holds the other roles together. By devising a supply chain strategy and undertaking intelligent inventory planning, the VP Supply Chain Management plays a decisive role in the team. They can ensure that unreliable suppliers or production facilities are covered by strategically deployed safety stock, ensuring that the company keeps its promises to the customers.

Each team member can make decisions individually, but as a team you need a good strategy to achieve the best results. It is not advisable, for example, for the VP Sales to agree high service levels with the customer while the VP Supply Chain Management is cutting back on stock! That's why it's essential that you always discuss your decisions with each other.

Gameplay. TFC takes a number of rounds to experience. Every round depicts half a year of TFC. A round starts with analysing the initial situation of the round, followed by decision making. As soon as you have finished a round, the round will be calculated and you will jump half a year in time. After that, results can be interpreted and analysed, and complemented with additional reflections about specific supply chain concepts. Then the cycle starts again, until all rounds of gameplay have been finalized. In a typical game setup, complexity will gradually increase throughout the game, meaning that when the rounds in the game advance, more decisions to be taken will be added.

Central indicator for team performance: ROI. The objective is for you and your team to achieve the best possible return on investments. In other words, the sole aim is not simply to make as much money as possible – managing your investments in a proper way also counts. After each round, your team's ROI can be compared to the scores of the other teams. Next to the team score there is also an individual score. These individual scores do not count towards the team score, but it's always nice to be the best in your field! After each round you can check your performance and compare it with the other teams.

Trade-offs. You will make many decisions during TFC. A trade-off is incorporated into every decision, so a decision will never have only positive effects, but will have negative ones too. The trick is to assess these consequences and to balance them against each other. Should you not make any decisions during a given round, the decisions made in the previous round will be reused.

Strategy and tactics. TFC is a tactical and strategic game. You will be assessed in terms of the long-term effects of your decisions, as expressed by your team's ROI. This means that you must gear your business towards long-term goals (as if your decisions will be in effect over many years). Given that we will measure the results in terms of their long-term effects, you will never suffer in the current round the negative consequences resulting from poor decisions in previous rounds. The advantage of this is that you can organize the business in a new way in every round, without having to take the decisions and results from previous rounds into account. But, of course, by analysing your results from the previous rounds closely, you can start making improvements.

Back to theory for a moment

In Chapter 1, a number of concepts were touched upon. Let's go back to some of those. First of all, we spoke about *definitions* and the importance of clarifying them whenever you are working with others, in order to avoid confusion. In TFC's system you will find a lot of specific terminology. Some of it might be very clear or straightforward, other wordings might be less familiar to you. In those cases, don't guess nor make assumptions about what things could possibly mean. Like in real life, go out and ask for clarification. In this case, you can do that by clicking on the ① symbol, which can be found next to many of the words on the TFC screens.

Second, the question was raised of how big our supply chain is, how many stages backwards or upstream in the supply chain we want to look and manage actively, and how many stages downstream. In TFC, since the company is in such big trouble, we start with looking only at direct suppliers and direct customers. As soon as we have fixed the most urgent issues there and get the company into more stable waters, we might start widening our scope, but for now we leave it at one stage upstream (direct suppliers) and one stage downstream (customers).

In Chapter 1 we also spoke about the fact that *size sometimes does matter* in supply chains. In the case of TFC, this might have an impact, for example when negotiations are at hand or when collaboration projects could be considered. Not all customers are the same size, nor are all suppliers. Some are more important to TFC than others and, to some, TFC is more important than to others, and this might influence the relationship. You will have detailed information available about all companies involved in TFC's supply chain, so be sure to analyse this aspect as well.

We finished Chapter 1 by looking at the pieces of the puzzle, the *building blocks of the supply chain*. In that context we spoke about the integral logistics concept, consisting of four different elements:

- *Physical infrastructure.* In the case of TFC, the physical network is fairly straightforward, as can be seen in Figure 6.3. Suppliers send materials to TFC, which produces (mixing and bottling) and ships out to customers.
- *Planning and control mechanisms.* In the case of TFC, you as the new management team have the task and responsibility of defining the appropriate planning and control mechanisms and the way you want to go about decision making as a

Figure 6.3   TFC's supply chain (linear)

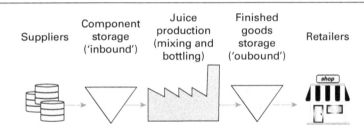

team: which information to analyse, which indicators and targets to put in place, how to align with each other in the team, and so on.

- *Information and subsequent systems requirements.* In the case of TFC, you will have the company's ERP system at your disposal, and you cannot make any choices about the type of system you want to have. In this case, the ERP system is very open, meaning that all team members have access to all parts of the system: every team member can see all screens and access all reports, including the ones corresponding to other functional areas. However, you can only actively touch and modify the decisions corresponding to your own role. Like most systems, the ERP system contains a wealth of data, some of which you might find relevant, while there might be other data that you might find, over time, that you hardly use. Also, as in most systems, there might be information you consider relevant, but it's not available, or not in the desired level of detail. As when these things happen in real life, you will simply have to deal with it.

- *Organizational setup.* In the case of TFC, you will be the local management of a single-factory company, so in that sense there is no real difference between central and local. Each of the team members has a functional responsibility for a specific area (sales, operations, supply chain, purchasing). On top of that, the team will have to decide how to deal with issues that are not strictly related to just one function, such as the definition of overall startegy and cross-functional co-ordination. This last point is pretty much intertwined with the aforementioned topic of planning and control mechanisms.

What's wrong with TFC?

A step-by-step approach to analyse the baseline

As you have seen so far, TFC is a company that's in big trouble. With your team, you enter as the new board of managers with the objective of turning the financial results around and make the company profitable again. This process of turnaround would obviously start with getting a very clear view on the current situation, so that on the basis of your observations you will be in the position to define corrective actions to improve the situation.

EXERCISE 6.1

Analyse TFC's initial situation

In the following pages, a step-by-step approach for the analysis phase is presented. Besides getting a first view on what needs to be done to improve things, you will also get to know the screens of the simulation, as well as the information you have at your disposal.

Referring back to the section *Guided Tour, web resources and business simulation game* at the beginning of the book, use the appropriate course code to enter the system via the game portal. Initially, focus your efforts on analysing the information corresponding to your own role in the team (sales, purchasing, operations, supply chain). This would be valid for Steps 1–4. Then, in Step 5, you bring your individual observations, conclusions and suggestions together with those of your fellow teammates, so that an integrated approach can be defined. Please note that the information you will find in the reports in the different screens represents the company's performance over the past six months.

The five steps presented in this chapter will help you to establish a thorough understanding of the initial situation in which TFC finds itself. Please note that Steps 2–5 can also be applied in exactly the same way after every single round of gameplay.

Step 1: supply chain infrastructure and flows

In Chapter 1 we spoke about different types of supply chain mappings and their importance for creating a clear view on a supply chain. Now take a piece of paper, or an empty PowerPoint presentation, and make a *network flow map* of the material flows of TFC. Your initial map should look something like the Figure 6.4, as prepared by Team SuperJuice.

Your map should include the following elements:

- 5 components and 1 supplier for each component;
- 1 inbound warehouse for components, with an external overflow warehouse next door in case the warehouse is full and new materials are still coming in from suppliers;

Figure 6.4   Template: TFC's supply chain (network)

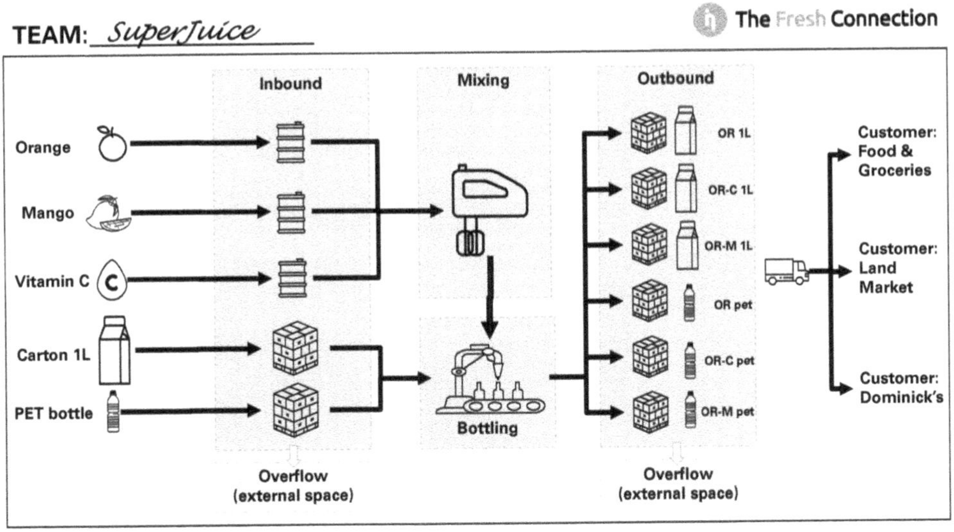

- 1 mixing line for mixing the ingredients of the juice;
- 1 botting line for putting the juice into the appropriate packaging: a 1-litre carton, or a 0.3-litre plastic bottle (PET);
- 1 outbound warehouse for finished goods, with an external overflow warehouse next door in case the warehouse is full and new goods are still coming in from production;
- 6 final products (3 flavours × 2 packaging types = 6 SKUs);
- 3 customers.

Step 2: what were the decisions taken by the previous management team?

According to Bob McLaren and his fellow co-owners of the company, the previous management team are the ones who brought the company to its disastrous current situation by making a series of bad decisions. The next step in the analysis is to understand which decisions they have made that caused such negative results for the company. Go to the screen of your role by clicking on the corresponding tab and analyse the information that can be found on the decision-making part of the screen (Figure 6.5).

Bring the most relevant information elements to the map you created in Step 1 and locate them where they belong on the map. Per role, for instance, take a look at Figure 6.6.

Please note that in case of Sales and Purchasing, the items mentioned might differ per customer or supplier, respectively, so should be analysed per each of those.

Your map should now be getting filled with information.

Figure 6.5   TFC screen: decision-making part

Decision screens

SALES	OPERATIONS	SUPPLY CHAIN	PURCHASING
Tabs for: • Negotiation of agreements with customers • Order management (priority rules)	Tabs for managing capacity of : • Inbound warehousing • Mixing • Bottling • Outbound warehousing	Tabs for planning of: • Components • Production • Products	Tab for: • Negotiation of agreements with suppliers

Figure 6.6   Past decisions: examples of items to analyse in the decision screens

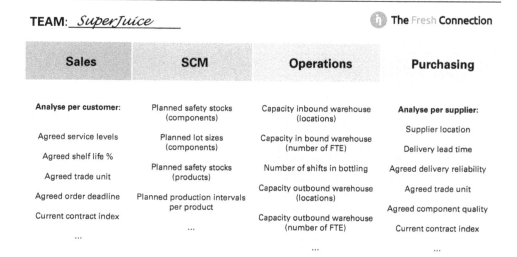

TEAM: *SuperJuice*   ⓝ The Fresh **Connection**

Sales	SCM	Operations	Purchasing
Analyse per customer:	Planned safety stocks (components)	Capacity inbound warehouse (locations)	**Analyse per supplier:**
Agreed service levels	Planned lot sizes (components)	Capacity in bound warehouse (number of FTE)	Supplier location
Agreed shelf life %			Delivery lead time
Agreed trade unit	Planned safety stocks (products)	Number of shifts in bottling	Agreed delivery reliability
Agreed order deadline	Planned production intervals per product	Capacity outbound warehouse (locations)	Agreed trade unit
Current contract index		Capacity outbound warehouse (number of FTE)	Agreed component quality
...	...	...	Current contract index
			...

Step 3: what happened as a result of the previous management team's decisions?

Obviously, it is possible that there is a big difference between the decisions made by the previous management team and the results they actually obtained. So, in the next step, we add the real results of their decisions to the analysis. Go to the screen of your role by clicking on the corresponding tab and analyse the information that can be found on the bottom left-hand side of the screen (Figure 6.7).

Here you will find a number of different reports, providing you with a wealth of information. Take a look at the different reports so that you know which information you actually have available. Bring the most relevant information elements to the map you created in Step 1 and locate them where they belong on the map. Per role, for instance, take a look at Figure 6.8.

Figure 6.7   TFC screen: report part

Report screens

SALES	OPERATIONS	SUPPLY CHAIN	PURCHASING
Reports about: • Customers • Products • Customer–product • Product–customer • Finance	Reports about: • Warehousing • Mixing and bottling • Finance	Reports about: • Components • Products • Finance	Reports about: • Suppliers • Components • Finance

Figure 6.8   Past results: examples of items to analyse in the report screens

TEAM: _SuperJuice_   The Fresh Connection

Sales	SCM	Operations	Purchasing
Analyse per customer:	Average stock levels (components)	Utilization rate inbound warehouse	**Analyse per supplier:**
Realized service levels	Variability of stock levels (components)	Utilization overflow inbound	Realized delivery reliability
Realized shelf life %	Average stock levels (products)	Flexible manpower inbound(FTE)	Rejection rates
Bonus / penalties (in EUR)	Variability of stock levels (products)	Utilization rate outbound warehouse	Purchase volume (in EUR)
Sales per customer (in EUR)	Obsolescence per product	Utilization overflow outbound	Demand per week (in units)
Demand per customer (in units)	Utilization rate bottling line	Flexible manpower outbound (FTE)	...
...	...	Utilization rate bottling line	
		...	

Please note that in case of Sales and Purchasing, the items mentioned might differ per customer or supplier, respectively, so should be analysed per each of those.

Step 4: what happened between decisions and results – gap analysis

Analyse the main differences between the planned performance and the real results. You now have the inputs from Step 2 (previous decisions) and Step 3 (previous results), brought together in the map that was created in Step 1. This allows you to form your own opinion about where the bigger issues might be. What has been happening and why?

At this stage, in order to get an even more complete picture, you might also want to create a *geographical flow map* of TFC's supply chain. Its retail customers are located in the same country as TFC (in The Netherlands, as you remember from a previous section), and information about the location of the suppliers can be found by clicking on the ⓘ symbol next to the name of a supplier in the purchasing decision screens. You could even try to adjust the thickness of the lines between TFC and its suppliers as a function of the amount of product flowing between them.

EXERCISE 6.2

Decide on the first action plan to turn the company around

Decide

As a last step of the initial work done to get a grip of the situation, it is now time to translate your findings into workable actions.

Step 5: what should be done now – action plan

Now bring your individual inputs, observations and suggestions together with those of your colleagues in your team. This will give you a complete and comprehensive insight into the overall performance of the company and potential causes for current losses. Go through the map together and get clarity on the observations of each one of you:

- Highlight, for example in red, all items that catch your attention in terms of discrepancy between what should have happened and what did happen.

- For each of the identified items, which specific actions can you think of to improve on the current situation? Write those down, per each of the functional areas of sales, operations, supply chain and purchasing.

Figure 6.9   Template: observations from diagnosis and proposed actions

TEAM: _SuperJuice_   The Fresh Connection

Functional area	Observations	Proposed actions
Sales	Penalties with all customers Low delivery reliability ...	Promise less service or increase performance (check how with OPS and SCM) ...
Operations		
Supply chain		
Purchasing		

Please note: make sure that you really focus on _concrete actions_. One of the more common mistakes I see is to mainly mention the desired outcomes, rather than corrective measures. For example, if achieved service levels are perceived to be too low, then avoid describing the corrective action as 'improve service level', because it just specifies the desired outcome without specifying how to actually achieve it (there are many different steps that can be taken to contribute to the improvement of service levels). See Figure 6.9 for a template from Team SuperJuice that you can use.

TFC gameplay: what you need to know

Your first analysis of the company's initial situation has been done and you're almost ready to go, but before going to the business dimension of TFC's supply chain, let's first take an additional look at TFC gameplay. Normally, you would be participating in a game in which different teams from the same school or university play together in the same game. The exact configuration of the game, meaning which decisions can be taken in which round, has been decided upon by the course instructor, taking into consideration the exact learning objectives of the course in which the game is used.

There is a wide variety of possibilities for course setups. Sometimes the game is played 100 per cent in class, with active presence of the course lecturer in terms of explaining concepts and being available to answer teams' questions. Sometimes the game is played 100 per cent outside class hours, with lecturers being available at given times to give feedback and/or clarify doubts. Also, more and more blended formats can be found. Again, the decision about how to set up a course using TFC is a choice by the course lecturer, depending on available time and course objectives, and would normally be communicated to you prior to the start of the course.

Whatever the format chosen, the sequence of activities is normally quite similar, pretty much following the learning cycle of Kolb as discussed previously in Chapter 1:

1 Profound analysis of the current situation by the team.

2 Decision making and implementation of decisions in the simulation.

3 Closing of the round by the instructor in order to calculate results.

4 Reflection on the results, typically complemented by some exercises in order to 'conceptualize' the reflections.

5 Back to Step 1, profound analysis, for the next round.

Please note that there are certain parallels between the steps above and the steps normally performed according to frameworks of continuous improvement, such as CAPD (check–act–plan–do). The main, but important, difference lies in Step 4, in which explicit reflection takes place with the aim of analysing relationships between causes and effects, as well as on the students' own actions. This step invites participants to take a step back from immersion in the gameplay and look at what has actually happened, from a distance so to speak. If well done, this should boost learning based on a much deeper understanding of the factors at play.

Depending on the exact size of the student group in a class, it is common for lecturers to request you to prepare your thoughts on the reflections and conceptualizations and send those in for feedback. Remember, it is in those reflections and their translation into new decision making that the real learning takes place.

A few words on decision making in the game: in the roles of Operations and Supply Chain, there are a number of different tabs each representing a different part of the functional scope for which decisions need to be made:

- *Operations* has separate tabs for:
  - inbound warehouse (goods reception and component storage);
  - mixing of ingredients;
  - bottling of juice;
  - outbound warehouse (order preparation and shipment).
- *Supply Chain* has separate tabs for:
  - component (ie raw material safety stock levels and lot sizes);
  - production (frozen period in production planning and scheduling);
  - product (finished goods safety stock levels and production batches).

Basically, on each of those tabs one or more parameters need to be defined, potentially changed and then saved by clicking on the 'save' button. Decisions (parameter changes) that haven't been explicitly saved will not have been implemented, so please make sure to check carefully that your decisions have indeed been saved. Please note that in the following pages and chapters a number of screens from the game will be shown, but in a slightly 'stylized' way. These screens are shown to illustrate relevant concepts, but they have been stylized in order to cater for the possibility of design changes that might take place on the real screens in the game.

In the roles of Purchasing and Sales, the decision making largely consists of negotiations with suppliers and customers, respectively. Negotiation takes place individually with each supplier and with each customer. In order to start a negotiation, the corresponding VP has only to click the 'yes' button in the agreement screen of a particular customer or supplier in order to access the negotiation screen. In that screen, the negotiable contract parameters can be seen, as well as the so-called *contract index*. The contract index is an indication of the price to be paid, either by your customer to you, or by you to your supplier.

If the index goes up, the resulting price is higher; if it goes down, the price is lower. If a change in a certain contract parameter is considered, it can be changed in the corresponding field in the negotiation screen and then, by clicking on the 'calculate' button, the new contract index will be shown, so that the difference in price becomes clear. If the new price is acceptable, clicking the 'deal' button implements it (see Figure 6.10).

Figure 6.10   Negotiation window (example from sales role)

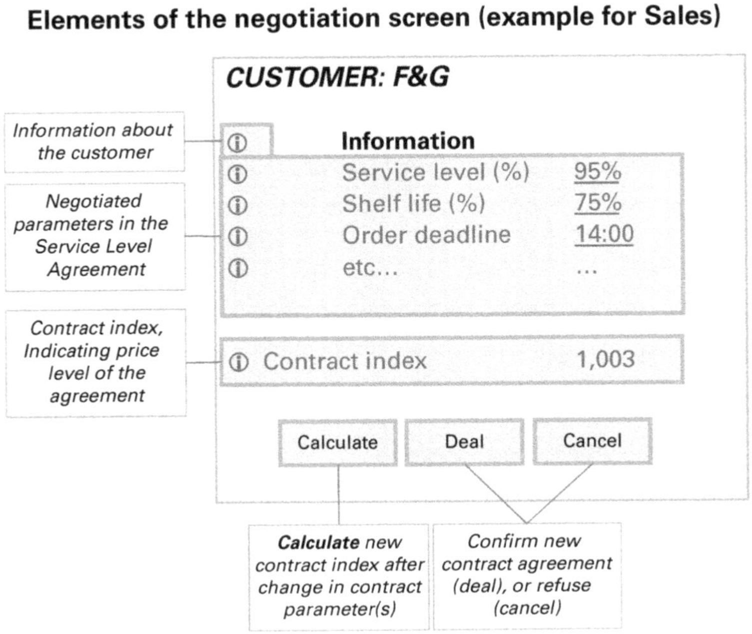

Elements of the negotiation screen (example for Sales)

CUSTOMER: F&G

Information about the customer	ⓘ	**Information**
	ⓘ	Service level (%) 95%
Negotiated parameters in the Service Level Agreement	ⓘ	Shelf life (%) 75%
	ⓘ	Order deadline 14:00
	ⓘ	etc... ...

Contract index, Indicating price level of the agreement — ⓘ Contract index   1,003

| Calculate | Deal | Cancel |

Calculate new contract index after change in contract parameter(s) | *Confirm new* contract agreement (deal), or refuse (cancel)

Please note that the resulting contract index in purchasing will be applied to the 'basic price' of components and the resulting contract index in sales will be applied to the standard 'sales price (retailing)'. Both these basic prices can be found in the 'information' tab. For example, if your contract indices with customers are lower than those with your suppliers, this doesn't automatically imply incurring losses, because both indices will be applied to different figures.

Also, be aware that in the case of all four of the roles, all decisions can be undone, changed, redone and so on as many times as you want during the gameplay of one round. Those parameters which are set at the moment of closing a round for calculation are the ones that will go into the calculation of the results of the round.

Please note that the TFC calendar is based on *working days*: five days per week. This is also valid for lead times from suppliers. If these are longer than one week, they are then expressed in the number of working days of lead time (a 30-day lead time would mean six weeks).

Summary

In this first chapter of mastering the fundamentals you have got to know TFC and the problems the company has. With your team you have done a step-by-step analysis and you have your ideas prepared for making changes in the first round of gameplay.

In the next four chapters, the journey will continue and we will go back to the business, technical and leadership dimensions of supply chain management, as well as the integral view on global complexity, and apply them to the case of TFC. For each of the topics, you and your team first analyse the current situation and the possible alternatives for improvement, and then decide on what needs to be implemented. All exercises will explicitly follow this sequence of analyse and decide. Each chapter will end with a final reflection on the combined topics of the chapter.

EXERCISE 6.3

Reflect on the way of working as a team during gameplay

Reflect

As a team you have now done your first analysis of the situation and you have defined your ideas on the way forward in terms of decisions to be made as soon as the gameplay starts. Similar to Steps 1–5 followed in this chapter, the analysis and decision making around most of the topics in Chapters 7 through 10 will be recurring and repeated in every round of gameplay, taking the results of the previous round into consideration while preparing decisions for the next round. Therefore, it is important to reflect upfront on how you will organize yourselves as a team during the gameplay, when normally some more time pressure will be there as well. Take some time to do that now.

Please note that that your course lecturer will typically guide you during the rounds of gameplay and assist in defining the focus for each round. The exercises within each of the chapters will be of help. As in real life, the company continues and decisions will have to be updated and made constantly, adjusting to previous results. The exceptions to this are the definition of corporate and supply chain strategies, which you will normally only do at the strategic level every once in a while, and the initial design of the overall S&OP decision-making process, which you would do once and then implement and gradually improve over time.

Mastering the business dimension of the supply chain

07

Now that the starting point of TFC's situation has become clearer from the initial overview created in Chapter 6, it is time to analyse in more detail some aspects related to the 'business' dimension of TFC's supply chain and master the fundamentals related to it. The topics in Figure 7.1 were introduced in Chapter 2, and in the following sections we will put our focus on three of them: competitive strategy, customers and value propositions, and supply chain and finance. We will come back to the complementary topics of competitive advantages, business models and the external environment in Part Three.

Together these topics form part of the main inputs to defining the adequate supply chain setup, as we know by now from the integral logistics concept (Figure 1.2, p 10).

Competitive strategy

In terms of the competitive strategy of TFC, we can be fairly brief at this stage. You can assume that the basic fruit juices that TFC offers are of sufficient quality that it can compete with other manufacturers in the industry and that it fits with the expectations of different market segments. Referring back to Porter's strategies in Chapter 2, for the sake of argument, we will leave out the niche strategy for the moment, which implies that we will focus on the choice to be made between a *cost leadership* strategy (low cost) and a *differentiation* strategy, based in this case on superior service and quality, as expressed in terms of flexibility of ordering, reliability of delivery and freshness of the product. In terms of Tracey and Wiersema's framework, the most accurate way of describing it would probably be as choosing between the *operational excellence* strategy on the one hand, with a clear focus on

Figure 7.1   Topics from the business dimension of the supply chain

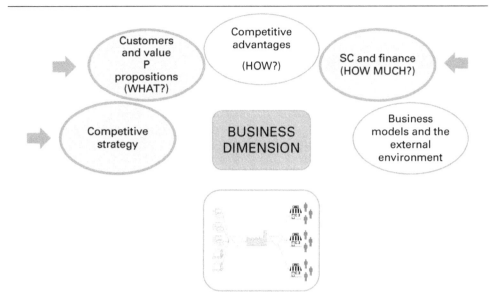

low cost, and the *customer intimacy* strategy on the other, with a clear focus on offering a no-stress, superior-freshness and highly flexible full service to the customer.

As can be deduced from the above, this means that competition is not so much based on the 'core product', but much more on the product/service surround, as discussed in Chapter 2. If you offer better or more service, your retail customers will be willing to pay you more money per litre of juice, and if you offer less service, they will pay you less.

EXERCISE 7.1

Analyse and decide on competitive strategy

Analyse

Since you cannot do a real market analysis at this stage, analyse whether there are any preferences in the team for any of the given strategies of cost leadership/ operational excellence (low cost) or differentiation/customer intimacy (full service and quality). If so, analyse what the reasons behind those preferences are.

Decide

As a team, decide on the competitive strategy you want to pursue: cost leadership/ operational excellence (low cost) or differentiation/customer intimacy (full service and quality).

Please note that with either of these two basic strategies you will be able to achieve good results in the simulation in terms of return on investment (ROI), as long as the strategy is implemented thoroughly and backed up by a well-aligned and coherent supply chain strategy. As noted also by DeSmet (2018):

> [D]ifferent strategies lead to different ways of reaching that same goal. The operational excellence leaders will work at lower margins but compensate with higher efficiency on the capital employed. The product leaders require more capital to lure customers to more high-end products, but they manage to compensate for this by higher margins... Different strategies lead to different levels of complexity, and each of them can be equally successful.

Customers and value propositions

TFC has three different customers. As the VP of Sales will probably already know by now, these three customers are not equal. They are different in terms of size (number of stores and therefore sales volume in litres of juice), locations and market share. But also, are they different in terms of their own competitive strategies? Some might be following a cost leadership strategy, or a differentiation strategy, or even a niche strategy towards their customers, in this case the consumers of the juice. By clicking on the ⓘ symbol next to the name of the customers in the sales screens, you can find more information about each of your customers, the retailers.

Another factor to keep in mind is that because of their own different competitive strategies, they will most likely react in different ways to the proposals you might present to them during sales negotiations. As in real life, each of them is probably sensitive to different elements of the service level agreements. For example, one of your customers might be willing to pay you 4 per cent more per litre of juice if you promise them an increase of 2 per cent in service level, whereas another of your customers might only be willing to pay you 1 per cent more for the same increase, simply because they are less interested in it, as it probably fits less well with their own competitive strategy.

EXERCISE 7.2

Analyse customer preferences and decide on value propositions

Analyse

With each customer you negotiate the same contract parameters as part of the service level agreement, but the value of the various parameters can obviously be very different for each of the customers:

Figure 7.2 TFC screen: sales contract parameters (example of one customer)

CUSTOMER: F&G

ⓘ **Information**
ⓘ Contract index   1,003
ⓘ Service level (%)   95%
ⓘ Shelf life (%)
          75%
ⓘ Order deadline   14:00
ⓘ Trade unit
          Pallet layer
ⓘ Payment term (weeks)   4 weeks
ⓘ Promotional pressure   Middle

ⓘ Negotiate | Yes |

- By clicking on the ⓘ symbol next to the names of the customers in their respective agreement overviews, open the profile of each of the three customers and compare the descriptions.
- Based on the information you find in their profiles, to which contract parameters would you expect each of them to be more sensitive (see Figure 7.2 for an example overview of the contract parameters)? Which contract conditions would be more critical to the pursuit of the commercial strategies of each of the retail customers and why?

Decide

What do you propose to do with these insights?

Supply chain and finance

As you will have seen, there is a tab called 'Finance' in TFC's ERP system, where you can find a financial statement (see Figure 7.3).

In terms of the finance statements, let's focus here on four concepts that were highlighted in Chapter 2:

- *Earn & spend (income statement)*. The part on the middle left-hand side of the diagram contains the elements of the income statement. Starting with the revenues, it then shows all the expenses. It allows you to analyse in detail of how the P&L is built up. The column with the comparison between the two most recent rounds enables a clear view on decisions taken and the financial results obtained.

Figure 7.3   TFC screen: financial statements

ROI (OVERALL ROI)			
EARN & SPEND (DETAILS OF THE INCOME STATEMENT)	Results of the last round (6 months)	Results of the next to last round (6 months)	Difference between last and next to last rounds
OWN (DETAILS ABOUT ASSETS)			

- *Own and owe (balance)*. In the financial overview of TFC, the focus in the 'own & owe' part is on the assets side of the balance sheet and doesn't emphasize the liabilities. This is because Bob McLaren and the other owners of TFC want you to dedicate your time and efforts to the execution of the business while they take care of the financing aspects themselves. Shown are fixed assets and machines (from Property, Plant and Equipment), inventories and the resulting investment due to payment terms.

- *Working capital*. Because of the way the finance statement in TFC is structured, and because in terms of the balance sheet the focus is on the assets, rather than on the liabilities, there is a large overlap between the balance sheet and the elements of working capital. As stated under the previous bullet point, inventories and the resulting investment due to payment terms can be found in the finance statement under the heading of 'Investments'.

- *Return on investment (ROI)*. On the upper line of the finance statement you can find the ROI. A truly powerful performance indicator, it combines the result of the income statement with the result of the investments to give an overall view on company performance. This indicator can also be objectively compared between different teams, since all are playing with exactly the same market circumstances.

EXERCISE 7.3

Analyse the finance statement and ROI and decide how to use this information

Analyse

Analyse the finance statement in detail, so that you become very familiar with what it contains. Most lines in the finance statement are directly connected to decisions in the different roles in the game. Go through the statement line by line and try to establish a link between the items mentioned and possible decisions in the game that might be connected to it.

Which are the elements in the finance statement that have most impact on the achieved ROI? If necessary, go back to some of the financial indicators dealt with in Chapter 2, such as the ones related to cost of goods sold (COGS), inventories, PPE and so on. What does this tell you in terms of priorities in decision making? You can also use data visualization software to get a grip of the current financials (see Figure 7.4 for an example).

Decide

How do you propose to use this information in the next round(s) of gameplay?

Figure 7.4   Analysis of P&L figures using data visualization software

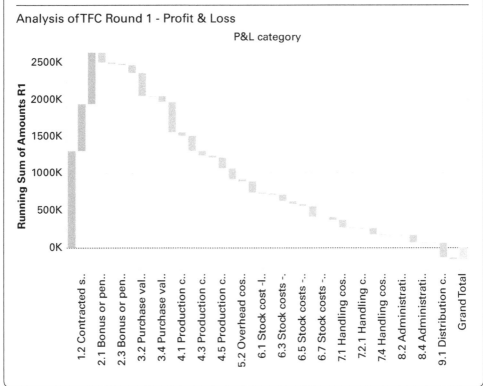

Analysis of TFC Round 1 - Profit & Loss

Please note that it is very recommendable to start each round of gameplay by going back to the finance statement and checking out the differences between the two last rounds played. With your colleagues, you should be able to explain each of the differences line by line, since they are all connected to decisions taken by the team in the

Figure 7.5 Topics from the business dimension of the supply chain applied to TFC so far

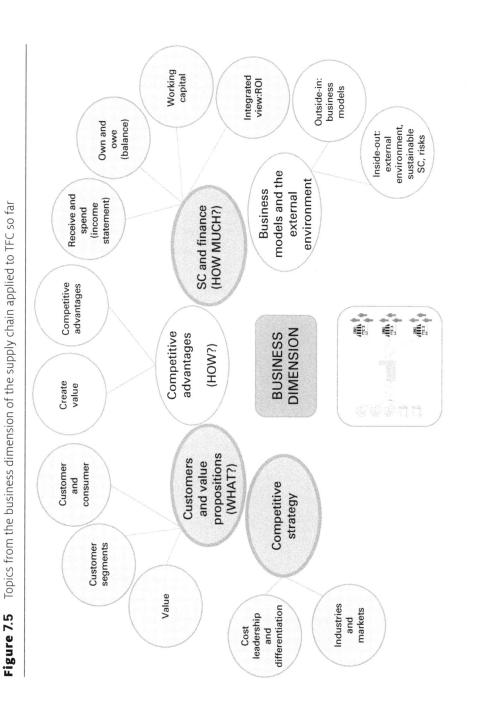

previous round. For example, if I were looking at the overview after finishing round 2 of gameplay, and I went to the line where it states *Pallet locations raw materials warehouse* and I saw under round 2 an amount of 80,000, under round 1 an amount of 100,000, and in the Difference column an amount of –20,000, I would need to be able to explain why the amount of money spent on the pallet locations in the raw materials warehouse has been reduced by 20,000. Which decision was taken in the round 2 gameplay that caused this reduction? Since decisions about pallet locations fall under the exclusive responsibility of TFC's operations manager, they would be in the best position to answer the question.

In this example, since we know that one pallet location has a cost of 200 per annum, or 100 per round, and the reduction in money spent has been 20,000, the conclusion needs to be that we reduced the number of pallet locations in the warehouse by 200. The operations manager should then be able to confirm that. You should follow the same logic for every line in the finance overview.

Please note that in the basic version of TFC gameplay, the cost of capital is set at 15 per cent per annum, that is, 7.5 per cent per round. This is relevant for calculating the interest costs associated with the stocks ('interest on stock value').

Summary

This brings us to the end of the application of the business dimension of the supply chain to TFC, in which the topics shown in Figure 7.5 in grey have been dealt with in more detail. Some of these will come back again in Part Three, as will the topics shown in Figure 7.5 in white.

EXERCISE 7.4
Reflect on topics from Chapter 7

Reflect

To properly close the chapter and follow the principles of the learning cycle of experiential learning, please go back to each of the topics from Figure 7.5 and reflect on what you have learned. Specifically, think about your learnings regarding:

- The different theoretical concepts and their practical application in real-life situations. To what extent are the concepts clear, and have you experienced the trade-offs involved? What would you do differently next time?

- The analysis and decision-making process. How did you go about the analysis so far? How has the decision making been organized in the team and to what extent was it difficult to reach agreements?

- Your team's behaviour. To what extent was everyone actively involved? If not, why not? What was done to deal with it in the best possible way?

Obviously, the story doesn't end here; we will take it right into the next part, which is about the application of the technical dimension to TFC. But remember, all business aspects remain relevant here as well.

The journey of mastering the fundamentals of the supply chain will now continue in Chapter 8 with the application of the technical dimension of the supply chain to TFC.

Mastering the technical dimension of the supply chain

08

In this chapter we will go back to many of the topics exposed in Chapter 3, in which the fundamentals of the technical dimension of the supply chain were explored. Now we connect the concepts of this dimension to TFC gameplay, so that you can start seeing the many challenges of their application in real life (Figure 8.1).

Referring once more to the overall concept as shown before, we will deal here with supply chain strategy, aspects of the physical infrastructure, planning and control, and information systems.

Supply chain strategies

Efficient or responsive supply chains

In Part One, we addressed different typologies of supply chain strategies and the underlying issues of choosing a particular typology in a particular situation. The aspects of predictability and volatility were highlighted as two very important inputs to the choice of supply chain strategy, 'efficient' and 'responsive' being the widely used extremes of the spectrum. We also said that, for the sake of argument, we would stick to applying either one of the extremes of the spectrum during gameplay, so that they become really clear to the reader in all their implications and serve, in a way, as the identified boundaries within which all other typologies can also be positioned.

In the previous chapter, you were asked to decide on a corporate strategy: low cost or differentiation (from Porter's framework), or operational excellence versus customer intimacy from Tracey and Wiersema's framework. In both cases, the second option applies mainly to the quality and service aspects of the juice business (freshness and flexibility). The chosen corporate strategy will obviously be the input

Figure 8.1   Topics from the technical dimension of the supply chain

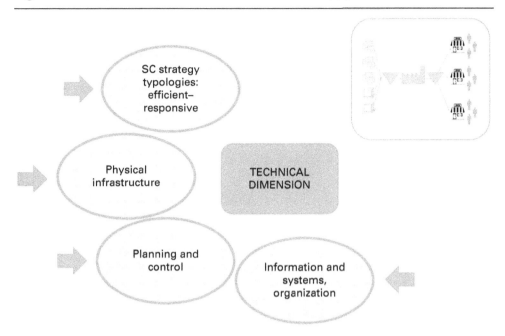

to the different functional areas and lead to defined functional policies: overall strategy will determine, for example, the commercial focus, leading to more or less predictability and volatility, leading to a better-suited supply chain typology. So, as a next step, take your chosen corporate strategy as a starting point for determining the details of your supply chain strategy.

EXERCISE 8.1

Analyse supply chain typology and decide strategy to be put into action

Analyse

Based on your chosen corporate strategy (cost leadership or differentiation), what would be the corresponding supply chain typology: efficient (low cost) or responsive?

Decide

On the basis of your answer to the previous question, use a template like the one from Figure 8.2 to determine the direction of specific actions per functional area.

Figure 8.2   Template: corporate strategy into supply chain action

Sales	SCM	Operations	Purchasing
TEAM: _SuperJuice_		STRATEGY: _Low Cost_ The Fresh Connection	

Sales	SCM	Operations	Purchasing
Service level ↓	Safety stocks Components	# Shifts	Delivery window
Order deadline ↓		# Pallet locations	Delivery reliability
Shortage rule	Safety stocks Finished goods	# FTE	
Shelf life	Lot sizes production	SMED	Trade unit
Trade unit	Lot sizes purchasing	Increase speed	
		Intake time	Supplier selection
		Prev. maintenance	Payment terms
Payment terms	Frozen period	'Solve breakdn.' training	Component quality
		Raw materials inspection	Transp modality

Please note that Figure 8.2 contains a number of decisions from a fairly standard configuration of the game. It can serve as a good starting point for defining what the elements of a chosen supply chain typology are. In the example in Figure 8.2, Team SuperJuice has chosen to pursue an efficiency/low-cost supply chain strategy. Now it has started to indicate, per each of the functional decisions from the table, in which direction they should go. For example, according to the team, in the case of a low-cost supply chain strategy they think that service levels promised to the customers should be on the lower end, indicated in the table with an arrow pointing down. Similarly, they think that the agreed order deadlines should be on the lower end. And so on.

Upon finishing the entire table, the team will have created a more specific plan for implementing the chosen strategy, thus giving a much clearer context for each of the VPs to work within for their individual decision making (strategy into action). In a way, with this activity you will have already set the scene for some of the aspects that will be dealt with in more detail in the coming sections.

Two more comments about this table, which can be extrapolated into any real-life supply chain, are:

- The table will be created by the team to the best of their current knowledge. As in real life, there might be some trial and error required before a solid final version is there. Maybe some of the arrows will change and will be pointing in a different direction later on, or perhaps they will be eliminated altogether because of insights that will be obtained during gameplay. This is perfectly fine and happens in the best companies. All new projects have an element of *ongoing discovery* and this is nothing to worry about. Just make sure to keep the strategic map updated as you go along.

- In addition, the table created obviously doesn't indicate how low 'on the lower end' is. It shows an arrow, not a number. These numbers might even vary between customers, suppliers and products, so will be part of the fine-tuning during actual implementation. Also in real life, this fine-tuning will be part of any implementation and will take some time before becoming really clear – another example of trial and error. Probably, by the end of gameplay you will be in a much better position to state to which range of values a downward arrow actually refers, because the experience of decision making in the various rounds and the corresponding results will have demonstrated that to you.

In the next section we will do a more detailed analysis of the different elements of the supply chain. But first, let's make a quick sidestep into the topic of data and reporting.

Averages kill!

Although, strictly speaking, more connected to the topic of information and systems, which will follow towards the end of this chapter, it is important to mention here one specific dimension related to it. Since in the coming sections we will be doing a lot of analyses using data from TFC's reports, it is important to have a good understanding of what these data actually represent. Particularly important is to make a clear distinction between numbers representing a total and numbers representing an average, and in both cases whether these totals represent, for example, a weekly or a six-month (one round) total or average. The definition of each item in the reports can be found by clicking on the ① symbol next to it, also specifying whether it's a total or an average.

In the case of averages, it's important to question what the behaviour around the average has been. This is also what quality improvement philosophies such as Six-Sigma focus on. And since, as in real life, the exact underlying data are not always visible to everyone, we need to make some assumptions here. But first, let's go to a very basic notion of averages, easy to understand but with serious implications. In the following six figures, the average demand per month over the total one-year period is the same: 100 units per month. This is easily calculated: total demand in one year, divided by the number of months, gives the average demand per month (Figure 8.3).

Figure 8.3 Average demand of 100 units per month

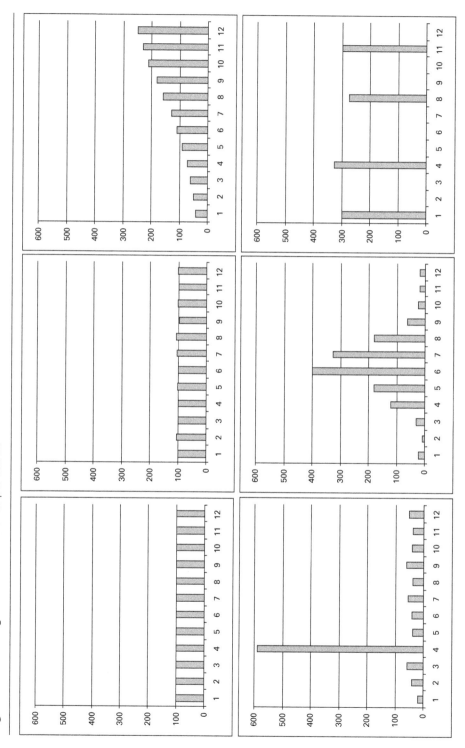

However, as can be easily understood, the real situation is totally different in each of the cases, for example leading to very different decisions regarding purchasing, production and inventories or even forecasting of future trends. Thus, be careful with averages – they might kill your future performance if interpreted incorrectly! Averages are interesting and useful pieces of information, but do not show the complete picture, only part of it. For example, an average doesn't reflect major or minor fluctuations, nor does it detect upward or downward trends, nor does it warn you about what are known as 'outliers' (exceptional one-time occasions).

Relating this to The Fresh Connection business simulation game, you can assume that most averages you will see in the reports will have an underlying pattern, as shown in Figure 8.3. Most of you will recognize it as the 'normal distribution', 'bell-shape' or Gauss curve, from basic statistics theory. Without going into the statistical specifics, for now just retain the message that most averages in the reports in TFC will show a similar underlying curve, meaning, roughly speaking, that approximately half of the values have been below the average, half of them above.

So, for example, even if the six-month average attained (ie achieved) shelf-life value as expressed in the customer sales reports looks OK to you in comparison to the value as agreed with the customer, be aware that a number of times this average wasn't reached and you actually achieved a shelf life that was a lot lower (ie not meeting customer agreements), and that in some cases you actually achieved a higher than average shelf life. In this particular example, you can contrast the attained shelf life with the amount of obsolete product, as can be found in the product sales report, to check the potential impact. You should make your interpretations accordingly.

Let's now look in detail to the elements of the technical dimension of the supply chain.

Physical infrastructure

In order to position the details of the different aspects of the physical infrastructure, it's important to highlight once again the importance of the global, holistic view. In the following sub-sections we will address, step by step, a number of concepts, all important in their own way, but none of them really independent of the others. We will deal with them here separately and sequentially, but with the understanding that they aren't separate, and should rather be dealt with iteratively than purely sequentially, as part of a larger global exercise.

Products: physical characteristics of components

In the starting situation, TFC deals with five different components, which have very different characteristics. Out of the many possible product characteristics, perishability is not really an issue: the shelf life of the various fresh components is two rounds (ie one year) for the fruit pulp, and even longer for the packaging materials. Also, the materials are not considered to be dangerous goods requiring special transportation or storage.

However, some components are solid, others are liquid, some are large, others small. Some are cheap, others more expensive, some are used in high quantities, others not. These characteristics do have an impact on how they can be managed in a smart way. Recall, for example, the concept of value density from Chapter 3 and the implications for how to use that in component segmentation and differentiating management priorities (see, for example, Figure 3.5, p 46).

EXERCISE 8.2
Analyse component characteristics and decide
on how to manage components

Analyse

Create an overview of the five components that TFC is using in order to manufacture their current product portfolio. You can use the template from Team SuperJuice (Figure 8.4) as a guideline. Part of the table is related to the physical characteristics of the components, part to their usage in terms of production or sales volume.

Figure 8.4   Template: component characteristics

TEAM: _SuperJuice_   STRATEGY: _Low Cost_   (i) The Fresh Connection

| Component | Component value density | | | Component usage | | | |
	Units per pallet	Price per unit	Value per pallet	Units per 6 months	€ per 6 months	Units per week	Pallets per week
Pack							
PET							
Orange							
Mango							
Vitamin C							

The corresponding information to populate the table can be partially found in the 'Information' tab in the simulation, and partially in the 'Component' report accessed via the purchasing VP's screen. Please note: the numbers you find are specific to your game's configuration and to your team's current performance.

As you can probably appreciate from the overview you have created, TFC's components are indeed very different in terms of size, value, quantities used and money spent. Now think about how you can use these insights to manage them in a more efficient and effective way and set smart priorities. Think about storage space utilization, transportation modes, trade units, lot sizes in purchasing, available capacity at suppliers, and so on. What are your conclusions? Write down your observations and conclusions per component by adding a column to the table you created.

Decide

What do you propose to do, based on these findings?

Products: physical characteristics of finished goods

The product portfolio of TFC, in the starting situation, consists of six products (six SKUs): three different flavours, sold in two different packaging types. All obviously contain liquid, but none is considered to be dangerous goods. Fragility doesn't seem to be an important issue, nor is the complexity of the bill of materials (the latter can be found in the 'Information' tab). However, there are two characteristics that deserve special attention in this case, perishability and physical volumes:

- *Perishability (shelf life).* As indicated earlier, the components that TFC is using have a long shelf life; however, as soon as water is added to the fruit pulp, the shelf life of the newly produced product changes. Shelf life is now only 20 weeks. This is what we call the *technical shelf life*, expressing that after this period the product is technically no longer usable, in the case of fruit juice meaning that you can no longer drink it. There is also another concept, called the *commercial shelf life*, which expresses the time that the product still has a commercial value. Sometimes products are technically still fine, but since new editions of the product have appeared on the market, their value has drastically reduced. As is normally the case for many retail products, the commercial shelf life is determined by a negotiation with the retail customer.

  TFC's VP of Sales negotiates with each customer a shelf life for the products, meaning that the remaining shelf life of any carton or bottle shipped to the customer can never be less than that particular agreed shelf life. As you can see, this is different from how drinkable the juice still is. The more shelf life promised to the customer, the more they are willing to pay, since they will have more time and therefore more opportunity to sell the product in their stores.

It is fairly obvious why this is relevant for the 'technical' dimension of the supply chain: the more shelf life I have to give to my customer, the less time I have between mixing and bottling the ingredients and doing the distribution. In other words, if my policy is to offer long shelf life to my customer, my supply chain setup should be relatively faster to make that feasible. Thus, it has consequences for my inventory policies, my production batch policies, my production capacity and machine choices, and so on. More about this later in the section about planning and control.

- *Physical volumes.* The second relevant aspect regarding physical characteristics of finished goods is their physical volume. Although the differences are not as large as in the case of the components, the finished products also have different physical sizes, for example expressed in the number of 1-litre cartons or 0.3-litre PET bottles that fit on a pallet. In addition, it might make sense to take a look at volumes in litres of juice sold and produced, for example per round, in order to put that into the perspective of number of pallets per SKU. These inputs are important when put into the context of defining, for example, the trade units, the lot sizes in production (production intervals) and the safety stock levels, which in their turn have an impact on, for example, warehousing capacity and production capacity. More about this also later in the section about planning and control.

As can be seen from the abovementioned aspects, product characteristics do have an important impact on the physical aspects of the supply chain, as well as on some of the planning parameters.

Push/pull: customer–order decoupling point

Recalling the diagram showing customer–order decoupling points (CODPs, Figure 3.6, p 49), and recognizing that TFC's supply chain is not 100 per cent identical to the one in the diagram, TFC's setup could be characterized as CODP 2, Make to central stock (MTS). Since this choice cannot really be challenged in the basic gameplay, we will just take it as a given and come back to the topic in Part Three.

Facilities: warehousing and production

The main facilities in TFC's supply chain are the factory and the two warehouses, for components and finished goods, respectively. For storage of the liquid components there is also the tank yard, which is used when these components are supplied in tank trucks. We can also add the other 'nodes' or 'hubs' in the network, as represented by the suppliers and the customers. The latter or, more correctly, the central warehouses of the latter, are located relatively close to TFC's manufacturing location, in order to facilitate fast delivery. Supplier locations are given in the supplier profile as well as in the overview of the purchasing agreements, and can be challenged as soon as the decision to change suppliers can be made.

The strategic decision of the location of TFC's own factory and warehouses, as well as of their overflow warehouses (additional storage with a third party next door in case their own warehouses are completely full at any given moment), will not be challenged in the standard setup of gameplay, but we will come back to that point also in Part Three. What you can challenge, though, is the size of the warehouses in terms of physical space, as well as their capacity in terms of human resources, and the machine capacity for mixing and bottling. Let's explore those a bit more in order to know what the situation is.

EXERCISE 8.3
Analyse production and warehouse capacity utilization and decide on actions

Analyse

As a starting point for deciding later whether to change warehousing and/or production capacity, thoroughly analyse the existing capacity situation:

- Go to the Operations reports of 'warehousing' and 'mixing and bottling'. Try to get a good understanding of what the different parameters and graphics are telling you. Click on the corresponding ⓘ symbol if any of the terminology is not clear.

- What is your interpretation of the situation? Has there been any underutilization of capacity or maybe any overcapacity and, if so, how much of it has there been? What could have been the reason(s) for this? Think about the patterns and volumes of the ingoing flows and the patterns and volumes of the outgoing flows, as well as the available capacity itself. What could be the causes of those patterns?

- What have been the consequences of underutilized capacity? What have been the consequences of overcapacity? What would need to be done to optimize the situation and become more efficient and/or effective?

Decide

What do you propose to do, based on your conclusions?

The exercise above has given you a clear image of the capacity status, but this is only part of the picture. Not only is it important to understand the current situation well, but also to have a very clear understanding of how capacity can be changed (ie increased or decreased) and what the implications of such changes might be. Let's take a look and analyse.

EXERCISE 8.4

Analyse options to change production and warehouse capacity and decide on actions

Analyse

Warehousing capacity for inbound as well as outbound goods consists basically of two different elements: space and people. Go to the Operations screens and find out the following information:

- What is the cost per year for one person (Full Time Equivalent – FTE) working in the warehouse? How much percentage increase in available capacity would one additional person give you? Please note that one round of gameplay represents six months, ie half a year. Most numbers in the reports represent one-round totals or averages.

- What is the cost per year for one pallet location in TFC's own warehouses?

- What is the cost per day for one pallet location in the overflow warehouse next door?

Capacity in the mixing stage of production consists basically of the mixing machine and its associated costs. By clicking on the ⓘ symbol next to the machine name, the machine fact sheet will appear. Check it out. If the configuration you're playing includes the option of changing machines, check out the other possible machines you could select and compare the cost and capacity aspects from the other machines' fact sheets as well. What are the strong points and weak points of each of the machines in terms of:

- capacity/speed;
- flexibility/changeover or cleaning time/minimum batch size;
- operating costs;
- investment.

In your opinion, in which cases would either one of the available machines become an attractive alternative?

Bottling capacity consists of machine capacity, including a fixed number of operators depending on the type of machine you are working with, plus a decision on the number of shifts you operate. Once more, the machine fact sheet will show you the information. Check it out and analyse the following, per each of the available machines:

- How many people are required to run the machine? Therefore, what is the labour cost associated with one additional shift of operation? How much extra capacity would that additional shift give?

- Total capacity.

- Operational fixed costs.

- Flexibility in terms of changeover times per formula (recipe) or packaging type.

- Tolerance for different-quality grades of bottles and cartons.

- Efficiency in terms of start-up productivity losses.

- Investments.

In your opinion, in which cases would either one of the available machines become an attractive alternative?

Bottling capacity can also be influenced by doing improvement projects, such as preventive maintenance, 'solve breakdowns' training, increase speed and SMED (single-minute exchange of die) action. For each of those, check out the associated costs as well as the expected benefits.

In your opinion, in which cases would either one of the optional improvement projects become an attractive alternative?

Go to the Finance statement and check out the cost components associated with the abovementioned topics to see how much they (would) represent of the total costs of operations. Now you would be in a position to make a fairly complete cost–benefit analysis for different scenarios. What are your conclusions on the basis of this?

Decide

What do you propose to do, based on your conclusions?

Transportation

In the case of TFC, as in real life, most transportation modes are to a large extent geographically determined. For TFC's specific situation, in the case of customers road transportation is the main mode, because of physical proximity. For suppliers it basically also depends on their location: delivering by truck from China to the

Figure 8.5   TFC screen: changing the transport mode for shipments from a supplier

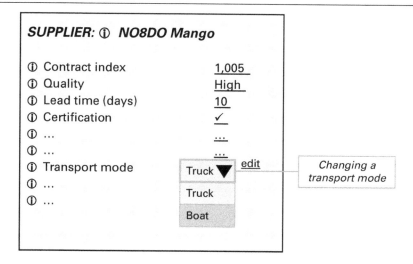

north-west of Europe is obviously a theoretical option, but in reality a very impractical and unrealistic one. There may, however, be some exceptions – suppliers for whom more than one transport alternative exists. You can see that information in the overview of the agreement in the Purchasing screens. Next to the transport mode there will then be the option to 'edit', and after clicking, the available options appear (Figure 8.5). A new mode can be selected and saved. The supplier lead time will change according to the newly chosen transport mode.

In the supplier profile that appears by clicking on the ⓘ symbol next to the name of the supplier, the costs associated with the currently chosen mode of transportation can be found. If another mode is selected *and saved*, and the profile is then opened again, the new transport costs appear, so that they can be compared with the previous costs (see Figure 8.6). The transport mode can be changed back at any time before closing the round of gameplay.

Outsourcing and collaboration

Part of the decisions about the physical infrastructure has to do with 'make or buy'. TFC has made such decisions, although in a fairly straightforward way. TFC doesn't own any fruit plantations, nor does it have any packaging manufacturing capabilities. During standard gameplay, this degree of vertical integration will not be challenged. However, this doesn't imply that there are no further choices to be made with respect to the setup with suppliers.

Figure 8.6   TFC screen: supplier profile, including transport costs associated
with chosen mode

Transport costs (can change in case transport mode is changed)

SUPPLIER SPECIFICATIONS

Name	No8DO Mango
Product range	Mango
Market share world market	8%
...	...
...	...
...	...
Costs per shipment	€ 100.00
Transport costs per pallet/Drum/IBC	€ 20.00
Transport costs per FTL/Tank truck	€ 500.00
...	...
...	...

Just as we saw earlier when discussing the characteristics of components and found that different characteristics may lead to different priorities in sourcing, transportation and warehousing, this might also have an impact on how we actually want to deal with the suppliers of those components. Some components may be more critical for our business than others, so our relationships with their respective suppliers might then also be critical to our business.

EXERCISE 8.5
Analyse components and suppliers' priorities and decide on actions

Analyse

Recalling Kraljic's framework from Chapter 3 (Figure 3.7, p 54), analyse the different components TFC is using, looking at how much money you spend on each of them, as well as how important they are to the total product mix you are selling.

Then look at the various suppliers for each of the components and try to evaluate the complexity of the supplier market for each component. How many alternative suppliers are there, what are their characteristics, are there large differences between them, and so on?

Taking the previous inputs, how would you position the different components in the framework? Which are the more strategic ones?

What does the above tell you about the way you might want to deal with the different suppliers, ranging from arm's-length purchasing to very close cooperation and joint development?

Decide

What do you propose to do, based on these conclusions?

In order to make the picture complete, we need to bring in another dimension we briefly touched upon before: size sometimes does matter. Obviously, you as the management team can have your own opinion about with which suppliers it makes sense to try to establish strategic relationships, but that alone doesn't mean that those suppliers also see the point to that. They run their own businesses and the fact that they are very important and strategic to you doesn't automatically mean that they think you are very important and strategic to them.

So, in addition to the supplier segmentation as done previously, we need to take a closer look at the suppliers we're particularly interested in.

EXERCISE 8.6
Analyse supplier characteristics and decide on actions

Analyse

For those suppliers you would consider to be strategic to you and with whom you would be interested in establishing more than just an arm's-length relationship, open their supplier profile by clicking on the ⓘ symbol next to their name or next to the word 'info' when looking in the supplier market. Read the profile and try to determine how important you could be to them. Which pieces of information tell you something about that?

You can do the same for the other suppliers in the market for the same component. What is the picture there?

What does the above tell you about the likelihood of being able to establish very close cooperation and joint development with the potential strategic suppliers?

Decide

What do you propose to do, based on these conclusions?

Network design

We will not challenge the current structure of TFC's network at this stage and will come back to that in Part Three. The only part we will look at from that perspective now is the one representing the supplier base.

EXERCISE 8.7

Analyse the geographical flow network and decide on actions

Analyse

If you haven't done so already in Step 4 of the mapping exercise in Chapter 6, this might be a good moment to draw a geographical network map of TFC's supply chain, focusing on the location of TFC itself as well as of its suppliers. You can also consider using the thickness of the lines connecting TFC with its suppliers as an expression of the volume and/or frequencies of the flows between them, potentially also adding the lead times along the lines.

What conclusions can you draw from this map?

Decide

What do you propose to do, based on your conclusions?

After having looked in this chapter at a number of very relevant aspects related to the physical infrastructure, we will leave this topic for the moment. We will return to it in Part Three, but we will now focus on the next area of attention in our overall supply chain concept: planning and control.

Planning and control

Before diving into the details of planning and control, it's important once again to highlight the importance of the global, holistic view. In the following sub-sections we will address step by step a number of different concepts, all important in their own way, but none of them really independent of the others. We will deal with them here separately and sequentially, but with the understanding that they aren't separate, and should be dealt with iteratively rather than purely sequentially. This will all fall into place at the end of the chapter when addressing the overall S&OP/IBP process.

Uncertainty and variability

As soon as the physical infrastructure has been defined, we can start looking at the decisions to be made within the given supply chain network, that is, our overall framework for planning and control. As you will remember from Exercise 3.7 (p 59), we looked first at sources of uncertainty, because a better understanding of the degree and sources of it would allow us to better determine how we want to deal with forecasting, inventories and production. In Chapter 3 we looked at it in a fairly generic way, but now it's time to apply the same concept to the specific case of TFC.

EXERCISE 8.8

Analyse uncertainty and variability and decide
on how to use this information

Analyse

Use the available reports per each of the four functional areas, as well as the different decisions that can be taken in each of those areas. Start at the market side of TFC's supply chain and work your way upstream towards the supply side of the chain. You could use a template like Figure 8.7 from Team SuperJuice.

Step by step, analyse the degree of uncertainty you find in reports and graphics. Even though the concepts of variability and uncertainty are not identical, as shown in Chapter 3, in this case you might also include variability in your analysis.

Figure 8.7   Template: analysis of uncertainty and possible actions

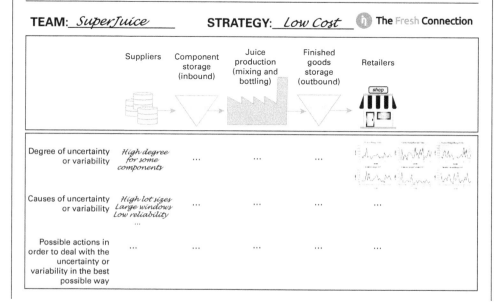

Try to determine the causes. Some of the causes of uncertainty or variability can be external, such as 'autonomous' customer behaviour, but some can also be induced because of decisions taken by your own TFC management team, such as the decision to participate in more or fewer promotions with your customers.

Try to determine, for each of the causes, what would be the best way of dealing with the uncertainty or variability. Please note: uncertainty and variability are not necessarily bad. In some cases, they can actually be the simple consequences of strategic decisions taken by the company itself. In those cases, reduction or elimination of uncertainty and variability might not be the best solution.

Decide

Although you probably don't have the complete picture yet, translate the outcomes of this first step in the analysis into possible decisions about actions to take and carry these forward to the coming steps before making your final choices.

Now that we have a clearer picture of the degrees of uncertainty and variability we must deal with, let's look at the implications of this on one of our major supply chain processes, the *demand to supply (D2S)* process, and particularly on the five keys to this major process we discussed in Chapter 3 (see Figure 3.10, p 58): forecasting market demand, capacity planning, production planning and scheduling, production and quality, and inventory management.

Key 1 to D2S: forecasting market demand

Forecasting is a critical activity, since it provides a starting point for upstream decisions about production, warehousing and transportation. Its impact is different in the case of more uncertainty compared to less uncertainty, more variability compared to less variability. Better forecasting doesn't impact variability, but might reduce uncertainty, depending on the causes of the variability.

Another important role of forecasting is with respect to the sales function in the company, which informs their colleagues in the operations areas about potential changes in expected sales volumes. Whenever decisions on promotions and/or product portfolio come into the picture, for example, forecasting gains in relevance, because the operational functions of purchasing, operations and supply chain might need to make changes accordingly (in production capacity, storage capacity, safety stock levels, and so on). For example, safety stock settings in TFC are expressed in weeks of demand, based on the expected demand per week coming from the forecast. Let's work our way step by step through the forecasting cycle.

Step 1 in forecasting is actually looking into the past in terms of achieved sales, but also in terms of delivery performance. Let's first look at past sales. In most basic configurations of TFC, there is a certain 'baseline' sales volume; call it the market size. This volume is pretty much the same in every round of gameplay, meaning that the *total amount of juice in litres* in one round is stable. Within this total six-month amount in litres a lot of day-by-day and week-by-week variability may exist, so total six-month demand may be stable, but it is not flat.

Now we should also look at past delivery performance; in other words, how did we deliver on the promises made? This should lead to conclusions about room for improving on the promises, or the need to make them less aggressive.

EXERCISE 8.9
Analyse sales performance and decide on how to use this information

Analyse

Taking the contract conditions as negotiated with each of the customers as a starting point, define which key performance indicators (KPIs) would best express your performance on each of the agreed conditions.

In the different sales reports, analyse your current performance based on the defined KPIs.

What gaps between promise and delivery do you see? How big are they? What have been the consequences of these gaps?

The gaps between promise and delivery can normally be closed either by improving delivery performance or by reducing the promises, or by a combination of both. Which options would you see as most feasible?

Also, analyse in detail the financial performance by product and customer in terms of contribution rate, margins and so on.

Decide

What conclusions do you draw from these analyses? Although you probably don't have the complete picture yet, translate the outcomes of this first step in the analysis into possible decisions about actions to take and carry these forward to the coming steps before making your final choices.

Step 2 would be to take into consideration any information already available about external future industry, market or demand trends as well as company decisions already taken in the past but still to be implemented, for example introduction of new products, new channels and/or new geographies. We will leave this topic for the moment and come back to it in Part Three.

Figure 8.8   Effect of sales promotions

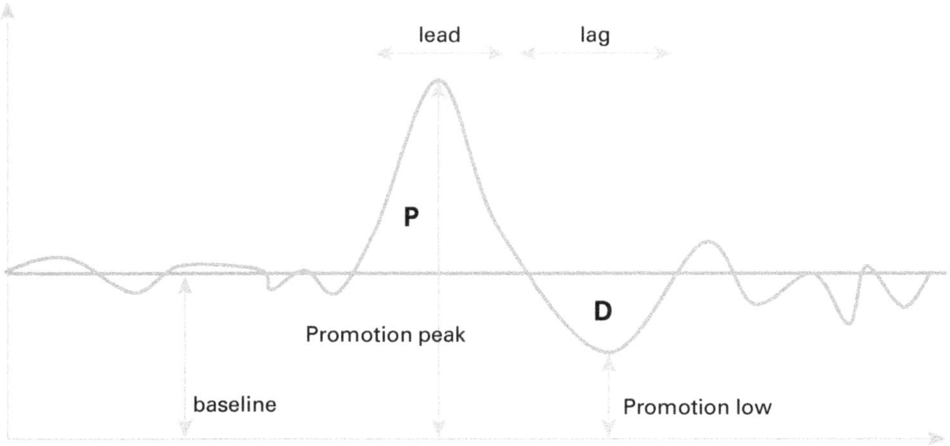

Baseline   = regular sales without promotions
Lift factor = promotion peak/baseline
Dip factor = promotion low/baseline
Net effect = surface P − surface D

Step 3 would then be to develop potential future scenarios, based on the previous historical analysis complemented by available information about the future. Scenarios may include changes in the product portfolio, for example eliminating a product because of bad margin performance, or because of continuous operational problems with the particular SKU; or considering participating in more promotions with one or more of the retail customers, trying to boost juice sales that way.

Both decisions will have an impact on the total amount of juice sales in litres (positive or negative), and in the case of more or fewer promotions, the degree of variability may also be affected: even though the net effect of promotions on sales is positive, more promotions do create higher peaks in sales, followed by longer slow periods (see Figure 8.8).

EXERCISE 8.10

Analyse sales scenarios and decide on their attractiveness

Analyse

Putting the input from the previous steps together, plus the options you have in terms of promotions and product portfolio, now develop scenarios for future demand, in order to close gaps between promise and delivery. Assess customer response, in terms of the contract index, to the changes you contemplate. How much increase or reduction in revenue do these changes imply?

If possible in the specific configuration of the game you play, include the possibility to do more or fewer promotions, to have more or less promotional pressure and to change the product portfolio. What are the (quantified) financial impacts you would expect from these decisions?

Decide

What are your conclusions on the different options you have looked at? Decide on which scenario you like best.

Figure 8.9   TFC screen: forecasting window

Product forecasting

Product	① Weekly demand	① Increase/decrease (%)			① Forecast
Fressie Orange 1 litre	67,400	(−)	0%	(+)	67,400
Fressie Orange/Mango 1 litre	42,200	(−)	+5%	(+)	44,310
Fressie Orange/C-Power 1 litre	11,400	(−)	0%	(+)	11,400
...					...
...					...
...					...

Finally, *step 4* would be to decide on the chosen scenario and create a final forecast, which can then be shared with colleagues in the company management team. Forecasting is done via the forecasting tab, as shown in Figure 8.9. In this screen, the VP Sales can indicate per each of the products in the portfolio, in steps of plus or minus 5 per cent, the expected increase or decrease in sales in the next round.

The updated forecast can now be consulted by fellow TFC management team members on the same screen used by the VP Sales to make the adjustments. In addition, the VP Supply Chain can use this updated forecast information in an analytical decision support tool, called the production interval tool, with which optimization of production intervals can be analysed (more about this tool under *Key 3 to D2S: Production planning and scheduling*).

EXERCISE 8.11
Analyse findings from the previous steps and decide on sales forecast

Analyse

Go back to your findings from the previous steps and check that your final conclusions are solid enough to move forward.

Decide

Based on the insights from the first three steps, now decide on your final forecast for each SKU.

There are two widely used performance indicators for measuring the 'forecast error' or 'forecast accuracy': MAPE and BIAS. Both aim to express the reliability of the forecast, although in slightly different ways:

- **MAPE** (mean absolute percentage error): MAPE is a measure of the forecast unreliability. It is determined by specifying the absolute forecast error (real demand minus forecasted demand) *on a weekly basis*. The sum of the forecast errors for all of the weeks is then divided by the sum of the demand of each week. A MAPE of 0 per cent is the ideal, in which case the demand has been equal to the forecast. But if the MAPE is high then the difference between forecast and reality has been large and the forecast apparently unreliable. Since the forecast in TFC is done on a six-month total, the forecasted demand per week is simply the average demand per week based on the forecasted total. MAPE will then be higher in case there is more variability in the demand per week (ie higher difference between average forecasted demand and peaks/valleys in demand).

- **BIAS:** the bias is calculated by evaluating the forecast after the previous round against the real demand in the current round, that is, *based on six-month totals*. The bias is the relative difference between these components. In other words, it is the six-month total forecast minus the six-month total real demand divided by demand. Using this definition, a positive bias means that the forecast was higher than demand, a negative bias means that the forecast was lower than demand. Both positive and negative biases are likely to lead to issues. A positive bias drives increased inventory. Clearly this is due to the fact that the predicted requirement is higher than actual sales. As a result, your inventory cost will increase and the potential for obsolescent products increases. A negative bias, on the other hand, can lead to low inventory cover, which may result in poor service delivery.

Figure 8.10 TFC screen: custom report generator ('Analysis')

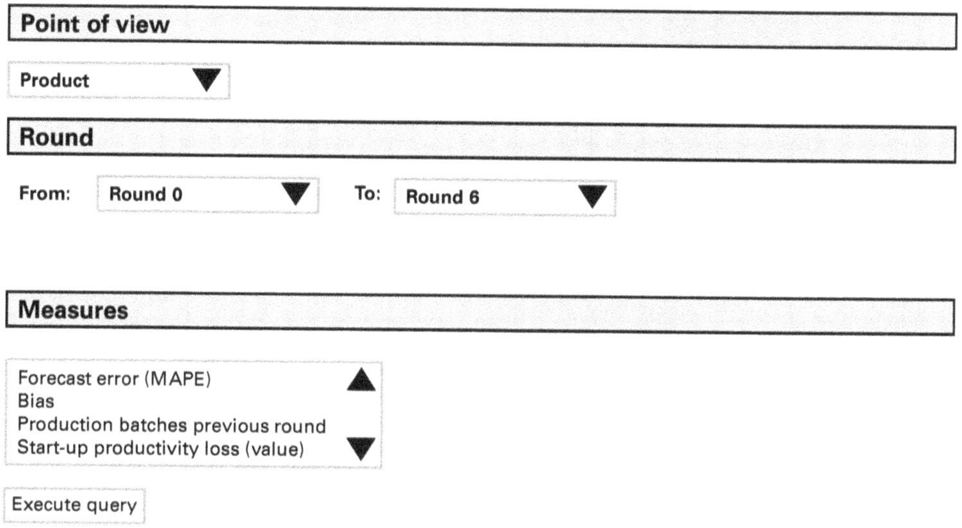

Point of view

Product ▼

Round

From: | Round 0 ▼ | To: | Round 6 ▼ |

Measures

Forecast error (MAPE) ▲
Bias
Production batches previous round
Start-up productivity loss (value) ▼

Execute query

When the round has been completed and calculated, MAPE and/or BIAS forecast performance can be checked either in the sales reports, or via the option to create custom reports by clicking 'Analysis' in the list of reports. A number of parameters can be set, thus specifying the desired report (see Figure 8.10). For each of the four roles a different set of parameters can be included in the reports.

Before closing this section on forecasting, please note the following very important comment: *a forecast is a piece of information; it is never a self-fulfilling prophecy*. In other words, a higher forecast is not a starting point that will automatically lead to higher sales. The process is precisely the other way around: the VP Sales contemplates a series of decisions and potential external market effects, as a consequence of which sales volumes might be affected. The forecast is then used to inform the other team members of those expected changes.

Key 2 to D2S: capacity planning

Taking the most recent version of the forecast into consideration, in terms of volumes as well as in terms of volatility, the VP Operations can now prepare the necessary changes regarding inbound storage capacity, mixing and bottling capacity, and outbound storage capacity. Since there is only one manufacturing facility, in this case there is no choice to be made in terms of allocating demand to different production sites.

Referring to the initial assessment of the current situation of available capacity as well as the costs and benefits associated with making changes in the available capacity, as done earlier in this chapter in the section on facilities, the analysis can now be extended by looking at future projected sales.

EXERCISE 8.12
Analyse sales forecast and decide on capacity changes

Analyse

Taking as a starting point the current status of capacity (shortage or overcapacity of production and storage capacity inbound as well as outbound), take a close look at the sales forecast by SKU.

If there are no changes in the forecasted sales, the focus can be on optimization of utilization of the existing available capacity. With regard to the defined corporate and supply chain strategy, what actions would you propose to optimize capacity utilization, either by increasing flexibility or increasing efficiency?

In the case of a changed forecast:

- By what percentage is sales per SKU forecasted to go up or down?
- How many litres of juice does that imply?
- What is the expected impact on variability of demand (increased or decreased)?
- What are the implications versus the existing available capacity for:
  o inbound warehousing: space and people;
  o mixing and bottling: machine utilization and number of shifts, improvement projects;
  o outbound warehousing: space and people?

Decide

From the different possibilities for changing capacity in storage and production, as analysed above, what actions would you propose to adjust available capacity to make it match the forecasted sales volumes and variability in a cost-efficient way? What arguments in favour of your choice can you bring to the table in case Bob McLaren asks you about it?

Key 3 to D2S: production planning and scheduling

In Chapter 3 the concepts of production batch sizes and the frozen period were mentioned as part of the wider topic of production planning and scheduling. In terms of the frozen period, we leave the implementation question here to be aligned with the chosen strategy: efficient or responsive. Think of what makes sense and try to optimize the exact length of the frozen period within the chosen strategy.

In terms of detailed production planning and scheduling, where you have multiple machines for either mixing or bottling, a decision needs to be made about which SKUs will be allocated to which machines. For example, each machine could have a different operational focus (efficiency or flexibility), thus differentiating between large volume production and smaller batches. Obviously, this is only useful if total machine capacity and total investment are justified by the total volume of demand.

EXERCISE 8.13

Analyse changes in machinery and decide on actions

Analyse

Recall the earlier analyses of the current capacity situation, the forecasted changes in volume and variability, and your suggested actions to deal with these. If you opted for a second machine, in mixing and/or in bottling, which products would you allocate to which machine and why?

What would be the expected new capacity utilization of the chosen machines? What conclusions do you draw from this?

Decide

Which adjustments, if any, would you propose to make in the next round?

Moving on to another important decision within the context of production planning and scheduling, the size of the production intervals, let's first analyse their current status and the resulting impact.

EXERCISE 8.14

Analyse changes in production intervals and decide on actions

Analyse

Go to the Supply Chain screen that specifies the current production intervals. What has been your reasoning behind the current parameter settings? Has any differentiation been done between the intervals of the different SKUs? Why or why not?

Go to the Supply Chain reports on finished goods ('Product'). What is the situation with respect to inventory levels and service levels (in order lines)?

Now go to the Operations report on mixing and bottling. How have the parameter settings for the production intervals impacted on machine capacity in the bottling line?

Referring back to the pros and cons mentioned in Chapter 3 regarding production batch sizes, and taking into consideration the chosen supply chain strategy, to what extent have the decisions so far given the expected results?

Decide

What adjustments, if any, would you propose to make in the next round?

Figure 8.11   TFC screen: opening the production interval tool

Button to access the 'production interval tool'

Just as production and storage capacity might be impacted by changes in demand variability and/or demand volumes, the same might be true for production intervals. Depending on the exact configuration in the game, you might now have the option to use the production interval tool, which can be accessed by clicking on the symbol shown in Figure 8.11.

Using the production interval tool, the VP Supply Chain can model different scenarios, by changing the production interval settings and calculating the impacts on both production costs and overall bottling capacity. The tool works in a fairly linear way, for example not taking into consideration the degree of variability in the demand, machine breakdowns or time spent on preventive maintenance, but may still provide very useful insights into the comparison of different scenarios that the VP Supply Chain may have in mind. Figure 8.12 shows what the production interval tool looks like and the steps that can be taken to use it.

Please note that the production interval tool is a 'decision support tool', a topic we will touch on a bit more towards the end of this chapter. In other words, the tool is a simulator to help you understand the sensitivities of changing certain parameters. Such an analysis can help in coming to a decision, in this case about which

Figure 8.12 TFC screen: using the production interval tool

Production interval tool

Select bottling line

		Swiss Fill 2 ▼			*One of the available machines can be chosen*

	Demand	**Production interval**	
Fressie Orange 1 litre	67,400	10	*Production intervals on the chosen machine for the products assigned to this machine can be changed*
Fressie Orange/Mango 1 litre	42,200	10	
Fressie Orange/C-Power 1 litre	11,400	10	
...	...	...	
...	...	...	
...	...	...	

Calculate

Costs/year		**Capacity/week**		*Impact of the defined intervals on estimated costs per year and capacity utilization per week can be calculated, after which a decision can be made*
Stock costs	€ 62,064	Run time	57.1	
Start up loss	€ ...	Changeover time	...	
Changeover cost	€ ...	...	...	
...				
Total costs	€ ...	**Total utilization rate**	...%	

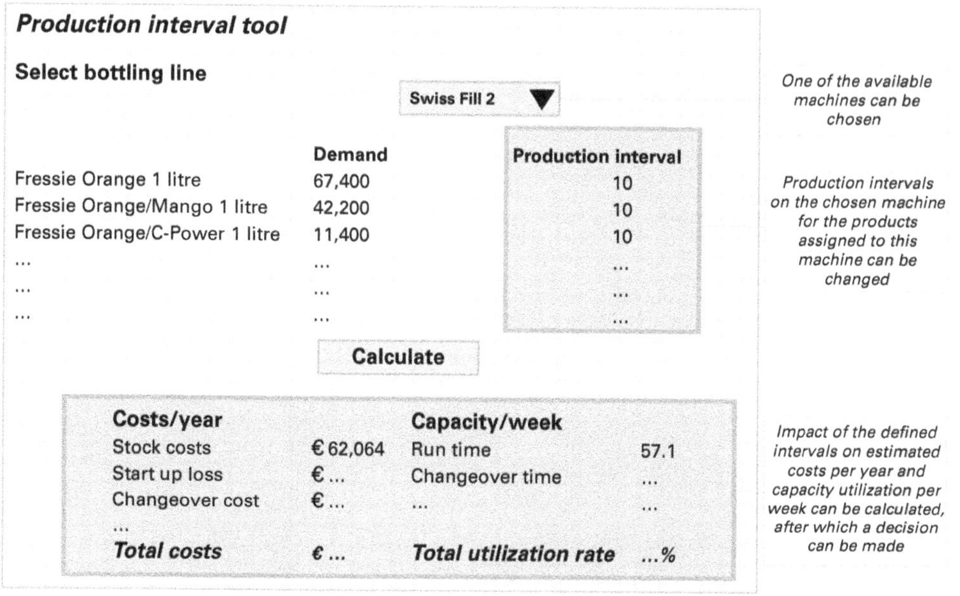

production intervals to choose. As such, the tool doesn't make any decision, nor does it implement the decision. That still needs to be done by the VP in question in the corresponding decision screens.

Please note that the first numerical column in the production interval tool shows the forecasted sales volume per product. This information comes directly from the forecasting screen as adjusted by the VP Sales. This means that if the VP Sales has not (yet) updated the forecast, the VP Supply Chain might be analysing the wrong information.

EXERCISE 8.15

Analyse changes by using the production interval tool and decide on actions

Analyse

Taking the current production interval settings, capacity and cost situation into consideration, as well as the chosen supply chain strategy, use the production interval tool to analyse different scenarios. Make sure you work with the most recent forecasts before making a final decision.

What is your conclusion on the basis of these analyses?

Decide

What would you propose to do next? Which compelling arguments would you bring to the table if Bob McLaren asked you to defend your choices?

Key 4 to D2S: production and quality

This brings us to the next key in the Demand to Supply (D2S) process: production and quality. Some of the execution steps in production have very clear operational day-to-day aspects, which are less visible in most basic setups of the gameplay (strikes, absenteeism, weather, traffic, and some others to which we will return in Part Three). However, there are some other aspects of production which have a clear relationship to tactical decisions made in purchasing, operations, or the supply chain.

As mentioned in Chapter 3, one of the main indicators used to express 'hiccups' in production is the 'production plan adherence'.

EXERCISE 8.16

Analyse production plan adherence and decide on actions

Analyse

Go to the Mixing and Bottling report in Operations and check the current level of production plan adherence. If it is 100 per cent, that means it has been possible to produce according to the established production plan.

If production plan adherence has been below 100 per cent, what could have been the exact causes for it in your particular case? Similar to the discussion about production capacity, you would need to look at the variability and uncertainty of the patterns of flow going out of production, the variability and uncertainty in the patterns of flow going into production, and inventory performance in between, as well as the available production capacity and the real capacity utilization in relation to demand volume and variability. All of these aspects might have had an impact on production plan adherence, and since each of them corresponds to a different functional area, different reports would need to be consulted in order to get a clear overall picture. Start at the downstream end and work your way upstream, identifying relevant indicators in every step of the supply chain, functional area by functional area. You can use the template shown in Figure 8.13, from team 'SuperJuice', who, as you can see, experienced a production plan adherence of 72 per cent.

Figure 8.13 Template: analysing production plan adherence

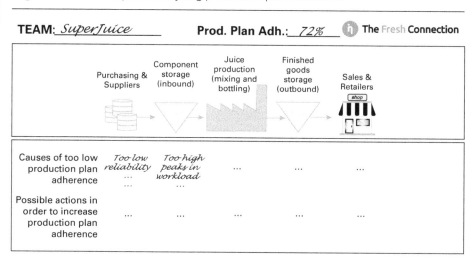

TEAM: _SuperJuice_   Prod. Plan Adh.: _72%_   The Fresh Connection

	Purchasing & Suppliers	Component storage (inbound)	Juice production (mixing and bottling)	Finished goods storage (outbound)	Sales & Retailers

| Causes of too low production plan adherence | _Too low reliability_ ... | _Too high peaks in workload_ ... | ... | ... | ... |
| Possible actions in order to increase production plan adherence | ... | ... | ... | ... | ... |

What consequences has your achieved production plan adherence ultimately had on delivery performance to your customers? And on internal performance in terms of efficiency and effectiveness? Which of these aspects can be quantified and how large has been the impact? These figures should give you a clear view on the 'urgency' of getting it fixed.

Decide

What actions would you propose to increase production plan adherence? Try to quantify the costs of these actions and evaluate how they offset the negative implications of poor adherence so far. What is your conclusion and how do you propose to move forward?

Key 5 to D2S: inventory management (warehouse replenishment)

In Chapter 7 we looked in more detail at the financial impact of inventories, from the point of view of interest to be paid, but above all as an asset appearing on the balance sheet and thus having an impact on the central indicator of ROI. You can take your observations from Chapter Seven as a starting point for what follows now. Recalling the main key concepts from Chapter 3 (see for example Figure 3.12 (p 63) showing the sawtooth diagram of inventory management), let's first look at the logic of inventory management and how it is integrated in TFC.

For *finished goods inventory*, an (R,S) policy is followed, in which the review period R is set to the length of the production interval. So if the production interval of a given product is five days, it means that the review for this product takes place every five days. The order-up-to level S (expressed in days) is defined as the safety stock for that product, plus the production interval, plus the specified frozen period. This quantity in days is then multiplied by the forecasted demand per day in order to express S in quantity of product. This quantity S is then compared to the economic inventory in order to define the exact production batch needed. One more thing to keep in mind is the minimum batch size of the machine used. If this minimum batch size is larger than the production batch needed from an inventory point of view, the machine's minimum batch size will be the dominant factor.

For *component inventory*, an (R,s,S) policy is followed, in which the review period R is set at one week; that is, inventory for components is checked once per week in order to know whether a replenishment order is required. The re-order point s is defined as the safety stock level (covering uncertainty), plus the lead time from the supplier (the bridge stock). The order-up-to level S is defined as the re-order point s, plus the component lot size as specified by the supply chain manager. Similar to the logic with finished goods, this quantity S is then compared to the economic inventory in order to define the exact quantity to be ordered. One more thing to keep in mind in this case is the trade unit as negotiated with the supplier by the purchasing manager. If this trade unit is larger than the component lot size as desired from an inventory point of view, then the negotiated trade unit will be the dominant factor.

Please note the chosen inventory policies in TFC, so (R,S) for finished goods and (R,s,S) for components cannot be challenged in the game.

Let's try to break down the abovementioned inventory policies to enable tangible decision making in the game. The VP Supply Chain decides on the component lot size, as well as on the component safety stock, both parameters included in the (R,s,S) policy. The amount of bridge stock per component is calculated automatically by the simulation tool, on the basis of the lead times of the chosen suppliers (as decided upon by the purchasing manager).

EXERCISE 8.17
Analyse component stocks and decide on actions

Analyse

An analysis of potential sources of uncertainty in supply was done in the section on 'Planning and control' in Chapter 3. Go back to that overview and then check out the 'stock development' graphics of components in the corresponding report in Supply Chain, as well as the KPI for 'component availability %' for each component.

On a performance level, to what extent have the defined levels of safety stock been justified by the identified uncertainty and the achieved component availability?

From a cost point of view, what have been the costs associated with the chosen levels of component inventory? From a global point of view, do the costs seem justified by the achieved performance?

Decide

What do you propose to do next in order to further optimize?

Now let's take a look at the finished goods inventory. Here the VP Supply Chain decides on the production intervals for each of the SKUs, the length of the frozen period, and the safety stock levels to cover demand uncertainty and the potential uncertainty caused by production performance. All these parameters are part of (R,S) policy.

EXERCISE 8.18

Analyse finished goods stocks and decide on actions

Analyse

An analysis of potential sources of uncertainty in demand and production was done previously in the section on 'Planning and control' in Chapter 3. Go back to that overview and then check out the 'stock development' graphics of finished goods ('product'), as well as the KPIs for each SKU for 'Service level (order lines)' and 'Obsoletes (%)'.

On a performance level, to what extent have the defined levels of safety stock been justified by the identified uncertainty and the achieved service levels and levels of obsoletes?

From a cost point of view, what have been the costs associated with the chosen levels of product inventory? From a global point of view, do the costs seem justified by the achieved performance?

Decide

What do you propose to do next in order to further optimize?

O2C and P2P processes: payment terms

As a last reflection, more oriented towards the financial flows as dealt with in the *order to cash (O2C)* and *purchase to pay (P2P)* processes, let's look at the financial impact of variability and uncertainty, and particularly those aspects that refer to the accounts payable and accounts receivable that you can normally find in the balance sheet of the company. Since in the case of TFC you do not have a separate balance sheet, the combined result of the payables and receivables can be found together under the heading 'Payment Terms' in the Investment part of the finance statement. You can use the templates shown in Figures 8.14 and 8.15 in the following exercises.

EXERCISE 8.19

Analyse payment terms and decide on actions

Analyse

P2P: in the profile of each supplier, check when the payment terms start counting, for example at the moment of ordering or at the moment of delivery. If relevant, check the lead time of the corresponding supplier as well as which uncertainties might have an impact on the actual delivery of the components taking place.

O2C: since delivery is next day in the case of having ordered product available in stock, the real payment term is fairly straightforward.

The two partial views analysed above should give you a clearer understanding of the need to finance the time gap between spending and receiving (ie the cash-to-cash cycle as introduced in Chapter 2). For which customers and suppliers, respectively, is the impact on the need for financing bigger? Take into consideration that in the total 'cash conversion cycle', the time that components and finished goods spend in inventory and production will need to be taken into account. This part is visualized in the customer payment term template (Figure 8.14).

In the Finance statement, under 'Investment', now check the total investment due to payment terms, which is the result of payment terms agreements with suppliers and customers. Also, check the amount of 'interest' paid in the last six months ('interest' as found separately in the Finance statement refers only to the financing of payment terms; the interest paid in relation to the amount of inventory of components or finished goods is mentioned under the heading of 'stock costs'). Now you have a starting point for setting priorities on managing the payment terms.

From an investment or financial cost (interest) point of view and in relation to improving overall ROI, to what extent are any changes in payment terms justified, either for (some specific) customers and/or for (some specific) suppliers?

Check the impact of changes in the payment terms on those (specific) customers and/or suppliers (Figure 8.15). How sensitive to price setting, as expressed by the

Figure 8.14 Template: analysing supplier payment terms

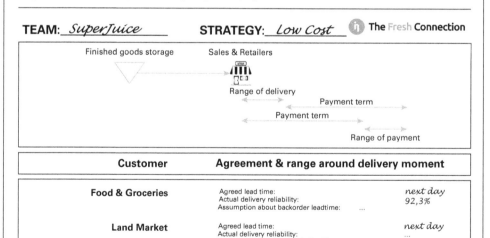

TEAM: _SuperJuice_   STRATEGY: _Low Cost_   The Fresh Connection

Component	Supplier and agreements	Range around delivery moment	
Pack	Mono Packaging Materials (France) Start payment term: at delivery Agreed payment term: 4 weeks	Agreed lead time: Agreed delivery window: Actual delivery reliability:	15 days 4 hours 92,3%
PET	Trio PET PLC (Spain) Start payment term: at delivery Agreed payment term: 4 weeks	Agreed lead time: Agreed delivery window: Actual delivery reliability:	10 days ... ...
Orange	Miami Oranges (USA) Start payment term: when ordering Agreed payment term: 4 weeks	Agreed lead time: Agreed delivery window: Actual delivery reliability:	... ...
Mango	NO8DO Mango (Spain) Start payment term: when ordering Agreed payment term: 4 weeks	Agreed lead time: Agreed delivery window: Actual delivery reliability:	... ...
Vitamin C	Seitan Vitamins (China) Start payment term: when ordering Agreed payment term: 8 weeks	Agreed lead time: Agreed delivery window: Actual delivery reliability:	... ...

Figure 8.15 Template: analysing sales payment terms

TEAM: _SuperJuice_   STRATEGY: _Low Cost_   The Fresh Connection

Customer	Agreement & range around delivery moment	
Food & Groceries	Agreed lead time: Actual delivery reliability: Assumption about backorder leadtime: ...	next day 92,3%
Land Market	Agreed lead time: Actual delivery reliability: Assumption about backorder leadtime: ...	next day ...
Dominick's	Agreed lead time: Assumption about backorder leadtime: ... Actual delivery reliability:	... ...

contract index, are your customers and suppliers to changes in the payment terms? To what extent does that offset gains in interest paid or total investment, thus affecting overall ROI?

Decide

What do you propose to do and why?

Information and systems

As a last topic in this chapter on the technical dimension of the supply chain, we go back to information and systems, the logic being that as soon as the physical infrastructure is determined and the processes for planning and control to manage the flows going up and down the infrastructure have been designed, as a last step we can then define data that need to feed into the processes and the IT systems to provide this information.

ERP system, reporting and data availability

In a way, you can say that TFC's ERP system is the screens you're looking at in the simulation game. It contains information about the relevant functional areas and the decisions taking place in each one. But it also contains a number of predefined reports, which also exist in real life and would be prepared by systems experts using datamining or business warehousing tools. As touched upon briefly earlier in this chapter in the section on forecasting, TFC's system also contains a custom report generator allowing visualization of specific performance indicators, for example in a multi-round view (Figure 8.10).

As in any real-life situation with almost any kind of software, TFC's system contains a wealth of information; you might feel overwhelmed at the beginning, trying to get a good grip of what is available in all of these reports and in which format. It's fairly simple and straightforward and there are really not many excuses: *welcome to your first day at the new job!* The sooner you know what's there and what's not, the better.

At the same time, despite the overwhelming quantity of data available, you might also come to the conclusion that there are still some things missing, or that the format isn't the one you would prefer, or that the level of detail isn't what you want. Again, this is a perfectly normal situation, which you will encounter in any company using any kind of system. Make sure you spend enough time to find data, know what you do or do not have, and understand what data limitations there may be and how they can best be used in your analysis and decision making.

It will take some time before you know all the ins and outs, possibilities and limitations of the system and any potential workarounds that might be necessary to get the maximum out of the available data. How much time you need and how much success you have simply depends on those involved, how much expertise, competencies and/or support they might have, plus the amount of effort they actually put into it. This might be pure coincidence in the case where team composition has been randomly defined, but there is a choice: it's simply up to you to decide how much time to dedicate to which things.

Decision support systems, analytical and visualization tools

Within TFC, to a large extent you are responsible for creating your own decision support system(s). These could be Excel based, or if you have the clearance/permission, you could potentially tap into existing licences for planning software or decision support systems via your school or university or company. There is one exception to this situation, which is the 'production interval tool' already mentioned under the section on production planning and scheduling (Figure 8.12). As you will remember, this tool allows you to model different scenarios and compare the results on cost and capacity criteria as the basis for your decision making. It is important to highlight here that any decision support tool, however advanced it may be, never releases the user from their final responsibility of implementing a decision. Even if a suggestion from a planning system is implemented, whether automated or manually, there has still been a person deciding that the suggestion was fine and acceptable.

With technology advancing at a faster and faster pace, we see more and more tools appear at reasonable prices that allow users to create data visualizations for analytical purposes in relatively easy ways (Figure 8.16). Tools such as Tableau, IBM Watson Analytics or Microsoft Power BI, among others, provide interesting capabilities in this sense (Baker, 2018). At schools and universities, teachers are also putting these or similar tools at the disposal of students so that they get acquainted with them and learn how to use them in a productive way. If you have access to any of these tools, TFC could be a very good integral case for trying them out and using them to your advantage during gameplay.

Summary

With this chapter, we have come the end of the application of the technical dimension of supply chain management to TFC, following the sequence of Chapter 3. We have looked at subjects related to the physical infrastructure, planning and control, and information and systems, as well as some organizational aspects. The topics shown in Figure 8.17 in grey have been dealt with in detail. Some of these, plus the ones in white, will return in Part Three.

Figure 8.16 KPI dashboard created using data visualization software

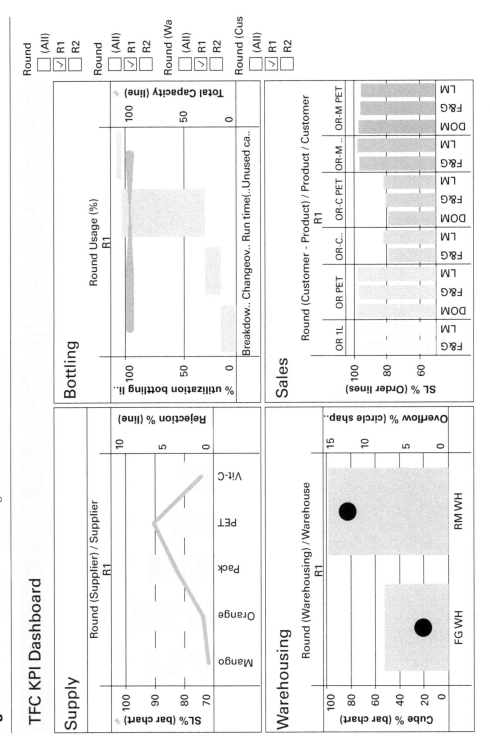

Figure 8.17 Topics from the technical dimension of the supply chain applied to TFC so far

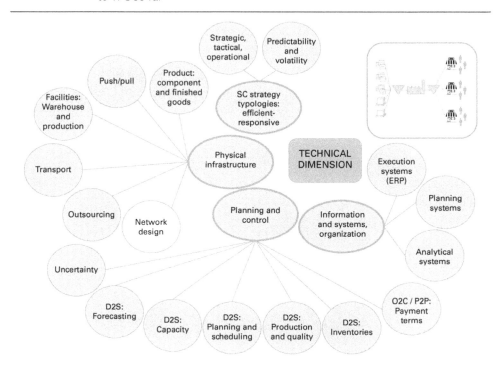

<hr />

EXERCISE 8.20
Reflect on topics from Chapter 8

Reflect

To close the chapter properly and follow the principles of the learning cycle of experiential learning, please go back to each of the topics from Figure 8.17 and reflect on what you have learned. Specifically, think about your learning regarding the following:

● The different theoretical concepts and their practical application in real-life situations. To what extent are the concepts clear and you have experienced the trade-offs involved? What would you do differently next time?

- The analysis and decision-making process. How has the decision making been organized? To what extent was the sequence of decisions clear? To what extent has the process been efficient and was any time lost in discussions that were not strictly necessary?

- Your team's behaviour. To what extent was everyone actively involved? If not, why not? What was done to deal with it in the best possible way?

After these final reflections related to Chapter 8, the journey of mastering the fundamentals continues in the next chapter, in which we look at the application of the leadership dimension to TFC.

Mastering the leadership dimension of the supply chain

09

In this chapter we will return to the leadership dimension of supply chain management and apply it to the management of The Fresh Connection. The chapter builds on the concepts exposed previously in Part One, Chapter 4, with a focus on performance management and target setting, stakeholder management, and team roles and dynamics (Figure 9.1).

Performance measurement and target setting

Indicators and targets are powerful instruments to influence people's behaviour and make them move in the desired direction. That's also why we cover the topic under the umbrella of the 'leadership dimension'. In order to understand where current company performance stands and to evaluate what corrective actions might be necessary so that instructions to collaborators can be given, clear key performance indicators (KPIs) need to be established. Since many decisions are taken by functional experts, KPIs in companies are typically also determined per functional area. Whether that really is always the preferable and most desirable way of doing things will be touched upon later, but for now let's focus on those functional KPIs.

EXERCISE 9.1
Analyse KPIs per functional area and decide
on how to use this information

Analyse

Taking the chosen supply chain strategy (low cost or responsive) as a starting point, think of 3–5 meaningful KPIs for each of the four VPs: Sales, Purchasing, Operations and Supply Chain Management.

Referring back to Chapter 4, to what extent you think each of them is SMART? Pay specific attention to the question as to why they are acceptable and realistic from the point of view of bringing something constructive to the evaluation of the successful implementation of the chosen strategy.

For the chosen KPIs per functional area, check by which functional decisions they are impacted. To what extent are these decisions the most important ones per functional area? Are there any gaps, that is, important functional decisions not covered by the KPIs? If necessary, reconsider KPIs.

Decide

Decide on a meaningful set of KPIs per role.

Figure 9.1   Topics from the leadership dimension of the supply chain applied to TFC

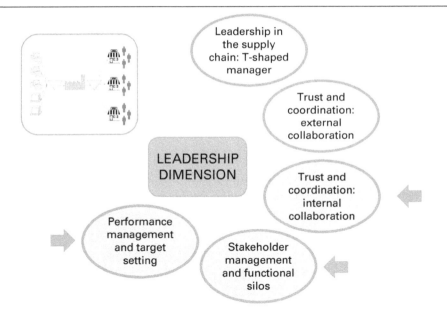

As mentioned briefly earlier, defining KPIs per functional area is no guarantee whatsoever of achieving cross-functional collaboration. It is therefore important to take this into consideration when designing the KPIs: they should be done in such a way that cross-functional alignment is secured in the best possible way. Now, to what extent do the functional KPIs, as part of the global KPI dashboard as you have defined it, stimulate collaboration and alignment and make the company as a whole move in the right direction, rather than pushing functional experts each in a different direction?

EXERCISE 9.2

Analyse alignment between functional KPIs and decide on the KPI dashboard

Analyse

For each of the KPIs currently on the list, one by one, check if pursuing their objectives would be potentially going against one of the other KPIs on the list. This would be particularly important for different KPIs between the functional areas. If necessary, reconsider KPIs.

For each of the defined KPIs currently on your list, think of a target value.

Decide

Decide on a global KPI dashboard with three KPIs per functional role, including target setting for each of the defined KPIs.

Decide how to use these KPIs and targets throughout gameplay.

If well designed in a global context, the currently chosen KPIs should to a certain extent be reasonably well aligned, or at least not be 'conflictive' between them. However, 'well-aligned' could potentially be taken a step further. As a complement to the purely functional KPIs, which can be used to 'judge' individual performance, it might be useful to think about some cross-functional KPIs as well: a small set of KPIs with the clear objective of actively stimulating internal coordination. Possibly, some of the KPIs you have just defined as functional KPIs already have such characteristics, but not necessarily (preferably not, because functional indicators should ideally be mainly related to decisions within that functional area).

EXERCISE 9.3

Analyse cross-functional KPIs and decide on their usage

Analyse

Try to define 4–5 truly cross-functional KPIs, meaning that they are each directly influenced by decisions from two or more functional areas. You can use the matrices from Figures 3.9 (p 57) and 3.14 (p 68) as a starting point, and add your own experience with the game so far into the equation. Set a target for each of them and make sure the KPIs are SMART.

Decide

Define and decide how these cross-functional KPIs can be productively used by the management team when aligning throughout gameplay.

One last reflection before moving on to the topic of trust and coordination: you have now been giving some thought to meaningful KPIs within the context of your chosen (supply chain) strategy. In the game, there is an option to check the 'rankings' (button in the top right-hand corner). Apart from being able to see team rankings based on ROI, per round or overall, it also allows you to visualize the individual rankings per round, based on the following KPIs:

- *Sales* – revenue (the more revenue the better).
- *Operations* – cost of operations (the lower the better).
- *Supply chain* – inventories (the lower the better).
- *Purchasing* – cost of purchasing (the lower the better).

First, it can be stated that these KPIs are very widely used in businesses, often connected to financial incentives (bonus systems). In other words, people are being rewarded for pushing in the direction of the targets associated with these KPIs.

Second, keeping in mind that these are very widely used KPIs, to what extent do you think they go well with the supply chain strategies of low cost and responsiveness? Do they make sense in both cases? In either case?

Third, after each round of gameplay, check to what extent the individual leaders, based on the rankings per role, are also part of the best-performing teams in terms of ROI. What does this tell you?

Stakeholder management: functional silos

Beyond purely measuring the individual performance of the different roles, another reflection is useful at this stage. Each team member has assumed a different functional role in the game and by now you have some experience of how that works out during gameplay. The following reflections deal with functional silos as introduced in Chapter 4.

EXERCISE 9.4
Analyse functional specialization and decide on actions

Analyse

To what extent has the functional specialization of having one person dedicated to each role had a positive impact in terms of causing a role-specific learning curve, enabling a better view and better individual judgement from a functional point of view within the silo?

To what extent has functional specialization emphasized the functional silos in the team in a negative way, for example by creating tension if a person from one role tries to tell a person in another role which decisions to make? Or by creating more misunderstanding because of specific functional expertise that team members from another role were lacking?

Decide

Decide how best to exploit the benefits of functional specialization while limiting the potential negative impact of silos in the team to a minimum.

Trust and coordination: internal collaboration and team performance

Measuring performance is a necessary first step for knowing where you are and for having a basis for deciding what needs to be done next. However, KPIs are not going to do all the work. As soon as people start working together to achieve results, the people dimension of teams comes into play. Independent of each team member's functional role and responsibilities, we can speak of the team roles of individual team members.

The term 'team roles' refers to how individuals behave when put together in a team. For example, some people will be more likely to take the lead and push the team forward, others will act as the 'glue' binding the individual team members together, and some will be searching for relevant information and feeding that into the team. People's individual personalities and characters have a big impact on this aspect, and the particular mix of a set of team members might be more or less balanced. Although there is plenty of academic debate on the subject, not necessarily with everyone always agreeing, the general idea is that the more balanced a team is in terms of team roles, the more likely it is that its performance will be better.

Obviously, there is also another dimension related to personalities and characters, which together generate a more or less stable or explosive mix within a team. The concept of 'team dynamics' contemplates this by evaluating, for example, how good the atmosphere in the team is and the extent to which progress is made in the work at hand. In the following steps we will use two short and simple questionnaires as developed by Management Worlds, Inc (reproduced with kind permission).

EXERCISE 9.5

Analyse the task orientation of the team

Analyse

Using the template in Figure 9.2, assess your team's performance from the point of view of the 'TASK' at hand. Preferably, each team member should do this individually.

Figure 9.2 Template: analysing the 'TASK' dimension of leadership

TEAM: *SuperJuice*   **STRATEGY:** *Low Cost*   🇭 The Fresh **Connection**

Team Assessment: TASKS

T1   *Do you have clear direction and objectives?*

| 1 | 2 | 3 | 4 | 5 | 6 | 7 |

Goals and objectives are clearly understood and agreed on.   *Goals and objectives are unclear. Few members feel ownership.*

T2   *Do team members understand what each is to do?*

| 1 | 2 | 3 | 4 | 5 | 6 | 7 |

Roles, responsibilities, and assignments are clear, accepted. There is a good division of labour.   *Roles and responsibilities are unclear, unassigned. Team not fully utilized.*

T3   *How is the work organized and carried out?*

| 1 | 2 | 3 | 4 | 5 | 6 | 7 |

Procedures for working together are organized, efficient. Team is creative, flexible.   *Work procedures are lacking or inefficient. Team is rigid and does not experiment.*

T4   *How well do you plan and control your project efforts?*

| 1 | 2 | 3 | 4 | 5 | 6 | 7 |

Actions and decisions are planned ahead, anticipating problems and alternatives. Data is organized, balancing details with the big picture.   *Planning timeframe is limited and work is micro-managed. Data is scattered, unorganized, too detailed, or to vague.*

T5   *How do you come to decisions as a team?*

| 1 | 2 | 3 | 4 | 5 | 6 | 7 |

Consensus is sought and tested. An approach to decision making and problem exploration is set. Disagreements are explored.   *No agreed approach to decision making or problem solving. Decisions are delayed, made by chance, or default.*

EXERCISE 9.6

Analyse the team and relationship orientations of the team

Analyse

Using the template in Figure 9.3, assess your team's performance from the point of view of the 'TEAM dimension (RELATIONSHIPS)' in the team. Preferably, each team member should do this individually.

Figure 9.3   Template: analysing the 'TEAM' dimension of leadership

TEAM: _SuperJuice_   **STRATEGY:** _Low Cost_   The Fresh **Connection**

Team Assessment: TEAM (RELATIONSHIPS)

R1   **What is the quality of participation in your team?**

1	2	3	4	5	6	7

All team members are involved and contribute views and ideas. Different opinions and views are listened to and valued.

Involvement is limited. A few members decide. Some members are passive or even apathetic in providing views and ideas.

R2   **What is the degree of trust and openness between team members?**

1	2	3	4	5	6	7

Team members feel they can speak up and challenge each other. Problems, conflicts, concerns are discussed openly and respectfully.

There is little trust among team members. Conflict is avoided. Communication is guarded, closed or diplomatically polite.

R3   **How is team leadership handled?**

1	2	3	4	5	6	7

Leadership is shared. All members participate and are influential.

Leadership is autocratic and direct. Dominance by one or a few members.

R4   **To what extent are feelings important data?**

1	2	3	4	5	6	7

Feelings are valuable input, comfortably shared between team members.

Feelings are hidden or ignored and not treated as useful information.

R5   **Is your team having fun?**

1	2	3	4	5	6	7

Members feel good about working together. Success is celebrated and mistakes are learned from. Humour is energizing.

Team members do not enjoy working together. Team is overly serious and celebration is minimized.

As an interesting extension of the reflection, individual team members might be challenged to complete the questionnaires more than once, each time reflecting a different moment (round) during gameplay. In this way, development over time can also be expressed and interpreted.

EXERCISE 9.7

Analyse the combined task, team and relationship orientations of the team and decide on actions to improve team performance

Analyse

Using the template in Figure 9.4, express the outcomes from the two previous questionnaires in one combined graphic, showing the individual assessments of the different team members.

Figure 9.4 Template: analysing the 'TASK' and 'TEAM' dimensions of leadership

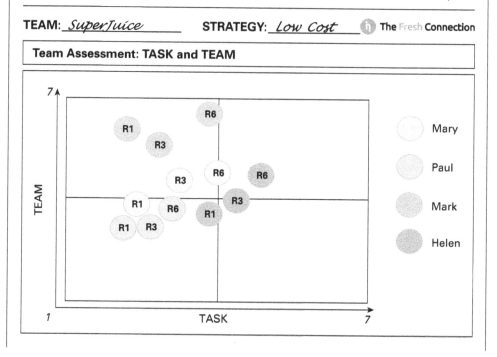

TEAM: _SuperJuice_   STRATEGY: _Low Cost_   ⓘ The Fresh Connection

If the previous questionnaires have been filled out multiple times by each team member to express development over time, this can also be incorporated into the graphic.

Decide

What are the conclusions you and the team can derive from this? Based on your observations as a team, what do you propose to do next?

Trust and coordination: external collaboration and transparency

In Chapter 4 we briefly touched on the topic of trust and coordination as part of the leadership dimension, aimed at establishing special relationships with suppliers and/ or customers with the objective of collaborating beyond pure buying and selling. Vendor managed inventory (VMI) was mentioned as an example. In some configurations of the gameplay, TFC's management team can also consider proposing such improvement projects to either customers or suppliers. In those cases, two possibilities exist:

- *Development projects with suppliers*: for each supplier you can specify whether you wish to implement a supplier development programme. For each period in which it is applied, a supplier development programme has a certain project cost associated with it (information about how much can be found in the system). This type of programme improves the performance of suppliers and facilitates certification of their production processes. Delivery reliability and the quality of the materials delivered by suppliers also improve, and their emission index decreases.

- *VMI with suppliers and/or with customers*: VMI can be employed for each supplier and/or customer. In implementing VMI, control of the stocks of the respective components is passed on to the supplier in question and the supplier ensures that sufficient stock is present (please note, in case of VMI with TFC's customers, TFC is the supplier; in the case of VMI with suppliers, TFC is the customer). Control limits for stock levels must now be specified by the customer, where the upper and lower limits indicate the scope available to the supplier for steering stock levels. The safety stock levels and lot sizes set by the VP Supply Chain are overruled by these upper and lower limits. Also, VMI has a recurring project cost associated with it. Please note, in the gameplay VMI cannot be employed for alternative suppliers (dual sources).

> **EXERCISE 9.8**
> Analyse VMI and decide on actions
>
> **Analyse**
>
> Go back to the criteria explored in Chapter 4 when discussing VMI, or in Chapter 3 when discussing supplier segmentation, as well as your observations in Exercise 3.5 (p 77) about outsourcing and collaboration. For which suppliers would you consider either VMI and/or supplier development projects? Why?
>> In the same vein, for which customers would you consider proposing VMI? Why?
>> What are the conclusions you and the team can derive from this?
>
> **Decide**
>
> Which decisions in terms of proposing development projects and/or implementing VMI do you take on the basis of the above? Please take into consideration that TFC is a medium-sized company with limited resources, so a maximum of three such projects in total can be proposed. Also due to TFC's size, and depending on the size of the customers and/or suppliers in question, your proposals might be declined by them. Should that be the case, you will be notified at the beginning of the next round after proposing the collaboration. In such cases, no project costs will be incurred.

Stakeholder management (direct stakeholders)

In the specific setting of TFC, most of the internal stakeholders directly involved in what is going on in managing the flow of goods actually form part of the team participating in the simulation game. We will come back to the stakeholders indirectly involved in Part Three. However, there is one other very important stakeholder we will have to address and to whom we haven't paid much attention since the beginning of this chapter: Bob McLaren is back and he wants some answers (Figure 9.5)!

Good reporting is an important and relevant skill in supporting effective stakeholder management. How you inform others, what exactly you tell them and how you tell them will create a starting point for the next steps in the process. It requires a healthy dose of empathy in order to understand what information your audience would be interested in, as well as a bit of creativity to make your report attractive to look at as well as easy to understand. Be aware that the people who are going to look at your report are probably short of time, so they need to be able to grasp your message quickly. Also, be aware that you might not be there with them when they see it, so you might not have an opportunity to explain anything until they explicitly ask you to do so.

Figure 9.5   Bob McLaren is back!

> Hello,
>
> I put you in charge of my company some time ago with great expectation.
>
> So please explain to me... what's happened since then?

EXERCISE 9.9
Analyse what has happened so far and create a report for the company's owner

Analyse

Using the template in Figure 9.6 as developed by Team SuperJuice, go back to your experience of the rounds played so far and create a management report for Bob McLaren.

Figure 9.6   Template: reporting for Bob McLaren

TEAM: _SuperJuice_   STRATEGY: _Low Cost_   The Fresh Connection

MANAGEMENT REPORT FOR BOB McLAREN

ROI

	R1	R2	R3	R4	R5
Situation at the beginning of the round	- 4,0% ROI Bad service levels High % obsoletes	...	...		
Main reason(s) behind decrease/increase of ROI vs. previous round	Inherited from previous mgmt	...	...		
Focus for the next round	Get rid of penalties	...	...		
Main decisions taken per area					
SALES:	Lower service level promise	...	...		
SC:	Diff. stock levels per SKU	...	...		
OPS:	...	...	...		
PUR:	...	...	...		

Decide

Decide which elements to focus on and create the report. Make sure that the report is accurate, to the point and self-explanatory.

Summary

With this chapter, we have come the end of the discussion of the leadership dimension of supply chain management, applied to TFC. We have dealt with performance measurement as a leadership instrument to influence behaviour, with internal stakeholders as evident via the functional silos, with internal collaboration and team performance and with external collaboration and transparency. We finished the chapter by looking at specific reporting for the owner of the company.

The topics shown in Figure 9.7 in grey have been dealt with in more detail. Some of these, as well as those in white, will come back in Part Three.

Figure 9.7 Topics from the leadership dimension of the supply chain as applied to TFC so far

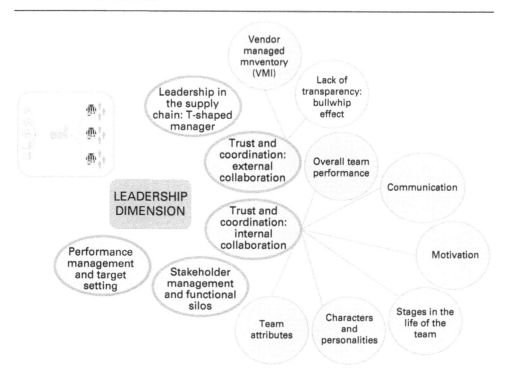

EXERCISE 9.10

Reflect on topics from Chapter 9

Reflect

To close the chapter properly and follow the principles of the learning cycle of experiential learning, please go back to each of the topics from Figure 9.7 and reflect on what you have learned. Specifically, think about your learning regarding the following:

- The different theoretical concepts and their practical application in real-life situations. To what extent are the concepts clear and you have experienced the complexities involved? What would you do differently next time?

- The analysis and decision-making process. How has the decision making been organized? To what extent was the sequence of decisions clear? To what extent has the process been efficient and was any time lost in discussions that were not strictly necessary?

- Your team's behaviour. To what extent did you share the same view when analysing team behaviour? Why was that, do you think? What would you do differently now that you are aware of this?

In the next chapter we will end our journey of mastering the fundamentals of supply chain, by going back for a moment to the topic of overall complexity due to the combination of the business, technical and leadership dimensions and their many elements, and the corresponding need for alignment.

Simple, but not easy (3)   10

Complexity and alignment

In the previous chapters the main concepts from the business, technical and leadership dimensions of the supply chain have been applied to TFC. Let's reflect on the overall picture that has emerged from gameplay during the journey of mastering the fundamentals.

Supply chain strategies revisited

Go back for a moment to Exercise 3.1 (p 47) and the template shown in Figure 8.2 (p 131) about translating corporate strategy into supply chain action. Reflect on how well your choices have worked out. To what extent have you been able to define and implement your chosen supply chain strategy well, whether low cost or responsive? To what extent have you actually revised your initial choices throughout the various rounds of gameplay? As said in Chapter 8, in real life the continuous adapting and fine-tuning of strategies is part of its implementation.

Now take the same template from Figure 8.2 and try to define the supply chain actions in line with the supply chain strategy that you did not choose. So if, like Team SuperJuice, you chose the low-cost supply chain strategy, elaborate the actions related to the responsive supply chain strategy and vice versa. Quite likely, some of the teams in your class have chosen a different strategy from yours, so, after completing the table, it is recommended that you discuss your findings with them, so that both visions and experiences can be put together.

Complexity!

So far throughout Part Two, many different concepts have been dealt with. Some of them may require a bit more thinking than others, or a bit more work to get to the bottom of them, but I hope you can agree by now that most of the concepts have

Figure 10.1 Complexity of the combined business, technical and leadership dimensions

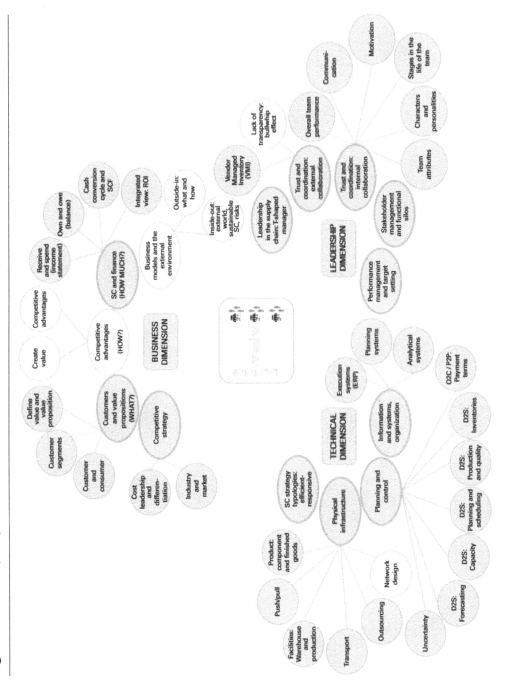

proven to be relatively straightforward. This was already noted at the end of Part One, but applying the concepts in a practical way to the gameplay with The Fresh Connection should have confirmed the message.

What I hope you have also experienced is that even though the concepts are relatively easy to understand, they don't make running an entire supply chain easy. The sheer quantity of them, the many interdependencies between them, the cross-functional dimension and the fact that sometimes there is room for opinion besides facts, as well as the fact that many things change all the time, make it anything but easy (Figure 10.1).

To get a clearer idea of the many interdependencies that exist between the different decisions per functional role, let's analyse and visualize this in more detail.

EXERCISE 10.1
Analyse interdependencies per functional area

Analyse

Using the template from Team SuperJuice in Figure 10.2, let the VP of each functional department list the top five most important decisions for their role.

For each of these five decisions, try to formulate how this decision might have an impact on another functional department and why.

Figure 10.2   Template: analysing interdependencies between departments (inputs)

TEAM: _SuperJuice_   STRATEGY: _Low Cost_   🛈 The Fresh Connection

IF I CHANGE...	I WILL INFLUENCE...	BECAUSE...
SALES Service level	Operations	Production capacity might need to be changed Machine capacity Number of shifts Warehousing capacity might need to be adjusted Number of locations Number of people
	Supply Chain	...
	Purchasing	...
Shelf life	Operations	
	Supply Chain	
	Purchasing	
...	Operations	
	Supply Chain	
	Purchasing	

EXERCISE 10.2
Analyse overall cross-functional interdependencies and decide
on actions based on the interdependency mapping

Analyse

When you have finished, try to put all the inputs together in one overall visual chart,
like the example in Figure 10.3 from Team SuperJuice, showing each of the
functional roles and the interdependencies as identified.

Decide

Now decide what you are going to do with this newly acquired insight.

Figure 10.3   Template: analysing interdependencies between departments
(visualization)

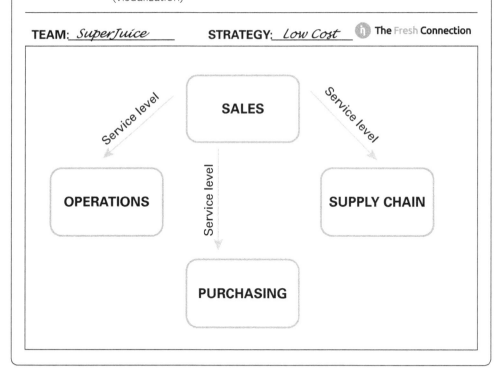

TEAM: _SuperJuice_   STRATEGY: _Low Cost_   The Fresh Connection

Making pros and cons explicit: business cases to support decision making

As you will have experienced during gameplay, as well as during the previous discussion on interdependencies, almost all decisions carry some sort of trade-off, the pros
and cons of which were also touched on in the earlier chapters. However, we need to

try to avoid speculating when contemplating changes. Intuition is, of course, fine as a starting point, but if possible a more thorough elaboration should be done to support decision making. In TFC's system, lots of information is available to support decision making and this is where so-called business cases come into the picture. The general idea behind a business case is to elaborate as far as possible the different pros and cons of a certain change, so that those responsible can make a well-informed decision.

EXERCISE 10.3

Analyse business cases and decide on actions based on them

Analyse

Using the template from Team SuperJuice (Figure 10.4), and taking a number of important decisions as an example, develop business cases for these decisions. Perhaps not everything can be quantified, but nevertheless make sure you create a picture that is as complete as possible. Examples you could think of are a change of

Figure 10.4 Template: decision support using structured business cases

TEAM: _SuperJuice_   STRATEGY: _Low Cost_   ⓘ **The** Fresh **Connection**

BUSINESS CASE FOR: _CHANGE OF ORANGE SUPPLIER FROM MIAMI ORANGE (USA) TO ARANCIA D'ESPAÑA (SPAIN)_

PROS (QUANTITATIVE):

Lead time from 30 to 10 days:
      Bridge stock 140 pallets less:
          ... EUR space saving
          ... EUR interest saving
....
....

CONS (QUANTITATIVE):

Standard contract index from 1,004 to 1,070:
      6,6% increase on current 409k spending:
          ... EUR additional purchase cost
....
....

PROS (QUALITATIVE):

Shorter lead time allows for smaller delivery window:
      less delivery uncertainty→less safety stock
....
....

CONS (QUALITATIVE):

....
....

PROPOSED DECISION: .....

supplier, the execution of improvement projects, changes in contract conditions with customers or suppliers, changes in production or purchase lot sizes, and so on.

As in real life, it makes sense for the VP in charge of the decision to take the lead in the preparation of the business case, or even prepares it alone. The result of the activity would be a well-prepared proposed decision.

Decide

Based on the proposed decision, discuss with the entire management team and make a final decision.

Cross-functional alignment: S&OP

If the objective is to make our supply chain perform well, taking into consideration the very different viewpoints of the technical, business and leadership dimensions, as well as the many interdependencies between the individual functional decisions, how can we make sure this is going to work in the best possible way? As mentioned on a few earlier occasions, cross-functional alignment via the process of sales and operations planning (S&OP) is one of the main keys to successful supply chain performance. So, let's try to develop an S&OP process in the following steps.

EXERCISE 10.4
Analyse the flow of decisions (decision-making process) and decide on actions

Analyse

Like Team SuperJuice, use the template in Figure 10.5. It contains one column per functional area. The team decided to use sticky notes to facilitate the activity. Figure 10.5 shows their diagram just after they started working on it.

Make a list of all the decisions per functional area which you have seen so far in the gameplay. You could write the decisions on sticky notes, one decision per note. Out of all of these decisions, create one global flowchart. In other words, for each decision, think of which other decisions provide an input to the decision. Please note that the flowchart doesn't necessarily have to go in only one direction: feedback loops are possible (some decisions have an iterative character rather than linear). Also, it could happen that you find decisions that have no clear relationship to other

Figure 10.5   Template: designing the decision-making process (S&OP logic)

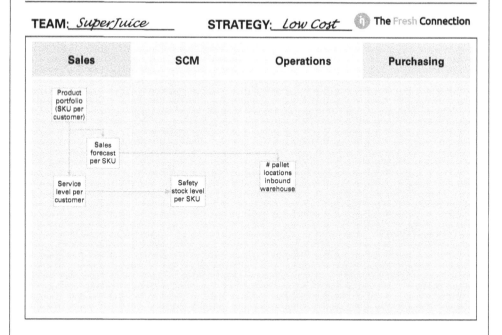

TEAM: _SuperJuice_   STRATEGY: _Low Cost_   The Fresh Connection

| Sales | SCM | Operations | Purchasing |

Product portfolio (SKU per customer)

Sales forecast per SKU

Service level per customer

Safety stock level per SKU

pallet locations inbound warehouse

decisions; that is they do not require input from another decision, nor themselves provide an input to other decisions.

Decide

Now decide how you can implement the findings of the S&OP flowchart in your team's decision making, the objective being to make the overall decision-making process more efficient (faster) as well as more effective (better and more well-informed decisions).

The keys to successful execution of the S&OP process are similar to those of any other business process. However, given the cross-functional nature of S&OP, some are put to the test much more intensively, thus becoming even more critical:

- Good process design.
- Clarity on roles and responsibilities in relation to each of the steps in the process.
- Solid preparation by each of the participants for each of the steps in the process. This is especially relevant before cross-functional meetings (doing your homework on time, with the correct level of quality, having information prepared that others need in order to be able to make progress).

- Discipline in the execution of the process.

- Focus on facts, not opinions.

- Make the assumptions behind proposed decisions explicit, as this will enrich the discussion.

- Constructive solution-oriented attitude in (cross-functional) meetings: critical but positive.

- Continuous evaluation and improvement of the process itself, trial and error being part of the implementation.

Please note that most of the abovementioned factors are very easy to say, very easy to understand, but practice shows that they are very difficult to achieve. You and your team, like any real-life company, have the challenge to make it work well!

Summary

This brings us to the end of Part Two and the coverage of the journey of mastering the fundamentals. Throughout gameplay, all of the dimensions dealt with in this part will be relevant in achieving good results in terms of ROI:

- the business dimension, covering competitive strategy, customers, value propositions and financial aspects;

- the technical dimension, covering supply chain strategies, the physical infrastructure, planning and control, information and systems, and organizational aspects;

- the leadership dimension, covering performance management and KPI target setting, functional silos, internal collaboration and team performance, external collaboration and top management reporting.

As in real companies, it's logical that it will take you and your team time to fully understand the complexities and learn how to deal with them in the best possible way. Go step by step, prepare and analyse well, reflect frequently and explicitly on what you are doing, keep the communication channels open and focus on continuous improvement. *It's simple, but definitely not easy!*

In the next part of the book, we will embark on yet another journey: imagining beyond the fundamentals.

PART THREE
Imagining beyond the fundamentals

Whereas Part One served as a general exploration of the many and diverse aspects of supply chain management, Part Two centred around the direct application of many of those concepts to gameplay in The Fresh Connection, focusing on mastering the aspects of running an established and relatively stable supply chain. In Part Three, we will look beyond such a stable environment and challenge the status quo to see clearly the impacts that changes might have on designing and managing a supply chain. The Fresh Connection will once again be at the heart of the analysis, but instead of focusing on gameplay, we will apply the company situation as a case study, wherever possible using relevant data from the system to support thorough analysis and decision making. As you will notice, a range of different types of exercises and formats will be used.

As you will remember, reflections and exercises have so far been grouped under the names of *explore* in Part One, and *analyze and decide* in Part Two. Even though a lot of exploring, analysing and deciding will still be required, reflections and exercises in the third part all fall under the umbrella of *imagine*, because the starting point is one of an uncertain future with many challenges ahead.

Please note that in terms of number of pages in the book, Part Three is relatively short, but don't be fooled by this, because you will find that the cases described require quite a lot of analysis, thinking and elaboration of alternative solutions. While dealing with a number of challenges related to the business, technological and leadership dimensions of supply chain management, in Chapters 12, 13 and 14 respectively, many potential actions, projects and initiatives for The Fresh Connection will be defined. In each of these chapters, after defining the potential paths forward for the company, we will park them for the moment, and return to them all in the closing chapter of the book: the conclusion.

The supply chain in a VUCA world   11

In order to have a solid starting point for imagining the impact of a large number of challenges throughout Chapters 12–14, in this chapter we will look at the main characteristics of the world around us and establish a view on TFC's current business model.

A VUCA world

The term VUCA was allegedly coined by the US Army War College when the Cold War in the 20th century came to an end, thus giving expression to the emerging of a new reality. Today, the term has become more widely used, in business and education as well as in other areas. The letters of VUCA stand for:

- *Volatile*. Expressing an *increasing rate of change* at all levels (political, economic, societal, technological, ecological, legal).

- *Uncertain*. Expressing an *increasing rate of unpredictability* about what might or might not occur in the future.

- *Complex*. Expressing an *increasing rate of complexity* due to more forces being at work at the same time.

- *Ambiguous*. Expressing, partially as a consequence of the above, an *increasing lack of clarity* about what's going on, what are the causes and what are the effects, and what the relationships between causes and effects may actually be.

Being an integral part of companies existing in this VUCA world, the supply chain area will clearly need to take these aspects into consideration as well. TFC and its supply chain are no exception: TFC as a company will constantly make decisions to move on in the VUCA world and its supply chain should be able to follow, or in some cases even able to lead.

Even though TFC's simulation has a number of specific configurations dealing with some of these forward-looking characteristics, in most educational environments these configurations are not used very often, typically because the focus of many courses is simply more on the fundamentals of supply chain management.

This doesn't mean, however, that we cannot use TFC's situation as a starting point for looking in more detail at a number of relevant trends and developments. We will do this in the next three chapters of Part Three.

Many of the topics covered in Part One were applied to TFC in Part Two. Most of those will come back in some shape or form in Part Three, but also the topics from Part One that were left out of Part Two, for practical reasons, will now be dealt with, thus completing the picture as shown in Figure 10.1 (p 182).

As the title of Part Three suggests, since we're dealing with possible future scenarios, a fair dose of your *imagination* will be required. This would be the same for any board of directors of a real company contemplating potential roadmaps for the future. But please note that imagination is not the same as pure speculation. On the basis of imaginative ideas, very concrete scenarios can be developed and evaluated, which is precisely what we will do in the coming chapters.

Visualizing the status quo: business model canvas

To be able to evaluate the potential impacts of the trends and developments we will consider, we need to create a clear view on the existing situation, the status quo. Based on the experience obtained with TFC during Part Two, we will assume that the ins and outs of TFC's current supply chain are by now well known. But we haven't really looked at TFC's overall business model. In order to establish a clear view on this, we go back to the concept of the business model canvas, introduced in Chapter 2.

EXERCISE 11.1

Imagine TFC's business model

Imagine

Go to the website www.strategyzer.com to download a copy of the business model canvas (you are allowed to do so, but please look at the exact Creative Commons licence conditions for its usage). You might also want to check out some of the other supporting resources for use of the canvas on the website.

Create a canvas for TFC. Like Team SuperJuice, use sticky notes when creating the canvas (Figure 11.1). This way, you will be more flexible when making adjustments.

Base yourself on the situation you know from the gameplay.

Figure 11.1 Template: business model canvas of Team SuperJuice

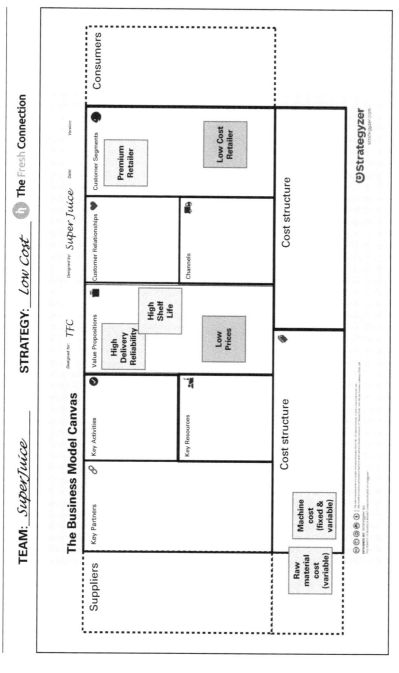

SOURCE Osterwalder (2010), www.strategyzer.com, with Team SuperJuice amendments

Please note that as kind of an experiment, Team SuperJuice has decided to take the liberty of making some amendments to the canvas:

● First, they have added a column called *Consumers* on the right-hand side, in order to be able to clearly express the distinction between TFC's paying customers and the consumers of TFC's fruit juices. Although TFC's current market is clearly B2B (business-to-business), they feel the consumer cannot be left out of the business model because TFC produces consumer products. In order to avoid confusion, for example between to customers and value propositions to consumers, the extra column was added.

● Second, they have added a column on the left-hand side called *Suppliers*, to be able to clearly express the distinction between key partners with whom a strategic relationship would be established and 'normal' arm's-length suppliers with whom there would be a more standard buying–selling relationship. They feel this would allow them to incorporate, for example, commodity suppliers from whom TFC might be buying a lot of money's worth of materials (ie important for the overall cost structure), but who would not be considered key partners, since commodities can be bought virtually anywhere. Accordingly, the cost structure box has been extended to cover the arm's-length suppliers also (replacing the revenue streams box).

● If you wish, you can try out Team SuperJuice's amendments and see if they also work for you. If not, just move along with the original canvas.

Please note that when creating the canvas, you shouldn't look only at operational and supply chain aspects but consider all elements of the business. When developing the canvas, keep the following checks in mind:

● Are all elements on the 'what?' side of the canvas (segments, value propositions, channels, customer relations) supported by one or more elements on the 'how?' side (key activities, key resources, key partners, suppliers)? If the answer is no, there are two options: either you might have missed something, or you have discovered a gap in the coherence of the business model.

● Are all elements in the canvas strictly necessary? In other words, if you take a specific element away, does that really weaken the coherence of the business model? If you find something that is not necessary, you might have discovered something that is redundant (ie it could be removed from the company without harming the strength of the business model).

Both checks can be done effectively in quite a 'mechanical' way, by simply going from sticky note to sticky note and checking one at a time.

Although, strictly speaking, it is part of the business dimension of the supply chain, let's look for a moment at what TFC's 'strategic secret' could be in terms of customers and value propositions on the one hand and competitive advantages on the other.

EXERCISE 11.2

Imagine TFC's value propositions and competitive advantages

Imagine

Since the simulation doesn't contain explicit information about the competitive landscape in which TFC is operating, you might need to use some imagination to think about what could be possible answers to the following questions. Your experience in the gameplay should also be helpful in answering at least some of the elements, but you would also need to think a bit beyond it:

- What is it that TFC is promising to its clients that makes them want to choose TFC (customers and value propositions)?

- What does TFC need to be particularly good at in order to consistently deliver on those promises day after day (competitive advantages)?

Summary

At this stage you should have a good understanding of TFC's overall business model and its critical elements as well as the competitive difference you can imagine it might have with other companies in the market. This would then give you the desired starting point for imagining and evaluating future trends and developments and their potential impacts. It is therefore highly recommended that you keep the designed canvas at hand while working on the coming chapters. In the next chapter, the journey of imagining beyond the fundamentals continues, and we will look what could happen if elements of the business dimension of the supply chain are challenged.

Imagining business challenges for the supply chain

12

In this chapter we will look at a number of business challenges that companies face, and in order to make them more tangible we will apply them to The Fresh Connection, so that ultimately we can analyse the potential impact they might have on the supply chain. We will be touching on some of the elements of the business dimension we have seen before and cover those that are still open (ie introduced in Part One, but not yet applied in Part Two). The focus will be on challenges related to market pressures and competition, business model changes, the trend of corporate social responsibility, changes in the external environment, and risk assessment (Figure 12.1).

Prepare for the return of Bob McLaren! Now that you have demonstrated that you have mastered the supply chain fundamentals of TFC, he is ready to open discussions with you about a wider variety of more advanced topics. In the remainder of this chapter he will be sending you a series of e-mails to get the conversation started. And he'll be waiting for your inputs....

Market forces: new entrants and tough competition

As you have noticed in Part Two, TFC has so far been operating in relatively stable market conditions. Demand variability existed, but total demand was fairly stable and competitors didn't seem to be much of an issue. Of course, this nice situation couldn't last forever. Competitive pressures are all around, not only because of new entrants from other territories. Also, existing incumbents can change their portfolios, they can acquire other companies and become much bigger and powerful in the market. Companies like TFC should continuously be alert to such pressures and have their plans ready.

Figure 12.1   Topics from the business dimension of the supply chain

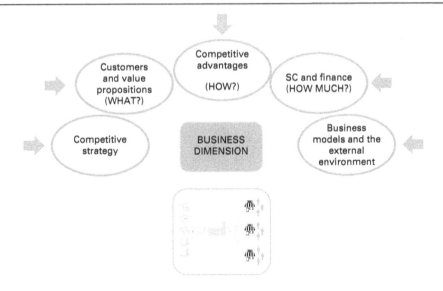

EXERCISE 12.1

Imagine changes in the competitive landscape

Imagine

Imagine you receive the e-mail shown in Figure 12.2 from Bob McLaren.

Figure 12.2   E-mail from Bob McLaren about new competitor

07-Dec 07:28AM
Bob McLaren <bobmcl@>
NEW MARKET INFORMATION

To: O TFC CEO ; O TFC Sales ; O TFC Operations ; O TFC Supply Chain ; O TFC Purchasing

M&I Flash
140kB

Hello all,

I'm happy about recent results, keep up the good work!
Just wanted to share something with you that has me slightly concerned.
Apparently, Chinese drinks giant JuiceCo has solid plans to enter the European market.
They are one of the largest Asian companies in the industry, seemingly very profitable and with a
wide portfolio of drinks, not only juices. Cash doesn't seem to be one of their issues. Don't know
much more at this stage. At the same time, we're seeing more and more organic drinks from (still)
relatively small brands entering the scene, and selling mainly to speciality stores
(for the moment, at least).

Obviously, these movements will most likely also affect us directly or indirectly, sooner or later.
I want you to analyse what this might mean to us and our supply chain and what you propose to
do. Have attached file with Market & Industry Flash FYI. We'll discuss your findings in our
upcoming meeting next week.

BRgds,
BMcL.

MARKET & INDUSTRY FLASH – JUICE BUSINESS

MARKET SITUATION:

- Global CAGR* at 1.3% over period 2012–2017.
- 100% fruit juice is largest contributor, and inreasingly popular.
- Nectar (25–99% fruit content), juice drinks (up to 25% fruit content), concentrated and powdered drinks make up the rest.
- Juice markets in developed economies are very mature and have very little growth. In developing countries there is still strong growth.

MAIN MARKET AND CONSUMER TRENDS:

- 100% fruit juice and smoothies are increasingly popular, as well as energy drinks and flavoured waters.
- Sodas are decreasing for the moment, to be seen what happens if alternatives with less sugar content appear.
- In some countries, governments are actively pushing consumption of low-sugar drinks.
- In some drinks segments, trends towards customized and individualized labeling.

CAGR: Compounded Annual Growth Rate

INDUSTRY AND SUPPLY SITUATION:

- Most of the traditional markets are supplied by either large global players or large local (national) players.
- Large retail remains the principal channel for sales.

MAIN INDUSTRY TRENDS:

- Industry consolidation going on at the top. Large Chinese corporations looking for international expansion, possibly via acquisitions of larger local players. Typically wide portfolios and looking for purchasing power in fruit markets.
- Small new local industry entrants at the bottom with strong focus on healthy drinks.
- Increasing competition from fresh squeezed drinks (smoothies).
- More volatile weather conditions lead to more unpredictable harvests and therefore less price stability for fruit purchase.
- The rise of megacities is causing increased importance of so-called nanostores.**

*** Fransoo et al (2018) Reaching 50 Million Nanostores*

First, take a look at the Market & Industry Flash Bob McLaren sent along with his e-mail (Figure 12.3).

Now it's up to you and the team to define what to do and report to Bob McLaren in the next meeting. For your analysis, you can use the template as developed by Team SuperJuice (see Figure 12.4).

In general terms, what are the impacts you could expect in a situation in which an important new company enters the market? Think of the impact on:

- the *industry* (eg competitive strategies of incumbents and new entrants);
- the *market* (eg customer segments, value propositions, customer behaviour);
- the *consumers* (eg consumer segments, value propositions, consumer behaviour);
- the *suppliers* (eg supply market, supply availability, supplier power).

Now relate your observations on the abovementioned factors to the existing business model you visualized in the previous chapter. Take the canvas as your reference point and check each of the areas in terms of potential impacts you foresee.

On the basis of your observations and assessment, try to formulate the implications for TFC as a company and its supply chain in particular.

For each of the functional areas in TFC's management team (sales, operations, supply chain and purchasing), define proposed actions to deal with and/or prepare for dealing with the identified market pressures.

Figure 12.4 Template: analysis of increased market pressures

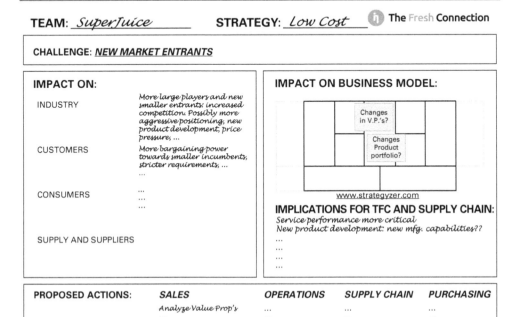

Probably, from the analysis, a number of actions have been defined. Let's park these for the moment and look at another business challenge.

The need for new business models

During gameplay in Part Two, TFC has been selling a small and stable product portfolio of six SKU. But because of competitive pressures like the ones analysed in the previous section, companies need to constantly innovate in products and services in order to keep customers and consumers happy in markets in which typically there is more and more choice on offer. Like others, TFC needs to think about new products, new segments, new channels, ...

EXERCISE 12.2
Imagine new product introductions

Imagine

Imagine you receive the e-mail in Figure 12.5 from Bob McLaren.

Figure 12.5　E-mail from Bob McLaren about new product introduction

---

17-Jan 09:49PM
Bob McLaren <bobmcl@>
NEW PRODUCT INTRODUCTIONS AND NEW BUSINESS MODELS

To: O TFC CEO ; O TFC Sales ; O TFC Operations ; O TFC Supply Chain ; O TFC Purchasing

Hello all,

As you may have heard, our Group's Research & Development team is in the final development stages before the launch of a new product: the *FressieCapsules*. This new product is building on the existing concept of individual coffee capsules, thus hoping to leverage on the positive experience that consumers already have with such devices. The idea would be to start selling capsules to our existing traditional retailers, in addition to the SKUs they are already buying from us. In addition, we are considering opening a direct sales channel to consumers via our own website. Launch is foreseen for Q4, initially with 1 SKU, to be expanded to 3 SKUs in Q1 next year. Current strategic projections are that during next year this should represent approximately 30% of our sales in volume. The juice in the capsules is the same as other current juices we produce, although juice in capsules is expected to have half the shelf life of juice in packs and cartons. Obviously, we would need to install a specific packaging line for the new product.

I'd like you to get organized for this new product introduction. We'll discuss your proposed approach in our upcoming meeting next month.

BRgds,
BMcL.

Figure 12.6   Template: analysis of new products, channels and business models

TEAM: _SuperJuice_   STRATEGY: _Low Cost_   ⓘ The Fresh Connection

CHALLENGE: __NEW PRODUCT INTRODUCTION, NEW CHANNEL, NEW BUSINESS MODELS__

IMPACT ON:

NEW SEGMENT(S)

EXISTING CUSTOMERS

MANUFACTURING & DISTRIBUTION

SUPPLY AND SUPPLIERS

IMPACT ON BUSINESS MODEL:

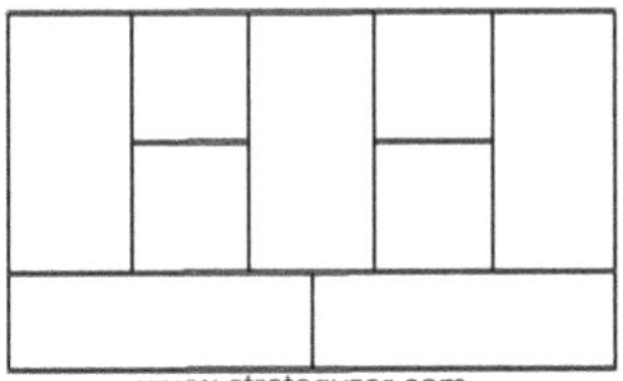

www.strategyzer.com

IMPLICATIONS FOR TFC AND SUPPLY CHAIN:
...
...
...
...
...

PROPOSED ACTIONS:	SALES	OPERATIONS	SUPPLY CHAIN	PURCHASING
	...	...	...	...
	...	...	...	...
	...	...	...	...

As in the case of the challenges associated with new market entrants, from this analysis of new product introductions and new channels a number of actions have been defined (Figure 12.6). Once again, let's park these for the moment and look at yet another important business challenge.

Transforming into responsible and green

During gameplay in Part Two, TFC's customers were mainly focused on getting a good service in terms of delivery reliability and shelf life, according to the promises and agreements made. In some industries, their carbon footprint and the wider topics of sustainability and corporate social responsibility (CSR) are gaining attention. TFC's business is no exception....

EXERCISE 12.3
Imagine the impact of carbon footprint

Imagine

Imagine you receive the e-mail shown in Figure 12.7 from Bob McLaren.

Figure 12.7 E-mail from Bob McLaren about carbon footprint

08-Feb 09:56AM
Bob McLaren <bobmcl@>
CARBON FOOTPRINT

To: O TFC CEO ; O TFC Sales ; O TFC Operations ; O TFC Supply Chain ; O TFC Purchasing

Hello all,

I met one of the higher managers of TFC's largest customer yesterday at a networking event. He was telling me about the fact that they have begun tracking and reporting carbon footprints of their suppliers. His expectation was that TFC would also soon receive their request to deliver carbon footprint reporting, however most likely in combination with some kind of target setting and linked somehow to the existing service-based bonus/penalty systematic. We need to figure out about our end-to-end supply chain where carbon emissions exist and how we could possibly measure the amounts. At the same time, it would be great to have a first shot at defining improvement areas in order to reduce the carbon footprint.

Sorry for the urgency, but I told him I would discuss internally and send him an input later on this week. Pls. let me know your thoughts and send me your inputs in the coming days.

BRgds,
BMcL.

Go step by step through all the activities in TFC's supply chain starting with distribution to customers, working your way upstream to suppliers (including the supplier production sites). It might be a good idea to use an empty version of the network diagram you created in Part Two (Figure 6.4, p 110) as the starting point for visualization:

- For each step, determine the potential sources of carbon emissions (there can be multiple sources per stage in the supply chain).

- See if you can identify public sources that can be of help in determining the quantities of emissions per stage in the TFC supply chain.

- Think about how carbon emissions could be measured in each stage of the TFC supply chain: who would have the information, or if it's not available, how could it be measured?

- For each of the stages in the supply chain, what kind of actions could you think of to reduce the carbon footprint? Who would be in charge of these actions?

- How can you get into the position of being able to identify the top-most polluting activities in TFC's supply chain, allowing priority setting?

Figure 12.8 Template: analysis of carbon footprint

TEAM: *SuperJuice*   STRATEGY: *Low Cost*   The Fresh Connection

CHALLENGE: *CARBON FOOTPRINT (MEASURE AND REDUCE KG CO2 PER LITRE OF JUICE SOLD)*

SOURCES OF CO_2:   HOW TO MEASURE? WHERE TO GET DATA? HOW TO REDUCE?
DISTRIBUTION TO CUSTOMERS
OUTBOUND WAREHOUSING
MANUFACTURING
INBOUND WAREHOUSING
SUPPLY AND SUPPLIERS

PROPOSED ACTIONS:	*SALES*	*OPERATIONS*	*SUPPLY CHAIN*	*PURCHASING*
	...	...	...	...
	...	...	...	...
	...	...	...	...

- What actions can you think of for each of the TFC management team members, to move this initiative forward?
- You can use Figure 12.8 to summarize your thoughts and report to Bob McLaren.

After this first exposure of TFC's management to the topic of sustainability and carbon footprint, it seems Bob McLaren isn't done yet.

EXERCISE 12.4

Imagine the impact of CSR, sustainability and TBL

Imagine

Imagine you receive the e-mail shown in Figure 12.9 from Bob McLaren.

Figure 12.9 E-mail from Bob McLaren about CSR, sustainability and TBL

10-Feb 04:14PM
Bob McLaren <bobmcl@>
CSR, SUSTAINABILITY, TRIPLE BOTTOM LINE

To: ○ TFC CEO ; ○ TFC Sales ; ○ TFC Operations ; ○ TFC Supply Chain ; ○ TFC Purchasing

Hello all,

Surprises seemingly never come alone. Just 2 days after my e-mail about carbon footprint, we had a meeting with our shareholders this morning and as it turns out, a number of them are becoming more and more concerned about the topics of corporate social responsibility (CSR), sustainability and the circular economy. Obviously I told them about our carbon footprint study, but they didn't want to leave it there. As they suggested to me, recommended reading on the issues are the books by Elkington (*Cannibals with Forks*), Braungart (*Cradle to Cradle*) and Raworth (*Doughnut Economy*), as well as the website of the Ellen MacArthur Foundation. I want you to (1) start elaborating on the concept of triple bottom line and (2) particularly also on the circular economy. My idea would be to see if we could launch a pilot-project on 'circular' still in Q2 or Q3 of this year. I have a meeting with the other shareholders in two weeks, so I need your inputs fast.

BRgds,
BMcL.

Step 1: operationalize the triple bottom line (TBL)

1 Per item of the TBL, define four KPIs related to the supply chain:

(a) *People*: think, for example, of TFC's own people, of suppliers' staff, of the local community of which TFC is part, of TFC's consumers, of the people in the world at large, and so on.

(b) *Planet*: think, for example, of air, noise and waste pollution, energy consumption, use of natural resources, water footprint, and so on.

(c) *Profit*: think of supply-chain-related costs, revenues, investments, and so on.

2 Check if they are SMART (see Chapter 4)

3 If you are convinced they are, create a factsheet for each KPI (see Figure 12.10), following the example of Team SuperJuice. As a start, they build on the work done after the previous question from Bob McLaren about their carbon footprint.

4 Now design an 'Integral TBL supply chain dashboard' with these 12 KPIs (see template in Figure 12.11).

Figure 12.10   Template: TBL KPI-design

TEAM: _SuperJuice_   STRATEGY: _Low Cost_   ⓘ **The** Fresh **Connection**

CHALLENGE: **_TRIPLE BOTTOM LINE KPI FACTSHEET_**

KPI NAME: *TFC Carbon Footprint*

DESCRIPTION: *Total end-to-end CO_2 emissions per SC*
                   stage, attributable to TFC decisions

FORMULA: *Total TFC end-to-end CO2 emissions in KG*
                   ―――――――――――――――――――――――
                   Total amount of litres of juice produced

DATA SOURCES: *Transport suppliers & carriers, Operations,*
                   Component Suppliers, Energy suppliers

HOW TO COLLECT: ...

FREQUENCY OF PUBLICATION: ...

PROPOSED TARGET: ...

TBL CATEGORY:

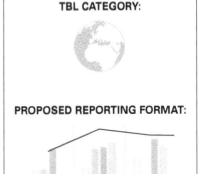

PROPOSED REPORTING FORMAT:

each bar represents 1 stage in the
supply chain. The line represents the
total end-to-end CO_2-emission

Figure 12.11   Template: TBL KPI-dashboard design

TEAM: _SuperJuice_   STRATEGY: _Low Cost_   ⓘ **The** Fresh **Connection**

CHALLENGE: **_TRIPLE BOTTOM LINE KPI DASHBOARD_**

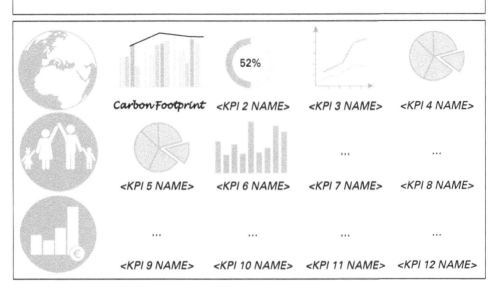

Step 2: definition of actions

- Saying that you want to become more socially responsible as a company is one thing, but those are just words until real actions are taken. Using Figure 12.12, for each KPI try to identify the *structural implications* for TFC of becoming more 'TBL-sensitive'. Which areas of the canvas are related to the KPI in a direct or indirect way? What are the implications of this? Ultimately, how could existing activities, resources and partnerships be affected? What new activities, resources and partnerships would need to be considered?

- What *actions* would you define in order to move forward and achieve the targets proposed for each of the KPIs?

Step 3: define a pilot project related to the circular economy

- Remember that Bob McLaren also asked you to come up with a proposal for a *pilot project* related to the concept of the circular economy. As a reference, go back to Figure 2.8 (p 34) showing the butterfly diagram of the circular economy

Figure 12.12   Template: definition of TBL actions

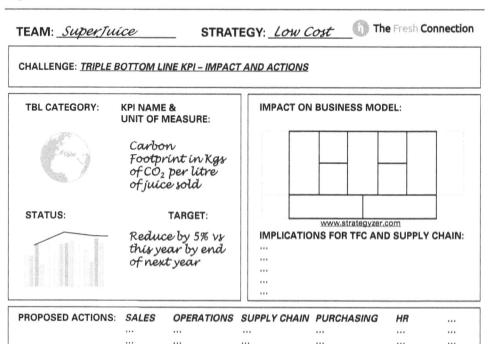

or check out the original version on the website of the Ellen MacArthur Foundation. Define a project around the circular economy that would be relevant for TFC. You can think, for example, about return and recycling of used bottles and/or cartons, the creation of a pallet return pool, reuse of waste, and so on.

- You can use the canvas as well as the diagram of TFC's supply chain network to analyse the potential impact that your proposed project has on the physical flows but ultimately also on the overall business model (from a strategic point of view, both are important). Describe the new process and the changes it implies using the template in Figure 12.13.

- In defining your project approach, think about what business process redesign thought-leader Michael Hammer wrote when addressing implementation of changes in processes. He stated that 'two principles are critical to success [...]. The first is "think big, start small, move fast". [...] The second principle is "communicate relentlessly" (Hammer, 2001).

- Create a compelling business case for the project based on TFC data and assumptions. For the business case you can go back to the template from Figure 10.4, which you have used previously. If relevant, make sure that you also include any potential one-off project or implementation costs and/or one-off investments.

Figure 12.13 Template: analysis of pilot-project circular economy

TEAM: _SuperJuice_   STRATEGY: _Low Cost_   🅗 **The** Fresh **Connection**

CHALLENGE: *CIRCULAR ECONOMY PILOT-PROJECT*

PROJECT NAME:

CURRENT FLOWS & PROCESS: FUTURE FLOWS & PROCESS:

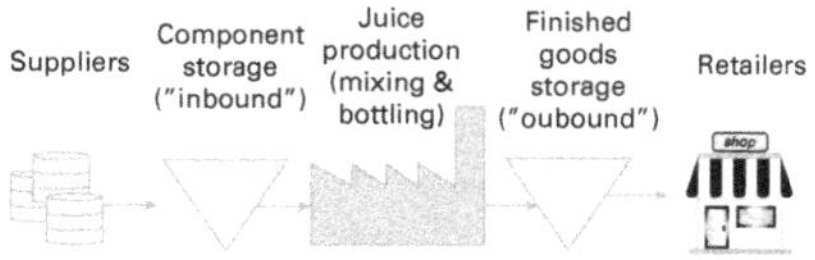

Suppliers Component storage ("inbound") Juice production (mixing & bottling) Finished goods storage ("oubound") Retailers

ADDITIONS AND CHANGES REQUIRED:

As you will have seen from the previous exercises, really becoming a more socially responsible company can have a lot of far-reaching implications, extending far into the supply chain. I'm sure that you have defined a large number of potential actions to be carried out by TFC management and staff. Once again, let's park these for the moment and come back to them at a later stage, and go on to yet another challenge.

Changes in the external environment: PESTEL

During gameplay in Part Two, you as TFC's management team have been focusing on turning around the company and returning to profitability given the status quo within the market. Obviously, companies do not live in isolation from whatever is going on in the world, from how industries, countries, technologies, people are changing over time. Like any company, TFC needs to get a view on changes occurring, evaluate what the implications might be and decide what to do....

EXERCISE 12.5

Imagine the impact of the external (macro) environment

Imagine

Imagine you receive the e-mail in Figure 12.14 from Bob McLaren.

Figure 12.14   E-mail from Bob McLaren about PESTEL analysis

26-Mar 11:04AM
Bob McLaren <bobmcl@ >
PESTEL

To: O TFC CEO ; O TFC Sales ; O TFC Operations ; O TFC Supply Chain ; O TFC Purchasing

---

Hello all,

Things seem to be moving in the right direction. I'm glad all is working out reasonably well, thanks for your efforts! I think we should take advantage of the positive momentum and take a more strategic look into the future. There are many things going on everywhere that might have an impact on TFC sooner or later. I want you to start getting your thoughts clear on them and start defining actions accordingly. Would be great if we could discuss first findings and conclusions in a breakout session end of next month during the Annual Conference of the Group.

BRgds,
BMcL.

Step 1: trends and developments

Identify trends and developments which might be relevant to TFC in terms of potential impact. Part of the identification might involve starting off with pure brainstorming, complemented by thorough desk research (fact finding) to ultimately support the proposals for Bob McLaren. If you run into gaps in the information, either make defendable assumptions or simply checkmark the identified gaps for further research and/or expert consultancy ('know what you don't know!').

Follow the PESTEL framework as briefly touched upon in Chapter 2. You can use the template from Team SuperJuice (Figure 12.15) to report on your findings from Step 1, as well as the upcoming Steps 2 and 3. Use a separate page for each PESTEL topic:

- **Political,** such as trade zones, political regimes, safety and security, political stability, trade embargos or bans. Look at TFC's entire supply chain network (so origins of flows, but also destinations and zones of transit), and so on.

- **Economic,** such as currency exchange rates, market upswings and downswings (look at markets for supply as well as for demand), the rise of emerging economies, and so on.

Figure 12.15   Template: analysis of PESTEL

TEAM: _SuperJuice_	STRATEGY: _Low Cost_	The Fresh Connection

CHALLENGE: _PESTEL ANALYSIS_

POLITICAL:
COUNTRIES OF SUPPLY
  France: ....
  Spain: ...
  USA: ...
  China: ...
ZONES OF TRANSIT
  Middle East/Africa: ....
  Atlantic
  Mainland Europe: ...
COUNTRIES OF MANUFACTURING

COUNTRIES OF DEMAND

GLOBAL POLITICAL CLIMATE

IMPACT ON BUSINESS MODEL:

www.strategyzer.com

IMPLICATIONS FOR TFC AND SUPPLY CHAIN:
...
...
...
...
...

PROPOSED ACTIONS:	SALES	OPERATIONS	SUPPLY CHAIN	PURCHASING	HR	...
	...	...	...	...	...	...
	...	...	...	...	...	...
	...	...	...	...	...	...

- **Social**, such as individualization, sensibility for the environment, but also demographics (growing/declining populations, ageing populations, millennials), the rise of megacities, increasing issues with traffic, sensibility for human aspects (labour relations, unionization, sweatshops in developing countries), and so on.

- **Technological**, such as artificial intelligence, robotics, drones, blockchain, Internet of Things (IoT), 3D-printing, virtual reality (VR), augmented reality (AR), material sciences (smart materials), renewable energies, nanotechnology, and so on.

- **Ecological**, such as climate change, weather, temperature, wet and dry periods, weather stability, fossil and alternative energy sources, air, noise and waste pollution, plastic soup in the oceans, raw material scarcity (precious metals, minerals, clean water), and so on.

- **Legal**, such as international trade laws and import/export quotas and taxes, customs regulations, (food) security legislation, cool and cold chain requirements, emission reduction targets, and so on.

Step 2: analyse potential impacts

For each of the identified relevant trends, you can use the canvas to analyse potential impacts on TFC.

Step 3: define actions

Define actions in order to move forward. Try to be as specific as possible, so that the company's management receives a concrete and compelling proposal from you.

Once more, a number of actions have now been defined, in this case as a consequence of the analysis of the external environment. Again, let's park these for the moment and move on to the next topic.

An emergency!

EXERCISE 12.6

Imagine managing an emergency

Imagine

Imagine you receive the message shown in Figure 12.16 from Bob McLaren, at 06:11 in the morning.

Figure 12.16   Message from Bob McLaren: urgency!

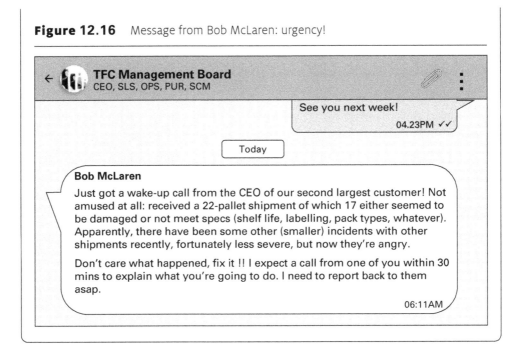

So far, you haven't had to worry about operational issues in TFC, but of course not everything will always work out according to plan. Bob McLaren has the customer waiting, so damage control is needed here. Analyse quickly what could have happened in the case of the 17 pallets. At the same time, think of an approach to the customer. They are very unhappy and you need to get some convincing information back to Bob McLaren so that he can report back to the customer and minimize the damage to the relationship. No time for templates, the clock is ticking....

Managing uncertainties: risk assessment

Imagine the issue with the customer has been settled and that it's back to normal business again. However, the incident has shown that TFC, like any other company, is vulnerable to unforeseen events happening. Maybe it's time for some solid risk management....

EXERCISE 12.7
Imagine managing supply chain risks

Imagine

Imagine you receive the e-mail shown in Figure 12.17 from Bob McLaren

Figure 12.17   E-mail from Bob McLaren about risk assessment

11-May 07:34AM
Bob McLaren <bobmcl@>
RISK ASSESSMENT

To: O TFC CEO ; O TFC Sales ; O TFC Operations ; O TFC Supply Chain ; O TFC Purchasing

Hello all,

Even though results in general have been quite OK lately, our recent incident with our number 2 client has shown that in fact we are quite vulnerable to disruptions and hiccups. I think it's become clear that we should be much better prepared and I want you to work on a thorough risk assessment of the entire end-to-end TFC supply chain. Identify risks, classify them and come up with mitigation proposals.

I'll be at your site for a quick visit probably in 3–4 weeks from now, let's discuss then. In the mean time, don't let such incidents happen again.

BRgds,
BMcL.

Go step by step through all of the activities in TFC's supply chain, starting with distribution to the customers and working your way upstream to suppliers (including the supplier production sites). It might be a good idea to use an empty version of the network diagram you created in Part Two (Figure 6.4, p 110) as the starting point for visualization:

- For each step, determine the potential risks you can think of. You might want to refer to Chapter 2 (Figure 2.9, p 36) for inspiration. Obviously, the previous exercises in this chapter may also provide useful inputs to the assessment.

- Then classify the identified risks according to probability, impact and detectability, thus coming to a list of risks ranked according to importance. Make sure to document the facts and/or assumptions underlying the risk classification.

- For your top five risks, define mechanisms to improve detectability, as well as potential mitigations for impact minimization. You can use the template from Team SuperJuice (Figure 12.18).

The actions required to move forward with risk management in TFC have now been defined. We will park these for the moment and come back to them at a later stage.

Figure 12.18   Template: analysis of risk assessment

TEAM: _SuperJuice_   STRATEGY: _Low Cost_   🔵 The Fresh Connection

---

CHALLENGE: **_RISK ASSESSMENT_**

RISK #1, DESCRIPTION:

RISK SCORE*:   48
P   - PROBABILITY (1–5):   3
I   - IMPACT (1–5):   4
D   - DETECTABILITY (1–5)**:   4

MAIN FACTS/ASSUMPTIONS BEHIND SCORES:
...
...
...

* Risk score = P x I x D
** Detectability (1–5): higher→score more difficult to detect
   before impact

POTENTIAL DETECTION MECHANISMS:
...

...

...

POTENTIAL MITIGATIONS:
...

...

...

...

PROPOSED ACTIONS: *SALES*   *OPERATIONS*   *SUPPLY CHAIN*   *PURCHASING*   *HR*   ...
                     ...   .
                     ...   .
                     ...   .

Summary

In this chapter we have been imagining beyond the fundamentals of managing a stable supply chain. We have addressed potential implications of challenges to the status quo from the perspective of the business dimension of supply chain: more intense market pressures, new products, channels and business models, the transformation into a socially responsible company, dealing with an ever more complex external environment, and finally, the wider topic of supply chain risk management. In the next chapter, the journey of imagining beyond the fundamentals will continue as we look at several challenges to the status quo from the perspective of the technical dimension of the supply chain.

Imagining technical 13 challenges for the supply chain

In this chapter we are going to look in more detail at what could happen to the supply chain if the status quo of the elements of the technical dimension is challenged. Since supply chain solutions by default are of an integral nature, the individual topics of the technical dimension are now not dealt with separately anymore, even though all of them will appear (Figure 13.1).

In the mini-cases in this chapter we will therefore look at the physical infrastructure (facilities, transportation, outsourcing and collaboration), planning and control, information and systems, and organizational issues from a holistic point of view. You will perhaps find that some of the mini-cases in this chapter are relatively open-ended. This is done on purpose, because questions and issues in real life do not always appear in a nice and clearly formulated way. In some cases, this is simply because the topic and/or its implications still aren't very clear to begin with. But that doesn't have to mean that they are then less relevant.

Please note that some, although not all, of the challenges dealt with in this chapter correspond to more advanced modules of TFC gameplay, which are normally only used in specific situations. In those cases, the elaboration here in the book is an adaptation of the game functionality and goes a bit beyond the pure gameplay version of the challenges.

Please note: I think that for all the challenges in this chapter, it is valid to say that no answers or solutions are written in stone here. There are always different interpretations and different solutions possible. You might want to consider evaluating various scenarios before deciding which one is most convincing in terms of outcomes, realism, likelihood, and so on. Just make sure that for whatever solution you finally propose, you have clear and compelling arguments in favour of it that can be explained and defended. If necessary, make reasonable and understandable assumptions. For most of the challenges, it would be a good idea to develop a template based on the one from Team SuperJuice, which we have already seen a few times in Chapter 12 (Figure 13.2). In addition, you might want to keep a copy of TFC's business model canvas as well as an empty canvas ready, just in case.

Figure 13.1   Topics from the technical dimension of the supply chain

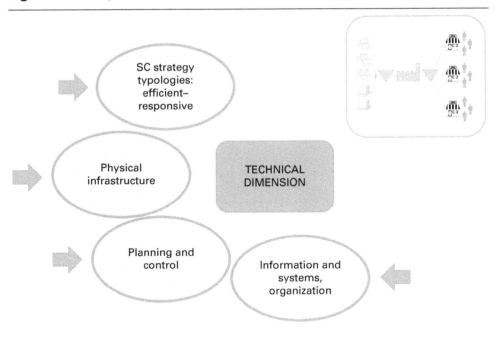

Figure 13.2   Template for analysing challenges

TEAM: _SuperJuice_   STRATEGY: _Low Cost_   Ⓗ   The Fresh Connection

CHALLENGE: _____

IMPACT ON:

NEW SEGMENT(S)

EXISTING CUSTOMERS

MANUFACTURING & DISTRIBUTION

PARTNERS, SUPPLY AND SUPPLIERS

IMPACT ON BUSINESS MODEL:

www.strategyzer.com

IMPLICATIONS FOR TFC AND SUPPLY CHAIN:
...
...
...
...
...

PROPOSED ACTIONS:	*SALES*	*OPERATIONS*	*SUPPLY CHAIN*	*PURCHASING*
	...	...	...	...
	...	...	...	...
	...	...	...	...

Challenging the push/pull setup

In the gameplay so far, we haven't questioned the way the products were produced, nor the decoupling point that was initially chosen by TFC. Basically, production has taken place straight from components to finished goods without interruption, on the basis of forecasts and corresponding inventory settings.

EXERCISE 13.1
Imagine challenging the push/pull setup

Imagine

Imagine an increasing commercial drive within TFC to jump on the trend of customization. For example, think of bottles with names printed on the label, bottles customized for specific events or campaigns, maybe even bottles designed in specific shapes. In addition, you could even think of customized flavours, customized packaging formats, packages combined with gifts or toys, and so on. A reconsideration of the customer–order decoupling point, touched on in Chapter 3, might be called for here.

Analyse from a business point of view what the impacts of customization can be on the business model. First, define a number of alternatives for how customization could be shaped. Then develop a template based on the one from Team SuperJuice in Figure 13.2, analyse the potential impact on the various areas of the canvas and reflect on the implications. Although you may have touch on it already during the elaboration of the template, make sure that you explicitly address the required implications for operations and for planning and control, potentially even for the organizational setup due to a potential change in the decoupling point.

For example, think of:

- What additional steps in the design/development and/or production process would be needed? What new competencies would need to be developed and/or subcontracted? How easy or difficult, and how time consuming, might that be?

- What new requirements would there be for the sources of components, for example customized labelling?

- What would be the implications for the machines used and potential new equipment required?

- In the case of new production steps, effectively a make-or-buy decision would come into play. What arguments in favour or against outsourcing would there be in this case?

- Due to potential changes in the decoupling point, what would be the implications for forecasting? Consequently, would there be any changes in who would be involved in the forecasting? And in the tools needed? The information needed?

- What would be the implications for the customer interface, for example key account management? How would the operational relationships with customers be affected, in terms of the design processes for customized products, obtaining of reliable forecasts in the case of continuously changing products, and so on?

Overall, what actions would you propose to deal with this new requirement? Keep a note of those actions for the moment, and we'll move on to the next issue: challenging capacity.

Challenging capacity

In most configurations of TFC gameplay, you don't have to worry about growth or capacity constraints. Demand is there and seems to be stable in terms of overall volume in litres of juice. And in terms of production or storage capacity, even though more expensive than regular capacity, whenever one of your warehouses is full, there is the overflow next door with unlimited capacity you can use. Whenever you run out of manufacturing capacity, there is always an unlimited amount of overtime available to finish production. In two subsequent steps, let's look at situations in which demand volume and capacity are challenged.

EXERCISE 13.2
Imagine challenging capacity in the case of expansion

Imagine

Imagine that Bob McLaren, together with the other owners of the company, are pushing for growing aggressively in the next few years, setting a target of 10–15 per cent year-on-year growth for the next 3–5 years, to be reached by having more direct and innovative sales approaches to competitors of your current customers. In other words, growth based on your current geographical scope and current product portfolio.

Reflect on the following:

- Considering short-term as well as longer-term solutions, what ways of expanding production and storage capacity can you think of (fixed staff, temporary labour, machinery and equipment, third parties, and so on)?

- For each of the options you have identified, list the pros and cons in terms of investments to be made, usage learning curve, speed of implementation, flexibility to upscale/downscale, temporary versus more permanent solution, easily reversible or not, risk against wrong forecast and/or wrong sales target setting, how easy/difficult to replace existing capacity, and so on.

- Based on your analysis, to what extent could you grow gradually, or to what extent would bigger incremental steps need to be taken at some point (Figure 13.3)? To what extent would you need to expand capacity in anticipation of expected growth, or could you be fast and flexible enough to 'grow with the flow'?

Park your observations for a moment.

We have still only considered unlimited flexible capacity as in TFC gameplay. In real life, you might at times have such a luxury as unlimited capacity, but it is not unlikely that someone in the company, for example the finance director, will tell you that overflow or overtime are fine, but that there is only a fixed amount of money that you can spend on it. In similar fashion, it might be that collective labour contracts, for example as negotiated with labour unions by the general management and the human resources department, only allow for a certain amount of extra hours per month.

Figure 13.3   Challenging capacity (some examples of capacity expansion strategies)

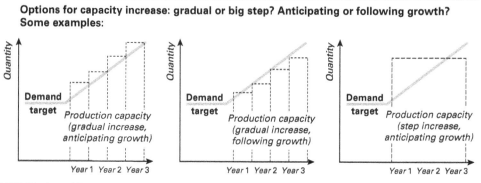

SOURCE adapted from Slack *et al* (2012) and Heizer and Render (2013)

EXERCISE 13.3

Imagine challenging capacity in case of capacity constraints

Imagine

Imagine that for budgetary or cost-efficiency reasons, only a ±10 per cent margin around the forecasted production volumes can be catered for in terms of flexible production and storage capacity.

Think about the following:

- As a starting point, you can compare figures from the gameplay in which you have used overflow capacity and/or overtime in production, to a larger or lesser extent. What implications would a hard-stop maximum on available capacity have had in those cases? What choices would you have been forced to make? How would you have made those choices, on the basis of what information and what criteria?

- Now enter the growth targets into the equation. What does it look like now? What issues could you potentially run into? How would you coordinate everything in order to make it work?

Overall, what actions would you propose to deal with this new requirement? Keep a note of those actions for the moment, and we'll move on to the next issue, that of machine life.

Challenging machine life

In The Fresh Connection gameplay you have had to deal with a certain number of machine breakdowns, against which you could protect yourself with preventive maintenance, and training your staff to solve breakdowns quicker. This is a normal fact of production life. For the duration of the gameplay you didn't have to worry about it much more than just that. At the same time, when you had the possibility of swapping one or both machines for other machines (bigger or smaller, faster or slower), you didn't have to pay attention to the investment aspects, specifically on how and where to get financing for buying the new machine(s), if the remaining market value of the old machines was very limited. Let's now introduce the element of machine life and machine investment into the equation.

EXERCISE 13.4

Imagine challenging machine life

Imagine

Imagine that the current machines for mixing and bottling were bought some 20 years ago when the company was founded. They are now getting towards the end of their technical lifetime (Figure 13.4). Regardless of technological developments that might have taken place during those 20 years, and the more technologically advanced machines that are surely available in the market right now, the existing machines will most likely start having more and more technical hiccups.

Figure 13.4　Challenging machine life

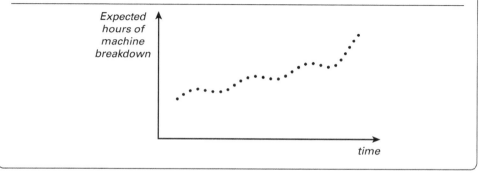

Reflect on the following:

- What would be the impacts you could expect if both your mixing and bottling machines started breaking down more often? Go back to the numbers of the game and work from the breakdown percentages you have seen there. What if these numbers doubled over the next year or two – what would be the consequences? What could be done to mitigate these impacts? How expensive and time consuming would that be? How would overall production volumes be affected? What would be the impact on the cost per litre of juice?

- If you decide that it's time to replace one or both current machines for mixing and bottling, what would be the possible scenarios and how would they compare? Consider, for example, simply replacing one machine with a new one. But you could also think of getting a strategic partner for mixing and/or bottling, or even start buying the mixing and/or bottling services from an arm's-length commodity supplier. Use the template from Team SuperJuice (Figure 13.2) as a basis for analysing the different alternatives, and also look explicitly at the business model implications using the canvas. What are the pros and cons of each of the alternative scenarios, in terms of strategic value, commercial aspects, required competency development, customer value, speed and flexibility, and so on?

Overall, what actions would you propose to deal with this new requirement? Keep a note of those actions for the moment, and we'll move on to the next challenge.

Challenging the network design

The supply chain network from TFC that you have seen so far has been stable and unchanged during gameplay: sourcing was done globally, whereas storage, production and distribution were local affairs. Let's see what could happen if that situation changes.

EXERCISE 13.5
Imagine challenging the network setup

Imagine

Imagine that TFC, as part of its growth strategy, is now considering geographical expansion, for example into Belgium, France and Germany (Figure 13.5). For the moment, consider a scenario of so-called organic growth, meaning by growing its own organization, not by mergers or acquisitions.

Figure 13.5   Challenging network design

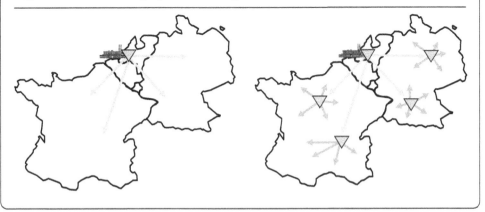

Elaborate two distinct scenarios:

- Delivery from finished goods inventory in TFC's home country directly to retail customers' storage facilities in the destination countries.

- Delivery from finished goods inventory in TFC's home country to TFC local storage facilities in the destination countries. Delivery to the retail customers from TFC's local warehouses.

Taking the situation and the numbers you know from TFC gameplay as a starting point, using the template from Figure 13.2 and making defendable assumptions where necessary, for each of the two scenarios evaluate the potential implications for:

- products and product portfolio (including labelling, packaging types, etc);
- demand (volume and variability);
- shelf life;
- production and production capacity (including options to upscale);
- inventory policies (central/local safety stocks);
- transportation (including outsourcing/subcontracting, risks);
- final distribution (including outsourcing/subcontracting, risks);
- potential return policies.

How do the two scenarios compare? Which one of the two would you propose? Or which one would you propose first and which one later on?

What actions would you propose? Keep a note of those actions for the moment, and we'll move on to the next challenge, related to changes in segments and channels.

Please note that in distribution network redesign, many detailed calculations can be made, comparing the many different possible scenarios. However, the key is to do this in an efficient way: start with high-level comparisons which can be done relatively quickly and only calculate in detail the (few) most promising scenarios. In this way, the majority of the time is saved for the detailed calculations of the really interesting scenarios, rather than calculating all possibilities in detail.

Challenging segments and channels

During gameplay you have basically been working with a fixed set of customers, representing different types of segments, a situation that wasn't challenged. Now let's see what could happen if that situation changes.

EXERCISE 13.6
Imagine challenging segments and channels (mini-case 1)

Imagine

Imagine that the marketing department of The Fresh Connection Group has an interest in entering the HoReCa segment (HOtels, REstaurants, CAfés). Specifically, they aim at smaller and larger restaurants and cafés (Figure 13.6). For the smaller-sized operators, the assumption is that glass bottles would probably need to be introduced as a new packaging type. For the larger operators, they are looking at the option of introducing refillable dispensers like the ones that many food retail chains are already using.

Figure 13.6 Challenging segments and channels (mini-case 1)

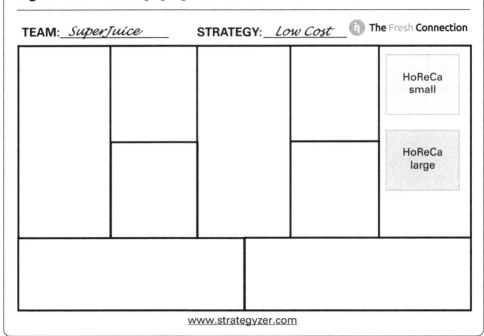

Taking the situation and the numbers you know from TFC gameplay as a starting point, and making defendable assumptions where necessary, for each of the two new segments evaluate the potential implications for:

- products and product portfolio (including labelling, packaging types, etc);
- the supporting equipment and potential maintenance;
- demand (volume and variability);
- shelf life;

- production and production capacity (including options to upscale);
- inventory policies (central/local safety stocks);
- transportation (including outsourcing/subcontracting, risks);
- final distribution (including outsourcing/subcontracting, risks);
- potential return policies.

EXERCISE 13.7
Imagine challenging segments and channels (mini-case 2)

Imagine

Imagine that you are contacted by a new player in the market, focusing on the emerging O2O market (Online to Offline) (Figure 13.7). In some countries this segment is growing very rapidly due to new online shops appearing, offering a wide variety of products, which the consumer can buy and later pick up, for example, at a local convenience store in the area where they live.

Figure 13.7 Challenging segments and channels (mini-case 2)

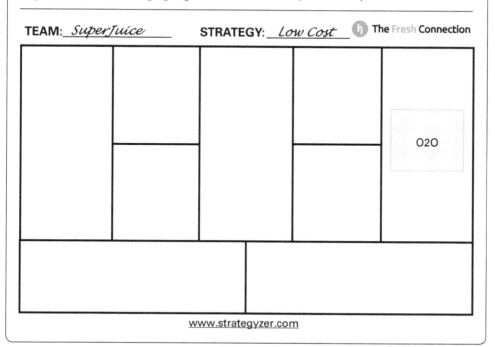

One of the disrupting elements of this new O2O market is that the retailer acts as a broker, without any physical locations of their own, but using local pickup points such as the aforementioned convenience stores, for whom this is a new source of revenue.

Going back to the template, including the business model canvas and taking the situation and the numbers you know from TFC gameplay as a starting point, and making defendable assumptions where necessary (for example, about the potential sales volume associated with this new market), evaluate the implications for:

- the overall business model of TFC;
- products and product portfolio;
- demand (volume and variability);
- shelf life;
- production and production capacity (including options to upscale);
- inventory policies (central/local safety stocks);
- final distribution (including outsourcing/subcontracting, risks);
- potential return policies.

Given the complexity and level of uncertainty in this second mini-case, you can focus mainly on raising relevant questions, potentially drafting some preliminary sketches for supply chain solutions.

Overall, what actions would you propose to deal with these two new requirements? Keep a note of those actions for the moment and we'll move on to the next challenge, which is related to the customers introducing new dimensions to the business.

Challenging the customer status quo

In the gameplay in Part Two, customers stayed pretty much the same throughout the various rounds, but obviously customers have their own path, their own visions for the future, and their own strategies.

EXERCISE 13.8
Imagine challenging the customer status quo

Imagine

Imagine that you receive a communication from your customer Dominick's that they are about to acquire a national competitor of theirs, which is a convenience store retail chain. The strategic fit that they see is that the retail chain is an expert in convenience stores, which are in fact very similar to the stores in the petrol stations of Dominick's themselves. As far as you are aware, the retailer has approximately the same number of stores as Dominick's, but without the petrol stations and located within cities (ie small stores with relatively small quantities of inventory of a wide number of different product categories).

Figure 13.8   Challenging the customer status quo

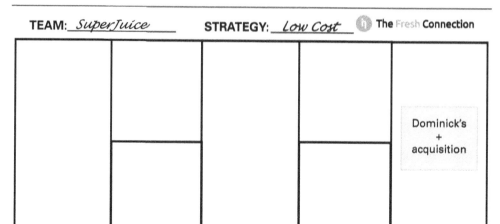

www.strategyzer.com

Develop a template based on the one from Team SuperJuice (Figure 13.8), analyse the potential impact on the canvas and reflect on the implications. Taking the situation and the numbers you know from TFC gameplay as a starting point, and making defendable assumptions where necessary, for each of the two new segments evaluate the potential implications for:

- products and product portfolio (including labelling, packaging types, etc);
- demand (volume and variability);
- shelf life;
- production and production capacity (including options to upscale);
- inventory policies (central/local safety stocks);
- transportation (including outsourcing/subcontracting, risks);
- final distribution (including outsourcing/subcontracting, risks);
- potential return policies.

Overall, what actions would you propose to deal with this new requirement? Keep a note of those actions for the moment and we'll move on to the next challenge, related to new requirements due to market developments at existing customers.

Challenging the value propositions

During gameplay you have basically been working with a fixed set of customers, representing different types of segments, to whom you were offering a particular value proposition defined by your own sales manager on the basis of a number of predefined elements. Let's see what could happen if 'the market' starts requiring new services.

EXERCISE 13.9
Imagine challenging the value propositions

Imagine

Imagine that there seems to be a new trend in the market in which some retailers are seemingly moving away from having very large warehouses. In practice, two different solutions seem to emerge. The first is a cross-docking scheme, in which retailers expect daily shipments from all suppliers into transport platforms at which the incoming shipments are reshuffled into outgoing shipments to retail outlets, carrying a mix of products from different suppliers. The second emerging solution is one in which retailers expect shipments to go directly from suppliers to their retail outlets. On top of that, imagine that retailers, because of their increasing purchasing power, are moving more and more towards agreements that include the introduction of end-of-shelf-life returns of unsold product.

Develop a template based on the one from Team SuperJuice (Figure 13.9), analyse the potential impact on the canvas and reflect on the implications. Taking the situation and the numbers you know from TFC gameplay as a starting point, and making defendable assumptions where necessary, for each of the two new segments evaluate the potential implications for:

- demand (volume and variability);
- inventory policies;
- distribution (including shipment sizes, shipment frequencies);
- warehousing (including picking and packing, order management, returns, merchandising).

Overall, what actions would you propose to deal with this new requirement? Keep a note of those actions for the moment; we will come back to them in Chapter 15.

Figure 13.9   Challenging the value propositions

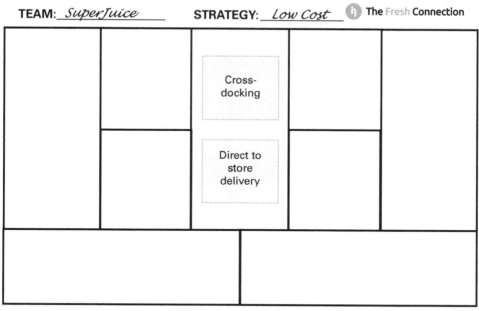

TEAM: _SuperJuice_   STRATEGY: _Low Cost_   The Fresh Connection

Cross-docking

Direct to store delivery

www.strategyzer.com

Summary

In this chapter we have seen many issues and developments in the company that might challenge the 'technical' status quo you have seen during gameplay. These challenges, of wide diversity and varying in complexity and urgency, have probably resulted in a large list of potential actions to consider. In the following chapter, the journey of imagining beyond the fundamentals of the supply chain will continue as we move on to some more potential changes, this time putting pressure on the leadership dimension and once again challenging the status quo we have experienced during gameplay.

Imagining leadership challenges for the supply chain

14

In this chapter we will return to the leadership dimension of supply chain management and focus on some challenges that were left untouched during the gameplay in Part Two.

Specifically, we will deal with the wider topic of stakeholders, leadership in the VUCA world, and external collaboration and transparency (Figure 14.1).

Managing many more stakeholders

So far, in the gameplay you have only had to deal with your own teammates as direct stakeholders, and with your suppliers, customers and Bob McLaren as virtual stakeholders. Let's expand the list a bit further by doing a more extended stakeholder analysis. Sometimes we also call this a 'force-field' analysis, since we're mapping out the various forces at play. This is a standard activity in project planning, but given the wide diversity of touchpoints it can also be very useful in the supply chain sphere.

EXERCISE 14.1

Imagine managing many stakeholders (stakeholder mapping)

Imagine

Imagine that as part of a wider analysis of the opportunities and threats for the supply chain, you are asked to carry out a full stakeholder analysis as the basis for defining actions affecting each of the main identified stakeholders.

Figure 14.1 Topics from the leadership dimension of the supply chain

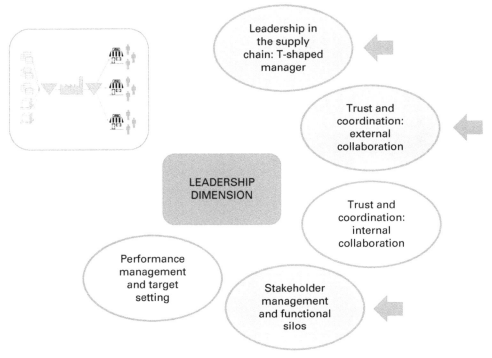

Step 1: Define a list of stakeholders of The Fresh Connection. For the moment, don't limit yourself too much:

- *Internal stakeholders*: for example R&D, legal & regulatory, IT, finance, HR, employees, and so on;

- *External stakeholders*: for example national and local authorities, local community, NGOs, labour unions, shareholders, customers, suppliers, other local companies, and so on.

The identified stakeholders could be put in a table, each one on one row in the table. See Figure 14.2 for an example by SuperJuice of what the template could look like.

Step 2: For each of the identified stakeholders, define the following (each of the points would be one column in the table started in Step 1):

- Directly or indirectly involved in the supply chain?

- Impact on which activities and/or which decisions in the supply chain?

- Relative importance to the supply chain (positive or negative)?

Step 3: Based on Step 2, create a ranking of the identified stakeholders in order of importance. For the top-priority stakeholders, define suggested ways to manage the relationship (Figure 14.3):

- What kind of activities to establish/maintain the relationship?
- To be organized with what frequencies?
- Who should be in charge?

Figure 14.2   Template: stakeholder analysis

TEAM: _SuperJuice_   **STRATEGY:** _Low Cost_   ⓗ The Fresh Connection

CHALLENGE: **_STAKEHOLDER MANAGEMENT_**

STAKEHOLDERS:	IMPACT ON WHICH AREAS OF THE SC?	RELATIVE IMPORTANCE FOR SC?
INTERNAL:		
R&D	_Product characteristics, process design (incl. production, transport & storage)_	++
...		
...		
EXTERNAL:		

Figure 14.3   Template: stakeholder action plan

TEAM: _SuperJuice_   **STRATEGY:** _Low Cost_   ⓗ The Fresh Connection

CHALLENGE: **_STAKEHOLDER MANAGEMENT_**

TOP PRIORITY STAKEHOLDERS:	SUGGESTED ACTIVITIES TO ESTABLISH/MAINTAIN RELATIONSHIP	FREQ?	WHO IN CHARGE?
INTERNAL:			
R&D	_Initial meeting to set the scene_ _Periodic visits/workshops about future developments_	_1x_ _6 months_	....
...			
...			

Keep in mind that in some of the identified cases, the relationship to the supply chain might be indirect and the stakeholders might not necessarily feel connected to it, potentially implying that extra attention and/or sensitivity might be needed.

As was done in Chapters 12 and 13, keep a note of the defined actions for the moment and we'll move on to the next leadership topic, related to internal collaboration.

Supply chain leadership in the VUCA world

During gameplay you haven't had to worry much about TFC staff, apart from specifying numbers of employees per activity in the supply chain. At this stage I think it might be interesting and useful to reflect for a brief moment on the role of staff in the supply chain in a VUCA world and to reflect upon what that might imply for leadership.

I remember an interview from years ago with Michael Dell, founder and CEO of the PC company of the same name. He was talking about how to deal with a company growing at a rate of approximately 25 per cent per year. Besides the more obvious aspects of how to keep up with increasing capacity of sourcing, assembly, storage and distribution, he was also specifically addressing the issue of managing a workforce under such circumstances as expanding to new countries, opening new call centres, more support functions, and so on. Basically, his point was that in a company that grows so fast, change is the norm rather than the exception, and you need a workforce that can deal with that, or even better, a workforce that thrives in such an environment. And of course those people exist, but reality is also that many people resist change. You cannot count on everyone getting a kick out of having new colleagues, new bosses and new procedures every so many months.

Following the logic of VUCA and looking at the world around us in general and the supply chains in it, it looks as if change will be more and more the norm and that in the supply chain we also need to get used to continuous change. The mini-cases of the previous chapters are proof of that – the supply chain is anything but stable.

EXERCISE 14.2
Imagine the impact of changes on people in the supply chain

Imagine

Imagine that changes in markets, industries, products, technologies, society, climate and so on, as identified earlier in your PESTEL analysis, are indeed going to take place in the foreseeable future. What would the impact be on people working in the supply chain area? Think of general support functions (staff), as well as operational people (line), shop floor as well as management.

- What are the implications of those changes for the profiles of the people needed in the supply chain in the different functions? Think of their technical profile as well as personality, behaviour and attitudes.

- What does that mean for recruitment and for training and education in the future?

- What does this all imply for future supply chain leadership? Also think back to the traits of the T-shaped supply chain manager. Which of the skills will be required, especially in order to deal with the aforementioned issues?

Let's move on to the last leadership topic of this chapter, related to external collaboration.

Managing trust and coordination: external collaboration

EXERCISE 14.3

Imagine managing external collaboration (mini-case 1)

Imagine

Imagine that your largest customer is in fact a large multinational retailer mainly maintaining arm's-length buying–selling relationships with small and medium-sized suppliers such as The Fresh Connection. They prefer to pay relatively little attention to these smaller companies, standardizing the ordering processes to the maximum possible, for example through automatically generated e-mails and limiting further communication to the minimum in order to have more of their resources available for shaping the relationship with their large suppliers, aiming at more large-scale improvements and synergies. So, effectively, for them, you seem to be one of the many. Too small to even ask them for reliable forecasts, or propose schemes such as vendor managed inventory (VMI). In practice, it's proven very difficult to talk to them. But they're big, pay reasonable prices and, not unimportantly, they pay on time. Now imagine that one day your finished goods warehouse manager tells you that orders from this customer now seem to be experiencing a 30 per cent increase across all of the SKUs in litres of juice over the normal volumes he's used to. Obviously he notices, since he and his team are the ones preparing the orders for shipment. In this case, since it's referring to the biggest customer, inventory levels are dropping faster because of the increased demand.

Since it can all be down to an exceptional week, in weeks 1 and 2 you think nothing of it, but when the higher demand continues in week 3, you need to decide whether you want to do something and, if so, what. Your options are the following:

(a) Do nothing; maybe it's something temporary and demand will go down later.

(b) Increase machine capacity to deal with the increased demand.

(c) Increase inventory levels to deal with the increased demand.

(d) Order more from suppliers to produce more and have more inventory.

(e) Two or more from the above (if so, which ones?).

(f) Other (please specify).

Write down your answer as well as the reasoning behind your decision. Now we go to another example.

EXERCISE 14.4
Imagine managing external collaboration (mini-case 2)

Imagine

Imagine that you are buying your oranges from a very large agricultural company. They're more than 10 times as big as you in terms of revenue and the relationship is distant at best. They have always been reliable suppliers to you, but you don't have a special relationship with them; they always seem to be busy with their other customers. Now imagine that the word is out that the growing season in the main country where you buy oranges is not looking very promising. Temperatures have not been good and there has been too much and more severe rainfall, and too little sunshine early on; it seems the climate is indeed getting crazy. For as big as they are, there is of course little your supplier can do about the weather. Although the situation might still turn around, since harvest is still some time away, almost everyone in the market buys from the same or other suppliers in the same country, and it looks as if some companies in the market are making moves to prepare.

Now you need to decide whether you want to do something and, if so, what. Your options are the following:

(a) Do nothing; maybe it will not be that bad after all.

(b) Pre-buy as much as you can from your supplier, just in case.

(c) Increase inventory levels to cover for more uncertain supply.

(d) Find alternative suppliers (including negotiation and getting them homologated to comply with your quality standards).

(e) Two or more from the above (if so, which ones?).

(f) Other (please specify).

Write down your answer as well as the reasoning behind your decision.

Let's go back to mini-case 1. Take the proposed action(s) you wrote down from the options in the list and assume that you would have gone in the chosen direction. Now elaborate each of the following scenarios:

1 After week 6 there is another increase, the average now being approximately 45% higher than initially.

2 After week 5 demand goes back to normal. Apparently, the higher demand was because some competitor of your customer had serious supply issues, leading to temporary higher demand to your customer, which now seem to have passed.

3 Demand stays at 30% above the previous average. Apparently, they have opened some new stores and/or reduced SKUs from competing stores on their shelves.

For each of the three scenarios and based on your proposed actions, try to elaborate the impact on each of your own activities (supply chain, operations, purchasing, sales), but also try to think of potential impacts on your business partners, such as suppliers, transport and distribution companies, external storage, temporary labour agencies, and so on (Figure 14.4). In addition, try to get a good grip on the timings involved; how much time would it take before your own decisions cascade down to other companies in the chain?

Figure 14.4   Template: scenario analysis – increased demand

TEAM: _SuperJuice_	STRATEGY: _Low Cost_	The Fresh Connection	
CHALLENGE: _STRONGLY INCREASED VOLUMES FROM LARGEST CUSTOMER_			
CHOSEN ACTION(S):			
IMPACT ON:	**SCENARIO 1:**	**SCENARIO 2:**	**SCENARIO 3:**
POSSIBLE RESULTS BASED ON CHOSEN ACTION(S):			

Let's now go back to mini-case 2. Once again, take the proposed action(s) you wrote down from the options in the list and assume you would have acted in the chosen direction. Now elaborate each of the following scenarios, four months down the road:

1 Harvest indeed turns out to be bad, and approximately only 60% of normal volumes are produced.

2 Harvest is not that bad after all, roughly the same volume as normal.

3 Your supplier communicates that increased speculation in the market has pushed demand and that in combination with the expected lower harvest volumes they will increase the price for orange by approximately 30%.

For each of the three scenarios and based on your proposed actions, try to elaborate the impact on each of your own activities (supply chain, operations, purchasing, sales), but also try to think of potential impacts on your existing business partners, such as customers, transport and distribution companies, external storage, temporary labour agencies, and so on (Figure 14.5). In addition, try to get a good grip of the timings involved; how much time would it take before your own decisions and events cascade down to other companies in the chain?

These two mini-cases show you once more the complexities in decision making and in scenario development when dealing with uncertainty. Second, they hopefully show you the potential impact of additional uncertainty due to difficult relationships

Figure 14.5 Template: scenario analysis – harvest problems

TEAM: _SuperJuice_   STRATEGY: _Low Cost_ 🍊 The Fresh Connection

CHALLENGE: *EXPECTED HARVEST PROBLEMS FOR ORANGES*			
CHOSEN ACTION(S):			

IMPACT ON:	SCENARIO 1:	SCENARIO 2:	SCENARIO 3:
POSSIBLE RESULTS BASED ON CHOSEN ACTION(S):			

with the customer and/or supplier, staying at the level of pure buying and selling. If the relationship had been of a different nature, then maybe other solutions would have been possible.

I think the following two reflections are appropriate here:

1 For each of the two mini-cases, from the overview of scenarios and your proposed decisions, how would they have played out? What would have happened? If you had done the scenario analysis before deciding on the basis of all of the possible choices, would you have chosen differently? What does that tell you?

2 Given the importance that the customer and supplier in question have for you, and given the complexities and risks associated with potentially changing either of them, what can possibly be done to create some sort of trust with them, enabling more coordination and transparency in the relationship than the simple focus on just buying and selling? What actions can you think of? Who should be involved? Who should take the lead?

One last thought before ending this chapter. Both mini-cases deal with situations that in practice might very well lead to the bullwhip effect as discussed in Chapter 4 (and remember the toilet-paper example from the beginning of Chapter 1!). An increased demand from a customer might lead to an overreaction by their supplier, who might be thinking that a new upward trend has begun, requiring increased inventories, capacity and so on. This, in turn, might lead to an overreaction by the supplier's supplier. Since the lack of transparency and potentially lack of trust between the different players in the chain lead them to speculate what's going on rather than know what's going on, practice shows that this normally results in covering with overcapacity and/or overstocking, leading to inefficiencies and potentially bad service.

Summary

This brings us to the end of this chapter about imagining what might happen to the leadership dimension if the status quo is challenged, thus almost ending the journey of imagining beyond the fundamentals of the supply chain. In the next and last chapter of this book, we will try to bring everything from the previous 14 chapters together, draw some final conclusions and identify points for further development.

Conclusion   15

Simple, but not easy (4): Complexity and alignment

In this closing chapter, we will come back to the various storylines that were opened throughout the book and we will close each of them with some final reflections and an outlook for your future continuous development.

Supply chain strategies revisited once more

The first storyline to bring home is about supply chain strategies. You will hopefully remember from back in Chapter 3 that we spoke about different typologies of supply chain strategies, to be applied as a function of overall corporate strategy, as well as supply and demand characteristics. A number of references were made to textbook authors presenting different frameworks for such typologies. As we said in Chapter 3: for the sake of argument as well as in order to make things manageable, and because they are in fact the cornerstones of the overall typology framework and therefore very important for any supply chain student and practitioner to know about, we worked for the better part of this book on the basis of the two extremes that all of the highlighted approaches have in common: the *cost-driven* and the *responsive* supply chain.

I hope that through the gameplay and the other exercises and reflections in the book you now have a better understanding of the buttons that can be touched in the supply chain, and how to touch them in the case of either of the aforementioned supply chain strategies. If that is indeed the case, you can then on the basis of your own experience and insights also form your own opinion about what those other typologies, most of them some form of 'hybrid' between the two extremes, would be like. Independent of the circumstances in which they would work best, you would have an opinion about what a supply chain strategy that is relatively low cost but at the same time somewhat responsive would look like, or a strategy that is mostly responsive, but at the lower-cost end of responsiveness. What do these hybrids mean in the context of physical infrastructure (warehousing, production, transport), for planning and control, for systems and for organizational models? With the information and experience you have obtained so far, how complex would it be to implement a truly hybrid strategy? How expensive would it be, how much time would it take? What are the implications and under which circumstances would such an implementation be justified?

At the same time, apart from looking at hybrid strategies as such, we can ask whether a company can have only one supply chain strategy at a time, either an extreme or a hybrid, or whether it might make sense to have multiple strategies in place at the same time. Referring back to the strategy compass from Figure 3.3, it would be reasonable to think that multiple supply chain strategies are sometimes justified. After all, different customer segments and different products might have very different characteristics. The key there is to be smart, as in any case of segmentation. Segregate strategies wherever it makes sense and combine wherever possible, in a context of dynamic markets and industries.

Hybrids and parallel strategies are extensive topics that we will not finish here because they are outside the scope and objectives of this book, but very interesting for you to explore further.

The Fresh Connection: now what?

The second storyline that we need to close is the one about TFC. In Part Two you found the company in a lossmaking situation and you had the opportunity, with your team, to turn the situation around and make the company profitable again. Then, in Part Three, we looked at a large number of challenges, for each of which you were asked to develop a list of potential actions, proposals and initiatives. If you were leading the company, there would be one final exercise to present to the boss: making sense of that long list of proposals and defining a feasible action plan for the next 2–3 years. Remember, TFC is a medium-sized company, meaning that time, money and resources are far from unlimited; in other words, choices will have to be made.

EXERCISE 15.1
Imagine defining a strategic plan

Imagine

Imagine that you have to come up with a list of strategic priorities for the coming 2–3 years. What would it contain?

Step 1: go back to all the actions, proposals and initiatives you listed in Chapters 12–14. Assume that all the challenges to which they are related are real and relevant in some way at this moment. As a reminder, the following challenges have been dealt with:

- Business dimension
  - New market entrants and tough competition
  - The need for new business models
  - Transforming to responsible and green
  - Changes in the external environment: PESTEL
  - Risk assessment
- Technical dimension
  - The push/pull setup
  - Storage and production capacity
  - Machine life
  - Network design
  - Segments and channels
  - Customer status quo
  - Value propositions
- Leadership dimension
  - Stakeholders
  - Internal collaboration
  - External collaboration

Step 2: Using the template from Team SuperJuice as shown in Figure 15.1, try to define priorities. Take your time and do it well. Make sure that you can defend your choices.

Step 3: Define where your priorities would lie. How many actions could you reasonably put on the priority list for the coming 2–3 years (Figure 15.2)? How much of the actual resources would that require? Consider that TFC as a medium-sized company probably doesn't have a dedicated project department, meaning that either projects would have to be staffed either by people who have a full-time tasks in parallel or by external (expensive) resources who would need to found and contracted.

So, now you should have a clear view on what TFC would be capable of doing in the next 2–3 years. Finally, let's meet the boss once more!

Figure 15.1 Template: project heatmap

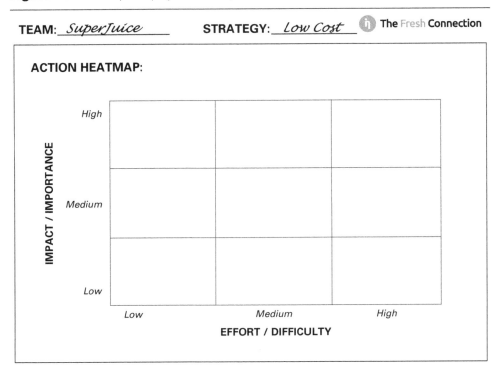

Figure 15.2 Project timelines

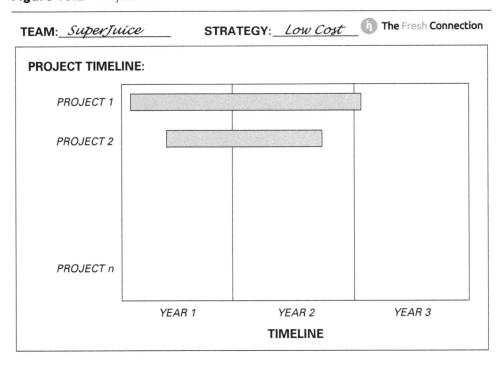

Bob McLaren is back

As you probably expected, Bob McLaren was going to show up once more before the end of this book.

EXERCISE 15.2
Reflect on the journey and report to the company's owner

Reflect

Bob McLaren seems to be in a mild, forward-looking mood, this time not asking about ROI, projects and the resolution of emergencies. Instead, he's asking for some self-reflection and is interested to know what you've learned from the experience and what you would do to continue learning from now on. Use the template in Figure 15.3 to list your findings. It might be interesting and enriching to do this first individually, and then put your inputs together with those of your teammates and discuss your points of view.

Figure 15.3   Template for learning points and takeaways

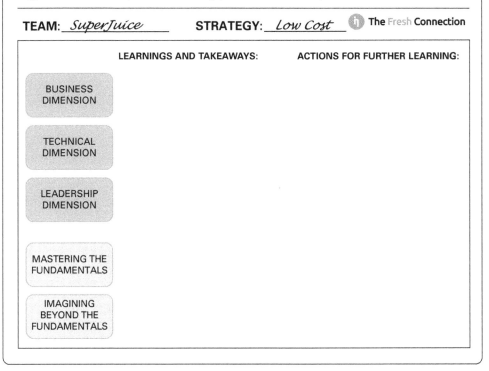

Listing your learning points and actions for further learning brings us back to the learning cycle of experiential learning.

Closing the loop: the learning cycle of experiential learning

The third storyline to finish in this last chapter is the one about experiential learning and the learning cycle. Recalling a phrase from the preface to the book, we expressed the hope that the learner 'would touch all the bases' of experiential learning by going through an experience, reflecting on what happened, conceptualizing the events and incorporating the findings into the next cycle of experience. As the subtitle of the book indicates, the focus has been on exposing the main *principles* of strategy, supply chain and leadership, *practising* the application of these concepts via gameplay and reflections, and imagining more *real-life applications* beyond the pure gameplay. Obviously, even though we're at the end of the book, the learning doesn't stop here. I would even argue that this is actually where the learning should really start to take off: you now have the basis and a view on where it might go. Now it's up to you to give that vision shape and form, and define how to continue the learning process.

One interesting reflection you can do for yourself at this stage is to take a close look at the concept of the T-shaped manager from Figure 4.3 and try to evaluate yourself on each of the elements, for example on a 1–5 scale. I'm sure that even though you would being doing this just for yourself, it would still give you a useful insight into where you stand during assessment. Based on your self-assessment, try to define some specific actions, things to work on over the coming months (try to set concrete goals as well as deadlines; remember the SMART KPIs!). And, of course, it would be interesting to go back to the chart every once in a while, to see where you have indeed developed, and then update your plans.

As we have said, the learning doesn't stop here; it has merely begun. It's up to you now to define your own continuous supply-chain learning path and find what works best for you: self-study using books, linking into web resources such as the sites of organizations and expert associations, subscribing to magazines and newsletters, following professionals' groups on social media such as on LinkedIn, finding mentors, reading general business and specific industry newspapers, doing project internships, and so on. There is a wealth of possibilities for you to tap into.

As mentioned when highlighting the supply chain manager's daily decathlon, 'supply chain managers need to be versatile, multi-skilled people, chameleonic in a way. A bit like the decathlon athlete, they need to perform well on a lot of different disciplines, not necessarily the best at each, but good enough to have a good shot at becoming the overall number 1 in the tournament' (Weenk, 2013b). I hope that in

Figure 15.4 Topics from the three dimensions of supply chain management

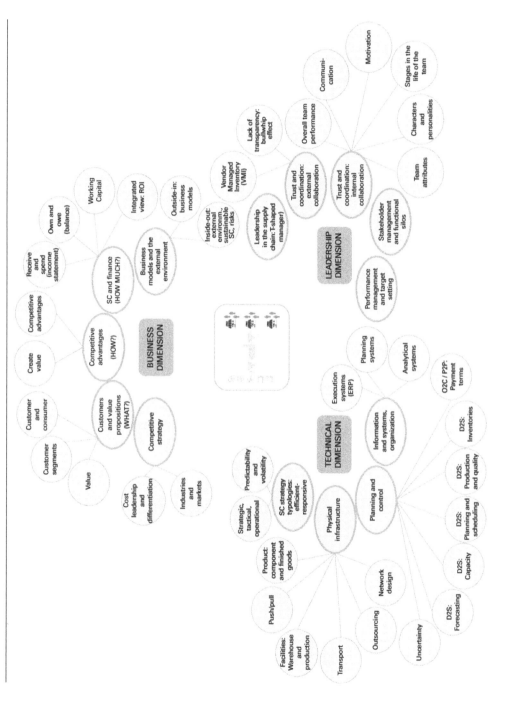

the spirit of the phrase from Ken Robinson and Lou Aronica at the beginning of this book, we have provided you with the conditions in which you can actively do things, that we have aroused your curiosity and have invited you to ask many questions, and that you have discovered new ideas and experienced the many exciting dimensions of supply chain management. Thus, I hope that it has contributed to your development of (part of) the supply chain manager's rich skillset and that you are getting ready to manage supply chains in the VUCA world.

So, congratulations on your journey through the business, technical and leadership dimensions of the supply chain (Figure 15.4): understanding the fundamentals, mastering them and even imagining beyond them. I hope it has been worth your while, and above all, that it has inspired you to move forward in supply chain management. Challenges are numerous, and I'm convinced that lots of brain power will be needed in the future. Many examples of such challenges have been dealt with throughout the book, and many more will appear wherever you go. But with a solid grounding in how to work and a good attitude, you are hopefully well prepared for whatever comes next. Remember, it's not about who has all of the knowledge; it's about who knows how to ask the right questions.

As you have seen in the book, the supply chain has many different angles, most of them simple but not easy. It's a wide, diverse and complex area, and that's precisely the fun part of it!

APPENDIX: EXPERIENTIAL LEARNING AND THE FRESH CONNECTION (EXTENDED VERSION)

The age of accelerations

Developments in the world are happening faster and faster and, as a consequence, the world is becoming less and less predictable. As an analogy for expressing this increasing speed of development, Brynjolfsson and McAfee (2014) cite a book by Kurzweil published in 2000, in which he alludes to 'the second half of the chessboard', based on a story from 6th-century India about the inventor of the game of chess.

As a reward for his invention, the inventor asked from his emperor nothing more than to 'place one single grain of rice on the first square of the board, two on the second, four on the third, and so on'. The emperor approves, thinking that that's a reward easy to fulfil, not understanding that the final amount of rice on the 64th square of the board would 'dwarf Mount Everest'.

Brynjolfsson and McAfee continue: 'Kurzweil's great insight is that while numbers do get large in the first half of the chessboard, we still come across them in the real world. [...] In the second half of the chessboard, however, [...] we lose all sense of them. We also lose sense of how quickly numbers like these appear as exponential growth continues.' They go on to argue that the rate of change in our world of today might well be reaching the second half of the chessboard soon, and 'like the emperor, most of us have trouble keeping up'.

Twenty-first-century skills

So if the rate of change keeps increasing and people have trouble keeping up, then the question arises as to what it is we can do to be better prepared for this uncertainty ahead of us. Both in business and in education, more and more people speak now about what has become known as '21st-century skills'. One of the thoughts behind this list of critical skills is precisely that the world is changing and that therefore changes are also required in people's skillsets, in order to best deal with this new normal.

The World Economic Forum (WEF) frequently publishes an overview of their view on the 21st-century skills, based on frequent surveys among a diversity of companies. The most recent list of top 10 skills that the WEF have come up with at the time of writing of this book is for the year 2020 (World Economic Forum, 2016):

1 Complex problem solving

2 Critical thinking

3 Creativity

4 People management

5 Coordinating with others

6 Emotional intelligence

7 Judgment and decision making

8 Service orientation

9 Negotiation

10 Cognitive flexibility.

Not surprisingly, an important number of skills are related to complexity and how to deal with it, and another important number of skills is dealing with human interaction. Apparently, one of the implicit expectations is that we will need to be working more and more in teams in order to deal with the increasing complexity in the world.

Fortunately, not only from a business perspective but also in the world of education, a similar view can be found. For example, education expert Sir Ken Robinson, in one of his recent books on the future of education (Robinson and Aronica, 2015), suggests:

> eight core competencies that schools should facilitate if they are really going to help students succeed in their lives [...] They are:
>
> CURIOSITY – the ability to ask questions and explore how the world works;
>
> CREATIVITY – the ability to generate new ideas and to apply them in practice;
>
> CRITICISM – the ability to analyse information and ideas and to form reasoned arguments and judgments;
>
> COMMUNICATION – the ability to express thoughts and feelings clearly and confidently in a range of media and forms;
>
> COLLABORATION – the ability to work constructively with others;
>
> COMPASSION – the ability to empathize with others and to act accordingly;
>
> COMPOSURE – the ability to connect with the inner life of feeling and develop a sense of personal harmony and balance;
>
> CITIZENSHIP – the ability to engage constructively with society and to participate in the processes to sustain it.

In other words, the key to solving problems and making decisions is no longer only in what you know, but in what you are able to do, especially in situations with less certainty. Factual knowledge lasts for less and less time, but well-developed skills will enable a person to find the most up-to-date inputs and answers whenever needed. Or as John E Kelly III, Sr VP of Research and Cognitive Solutions at IBM states, as cited in Thomas L Friedman's book *Thank You For Being Late*: 'In the 21st century, knowing all the answers won't distinguish someone's intelligence – rather, the ability to ask all the right questions will be the mark of true genius' (Friedman, 2016).

In a similar fashion, both Microsoft's CEO Satya Nadella and Amazon's CEO Jeff Bezos have said in interviews that they believe in the '*learn-it-all's*' over the '*know-it-all's*' (Bariso, 2017, 2018). Again, skills over knowledge. So, if in the 21st century skills are becoming more and more important in order to thrive in an ever-faster-changing world, how do we train these skills? If a shift of attention in skills is needed, what is the most appropriate way of learning?

Experiential learning

On the same webpage of the World Economic Forum as mentioned earlier, the list of skills for the 21st century is linked to the implications it has for education, advocating for example an increased need to focus on social and emotional learning as a required complement to more traditional cognitive learning (World Economic Forum, 2016). But let's try to make that a bit more specific.

Much has been written about the different ways people learn, and different schools of thought exist. What many agree upon, in one way or another, is that practical experience is a fundamental part of learning. Ken Robinson and Lou Aronica (2015) phrase it this way: 'many students learn best when they are actively doing things and not only studying ideas in the abstract: when their curiosity is aroused, when they are asking questions, discovering new ideas, and feeling for themselves the excitement of these disciplines.'

Also, I'd like particularly to reference the work of David Kolb (2015), whose book *Experiential Learning* is a classic book on the topic. Among other important contributions, such as for example the concept of individual learning styles, Kolb is well known for what is called the learning cycle (Figure A.1).

The main idea behind the learning cycle is that:

Knowledge results from the combination of grasping and transforming experience. Grasping experience refers to the process of taking in information, and transforming experience is how individuals interpret and act on that information. The experiential learning theory learning model portrays two dialectically related modes of grasping experience – Concrete Experience (CE) and Abstract Conceptualization (AC) – and two dialectically related modes of transforming experience – Reflective Observation (RO)

Figure A.1   The learning cycle

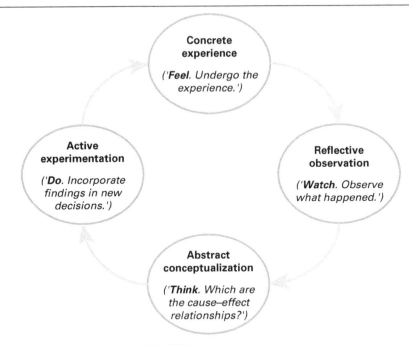

SOURCE after McLeod (2017), based on Kolb (2015)

and Active Experimentation (AE). Learning arises from the resolution of creative tension among these four learning modes. This process is portrayed as an idealized learning cycle or spiral where the learner 'touches all the bases'. (Kolb, 2015)

Even though the concept of the learning cycle and the connection to experiential learning were developed well before the start of the 21st century, their spirit seems to fit very well with the training and development of the aforementioned 21st-century skills.

In experiential learning, the focus is on going through a first-hand experience, which allows for reflection on what happened and why, leading to forming a conceptual view on the situation, potentially reinforced by existing theories and/or frameworks. This combination will then be the basis for an improved view on the situation, which can then be applied in the next experience, either in class or in another study environment, or directly in a real-world situation.

The link between experiential learning and 21st-century skills becomes even stronger if the experiences are based on problems or situations which the student will initially find 'unstructured' or 'new', in which they need to build up their own understanding of what's going on. Some would speak about getting the student 'out of their comfort zone'. This leads to what Robinson and Aronica (2015) phrase as:

'Effective learning in any field is often a process of trial and error, of breakthroughs punctuated by failed attempts to find a solution.'

Excellent and well-known methodologies for experiential learning in school settings are the case method, as championed by Harvard Business School, projects and teamwork, and business simulation games.

Mastering the supply chain

The objective of this book is to fully facilitate the '*learner touching all the bases*'. The Fresh Connection business simulation game is at the heart of this learning experience. In subsequent steps it serves as a vehicle for grasping experience, as well as transforming experience, by using the simulation of rounds of gameplay complemented by conceptual frameworks, as well as active reflecting by the student, leading into a new round of simulation, creating a steep learning curve based on first-hand experience. In addition, fields of direct application outside the simulation tool are touched upon, to widen the student's perspective even further.

Parts Two and Three of the book have a direct relationship to The Fresh Connection gameplay. Part Two: Mastering the fundamentals is built on the game's 'standard configurations', which are mostly used in schools and universities, thus allowing students to combine the book with active gameplay. In Part Three: Beyond the fundamentals, we build on some advanced configurations, which in practice are more widely used in specific corporate training situations. Here, The Fresh Connection serves to students as a 'real-life' case, filled with realistic data, which forms the basis of creatively thinking about future challenges, beyond the 'standard' management of a relatively stable supply chain.

REFERENCES

Ashkenas, R (2015) [accessed 31 March 2018] Jack Welch's Approach to Breaking Down Silos Still Works, *Harvard Business Review*, 9 September [Online] https://hbr.org/2015/09/jack-welchs-approach-to-breaking-down-silos-still-works

Baker, P (2018) [accessed 29 April 2018] The Best Data Visualization Tools of 2018, *PCMag.com*, 3 April [Online] https://www.pcmag.com/roundup/346417/the-best-data-visualization-tools

Bariso, J (2017) [accessed 31 March 2018] Microsoft's CEO Just Gave Some Brilliant Career Advice. Here It Is In 1 Sentence, *Inc.com*, 27 April [Online] https://www.inc.com/justin-bariso/microsofts-ceo-just-gave-some-brilliant-career-advice-here-it-is-in-one-sentence.html

Bariso, J (2018) [accessed 31 March 2018] Jeff Bezos Just Shared His 3-Step Formula for Success – and It's Absolutely Brilliant, *Inc.com*, 31 January 2018 [Online] https://www.inc.com/justin-bariso/amazon-jeff-bezos-healthcare-formula-success-1-sentence.html

BBC (2018) [accessed 31 March 2018] Chicken Chaos as KFC Closes Outlets, *BBC News*, 19 February [Online] http://www.bbc.com/news/business-43110910

Belbin, R M (2010) *Team Roles at Work*, 2nd edn, Routledge, New York

Braungart, M and McDonough, W (2002) *Cradle to Cradle: Remaking the way we make things*, North Point Press, New York

Brynjolfsson, E and McAfee, A (2014) *The Second Machine Age: Work, progress and prosperity in a time of brilliant technologies*, W.W. Norton & Company, New York

Campbell, D H (2011) [accessed 31 March 2018] What Great Companies Know About Culture, *Harvard Business Review*, 14 December [Online] https://hbr.org/2011/12/what-great-companies-know-abou

Chopra, S and Meindl, P (2016) *Supply Chain Management: Strategy, planning, operation*, 6th edn, Pearson Education, Harlow

Christopher, M (2016) *Logistics and Supply Chain Management*, 5th edn, Pearson Education, Harlow

Crawford, F and Mathews, R (2003) *The Myth of Excellence: Why great companies never try to be the best at everything*, Random House, New York

de Boer, R, van Bergen, M and Steeman, M (2015) *Supply Chain Finance, Its Practical Relevance and Strategic Value*, 2nd edn, Supply Chain Finance Community

De Bono, E (1999) *Six Thinking Hats*, rev and updated edn, Back Bay Books, Boston, MA

DeSmet, B (2018) *Supply Chain Strategy and Financial Metrics: The supply chain triangle of service, cost and cash*, Kogan Page, London

Dougherty, J and Gray, C (2006) *Sales & Operations Planning: Best practices, lessons learned from worldwide companies*, Partners for Excellence, Belmont, NH

Elkington, J (1997) *Cannibals with Forks: The triple bottom line of 21st century business*, Capstone, Chichester

Ellen Macarthur Foundation [accessed 09 May 2018] Butterfly diagram [Online]
    https://kumu.io/ellenmacarthurfoundation/educational-resources#circular-economy-
    general-resources-map/key-for-general-resources-map/butterfly-diagram

Financial Times (2017) Tesla hits bottleneck in drive to mass market, *Financial Times
    Weekend Edition*, 4–5 November.

Fine, C (1998) *Clockspeed: Winning industry control in the age of temporary advantage*,
    Perseus Books, Reading, MA

Fisher, M (1997) What is the right supply chain for your product?, *Harvard Business
    Review*, March–April

Fransoo, J C, Blanco, E E and Mejía-Argueta, C (eds) (2018) *Reaching 50 Million
    Nanostores: Retail distribution in emerging megacities*, CreateSpace Inc and Kindle
    Direct Publishing

Friedman, T L (2016) *Thank You For Being Late: An optimist's guide to thriving in the age
    of accelerations*, Farrar, Strauss and Giroux, New York

Gattorna, J (2015) *Dynamic Supply Chains: How to design, build and manage people-
    centric value networks*, 3rd edn, Pearson Education, Harlow

Guardian (2016) [accessed 31 March 2018] Hanjin Shipping Bankruptcy Causes Turmoil in
    Global Sea Freight, *The Guardian*, 2 September [Online] https://www.theguardian.com/
    business/2016/sep/02/hanjin-shipping-bankruptcy-causes-turmoil-in-global-sea-freight

Guest, D. (1991) The hunt is on for the Renaissance Man of computing, *The Independent*,
    17 September

Hammer, M (2001) The superefficient company, *Harvard Business Review*, September

Hansen, M T and von Oetinger, B (2001) Introducing T-shaped managers: Knowledge
    management's next generation, *Harvard Business Review*, March

Heizer, J and Render, B (2013) *Operations Management, Global edition*, 11th edn, Pearson,
    Harlow

Hoekstra, S J and Romme, J (1993) *Op weg naar integrale logistieke structuren* [*Towards
    integral logistics structures*], Kluwer, Deventer

Horton, C (2018) [accessed 31 March 2018] Toilet Paper Shortage Strikes Taiwan Amid
    Pricing Panic, *New York Times*, 27 February [Online] https://www.nytimes.
    com/2018/02/27/world/asia/taiwan-toilet-paper-shortage.html

Isidore, C (2018) [accessed 31 March 2018] Tesla Has a Problem. Maybe a Big Problem,
    CNN Money, 28 March [Online] http://money.cnn.com/2018/03/28/news/companies/
    tesla-model-3-cash-crunch/index.html

JWMI (Jack Welch Management Institute) (2015) [accessed 27 July 2018] What Is the Role
    of a Leader? *Published on YouTube* [Online] https://www.youtube.com/
    watch?v=ojkOs8Gatsg

Kaplan, R S and Norton, D P (1992) The balanced scorecard – measures that drive
    performance, *Harvard Business Review*, Jan–Feb

Klabbers, J H G (2009) *The Magic Circle: Principles of gaming and simulation*, 3rd and rev
    edition, Sense Publishers, Rotterdam/Taipei

Kolb, D (2015) *Experiential Learning: Experience as the source of learning and
    development*, 2nd edn, Pearson, Upper Saddle River, NJ

Kotler, P and Lane, K (2015) *Marketing Management*, global edn, Pearson Education, Harlow

Kraljic, P (1983) Purchasing must become supply management, *Harvard Business Review*, September

Kurzweil, R (2000) *The Age of Spiritual Machines: When computers exceed human intelligence*, Penguin Books, New York

Layall, A, Mercier, P and Gstettner, S (2018) The death of supply chain management, *Harvard Business Review*, June

Lee, H (2002) Aligning supply chain strategies with product uncertainties, *California Management Review*, Spring 2002

Lee, H, Padmanabhan, V and Whang, S (1997) The bullwhip effect in supply chains, *Sloan Management Review*, Spring

McLeod, S (2017) [accessed 31 March 2017] Kolb's Learning Styles and Experiential Learning Cycle [Online] https://www.simplypsychology.org/learning-kolb.html

Osterwalder, A and Pigneur, Y (2010) *Business Model Generation: A handbook for visionaries, game changers, and challengers*, John Wiley & Sons, Hoboken, NJ

Osterwalder, A *et al* (2014) *Value Proposition Design: How to create products and services customers want*, John Wiley & Sons, Hoboken, NJ

Pérez, H D (2013) *Supply Chain Roadmap: Aligning supply chain with business strategy*, CreateSpace Independent Publishing Platform

Phadnis, S *et al* (2013) Educating Supply Chain Professionals to Work in Global Virtual Teams, Working paper, MIT, first published at CSCMP Educators Conference Annual Educators Meeting, Denver, CO, 20 October

Porter, M (1980) *Competitive Advantage: Creating and sustaining superior performance*, The Free Press, New York

Porter, M (1985) *Competitive Strategy: Techniques for analyzing industries and competitors*, The Free Press, New York

Raworth, K (2017) *Doughnut Economics: Seven ways to think like a 21st-century economist*, Random House, London

Robinson, K and Aronica, L (2015) *Creative Schools: Revolutionizing education from the ground up*, Penguin Random House, London

Rushton, A, Croucher, P and Baker, P (2017) *Handbook of Logistics and Distribution Management: Understanding the supply chain*, 6th edn, Kogan Page, London

Schippers, M, Rook, L, and Van de Velde, S (2011) [accessed 13 June 2018] Crisis performance predictability in supply chains, Working Paper, Erasmus University/Rotterdam School of Management [Abstract Online] https://discovery.rsm.nl/articles/detail/47-crisis-performance-predictability-in-supply-chains/

Sharp, B (2010) *How Brands Grow: What marketers don't know*, Oxford University Press Australia, Victoria

Sheffi, Y (2007) *The Resilient Enterprise: Overcoming vulnerability for competitive advantage*, Massachusetts Institute of Technology Press, Boston, MA

Sheffi, Y (2015) *The Power of Resilience: How the best companies manage the unexpected*, Massachusetts Institute of Technology Press, Boston, MA

Silver, E A, Pyke, D F and Peterson, R (1998) *Inventory Management and Production Planning and Scheduling*, 3rd edn, John Wiley & Sons, Hoboken, NJ

Simchi-Levi, D (2010) *Operations Rules: Delivering customer value through flexible operations*, Massachusetts Institute of Technology Press, Boston, MA

Simchi-Levi, D, Kaminsky, P and Simchi-Levi, E (2009) *Designing and Managing the Supply Chain: Concepts, strategies and case studies*, 3rd edn, McGraw-Hill, New York

Slack, N *et al* (2012) *Operations and Process Management: Principles and practice for strategic impact*, 3rd edn, Pearson, Harlow

Stahl, R (2009) [accessed 31 March 2018] Sales and Operations Planning, Simpler, Better and More Needed Than Ever, *Foresight*, Issue 14, Summer [Online] http://rastahl.fatcow.com/-Final%20Summer%20Column%20.pdf

Stanton, D (2017) *Supply Chain Management for Dummies*, John Wiley & Sons, Hoboken, NJ

Tesla (2018) [accessed 13 April 2018] Tesla Q1 2018 Vehicle Production and Deliveries, *Tesla.com*, 3 April 3 [Online] http://ir.tesla.com/releasedetail.cfm?ReleaseID=1062670

Thalbauer, H (2016) [accessed 31 March 2018] Is Chief Supply Chain Officer Most Important Role In Executive Suite?, *Forbes.com*, March 25 [Online] https://www.forbes.com/sites/sap/2016/03/25/is-chief-supply-chain-officer-most-important-role-in-executive-suite/

Treacy, M and Wiersema, F (1995) *Discipline of Market Leaders: Choose your customers, narrow your focus, dominate your market*, Ingram Publishers, La Vergne, TN

Tuckman, B (1965) Developmental sequence in small groups, *Psychological Bulletin* **63** (6), pp 384–99

Visser, H and van Goor, A (2011) *Logistics: Principles and practice*, 2nd edn, Hessel Visser, 's Gravendeel, Netherlands

Wallace, T (2009) [accessed 31 March 2018] S&OP 101 [Online] http://www.rastahlcompany.com/10101.html

Weenk, E (2013a) *The Perfect Pass: What the manager can learn from the football trainer*, QuSL/Libros de Cabecera, Barcelona

Weenk, E (2013b) [accessed 14 June 2018] The Supply Chain Manager's Daily Decathlon, *SupplyChainMovement.com*, published between March and June 2013 as a series of six blogposts [Online] https://www.supplychainmovement.com/the-supply-chain-managers-daily-decathlon-part-1-of-6/ [Episodes 2–6 are available from there]

Weetman, C (2017) *A Circular Economy Handbook for Business and Supply Chains: Repair, remake, redesign, rethink*, Kogan Page, London

World Economic Forum (2016) [accessed 31 March 2017] What Are the 21st-Century Skills Every Student Needs?, World Economic Forum, 10 March [Online] https://www.weforum.org/agenda/2016/03/21st-century-skills-future-jobs-students/

INDEX

Printed in the USA
CPSIA information can be obtained
at www.ICGtesting.com
JSHW071129110524
62938JS00017B/875

9 780749 484484